I0793713

IMAGES
of America

NAVASOTA

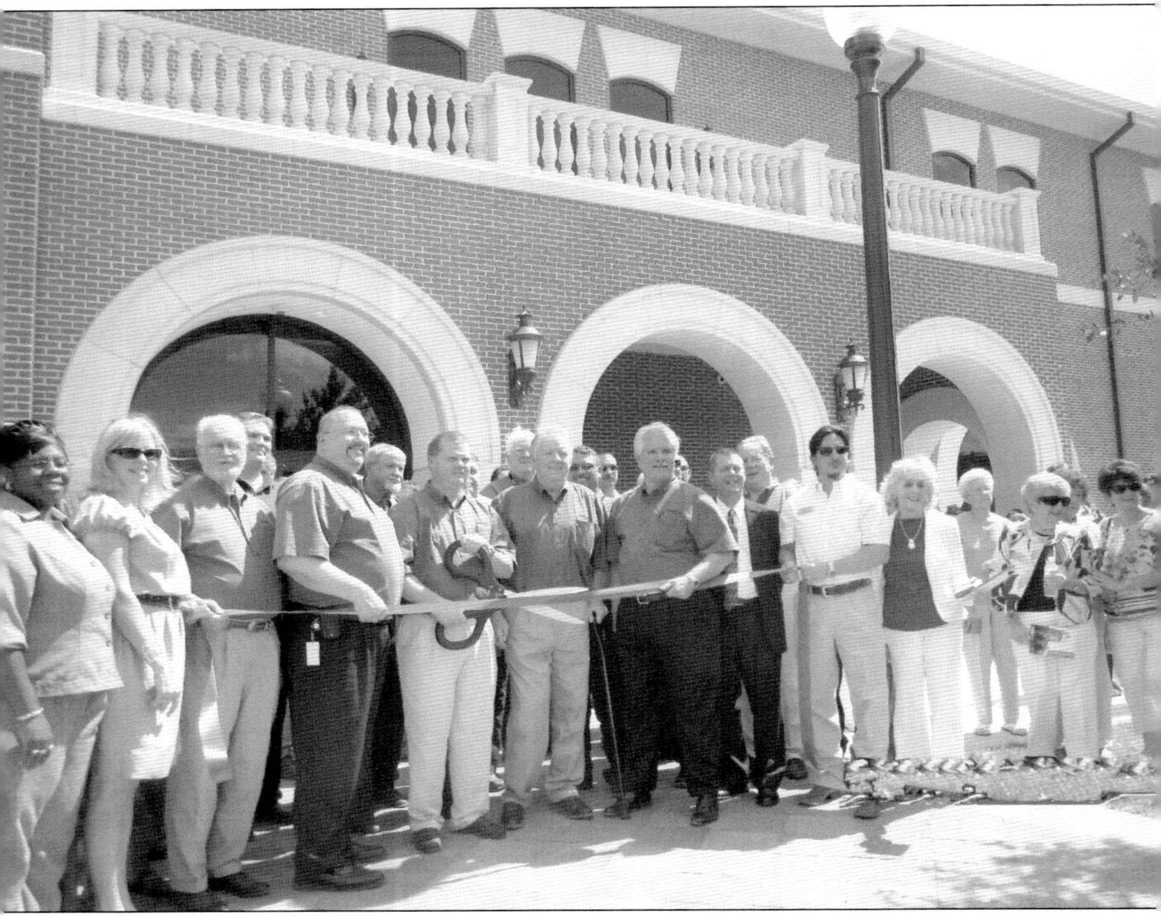

The Navasota City Hall was dedicated on September 1, 2011. Braced by the blue ribbon are members of the city council and the city manager. From left to right are councilman Bernie Gessner, mayor pro tem Peter Canney, Mayor William "Bert" Miller (with scissors), councilman Rance Barham, councilman Grant Hill; and city manager Brad Stafford.

On the Cover: On Thursday, October 9, 1891, citizens of Navasota gathered along Railroad Street for a parade. Navasotans have always been proud of their heritage, and parades remain one of their favorite ways of exhibiting that pride. The parade route along Railroad Street is significant, since railroads have fundamentally molded the socioeconomic character and heritage of the city.

IMAGES
of America

NAVASOTA

Robin Montgomery and Joy Montgomery
with the Texas Center for Regional Studies

ARCADIA
PUBLISHING

ISBN 978-0-7385-9502-3

Published by Arcadia Publishing
Charleston, South Carolina

Printed in the United States of America

Library of Congress Control Number: 2012930957

For all general information, please contact Arcadia Publishing:
Telephone 843-853-2070
Fax 843-853-0044
E-mail sales@arcadiapublishing.com
For customer service and orders:
Toll-Free 1-888-313-2665

Visit us on the Internet at www.arcadiapublishing.com

This book is dedicated to Navasota native Roy M. Horlock, a distinguished representative of one of the most prominent families in Navasota history. Mr. Horlock, his entire family, and the Horlock History Center have extended immeasurable support to the study and preservation of Navasota's history.

Contents

ACKNOWLEDGMENTS

It is impossible to accomplish a task such as this in a vacuum. The help of many people was needed, both organizationally and individually. At the top of our list are four people without whom this work would, truly, have remained ever a dream. These are Carl Smith, Betty Dunn, Evelyn Barden, and Beverly Montgomery. Smith and Dunn are members of the executive committee of the Center for Regional Studies. Barden and Montgomery did yeoman service domestically, buying us all precious time.

Besides our organization—the Texas Center for Regional Studies—other organizations were most beneficial, starting with Navasota city manager Brad Stafford, Mayor Bert Miller, and many other officials of the city, especially Kourtney Gruner. And indispensable to our task was the most gracious and helpful Rosemary Smith, managing editor of the *Navasota Examiner*. Equally indispensable was Russell Cushman, former city councilman and artist extraordinaire, whose collection of photographs was sourced throughout this book. Russell also provided valuable information and inspiration. The same may be said of the universally acknowledged premier historian of Grimes County, Marcus Mallard. Also high on our list are the Zuber-Hadley chapter of the Daughters of the Republic of Texas (DRT), the Navasota Public Library, and the River of Culture.

Individuals who have graciously provided information and photographs include Alton Aga, Latham Boone III, Leon Collins, Sandi Costa, Kathy Day, J.D. Dickenson, Mildred Edwards, Linda Evans, Joe King Fultz, Johnny Keown, Jose Maldonado, Bert Miller, Nancy Perry, Pastor Henry Sanders, University of Oklahoma professor Rich Taylor, Bill and Kathleen Terrell, Pamela Vance, and the proprietors of the Johnbellhood.org website.

INTRODUCTION

In 1682, René Robert Cavelier Sieur de La Salle claimed the Mississippi River Basin and all that it drained for France. Three years later, sailing from France with four ships at his command, he mistakenly bypassed the mouth of the Mississippi and anchored off Texas's Matagorda Bay. From there, he led several expeditions seeking to find the Mississippi. On the last of these, his men mutinied, ambushing and murdering him near Navasota.

La Salle was trespassing on territory that Spain claimed as its own. Five sea and six land expeditions of Spaniards searched for La Salle's headquarters, finally meeting success after the Frenchman's death. Still alarmed, the Spanish sent an expedition to the east to build a mission, with an accompanying military presence, to officially mark its claim to territory adjoining French Louisiana. The Caddo Indians greeted them with the word *tayshas*, meaning "friends." The word in Spanish was *tejas*, and the Spanish took that as the name for the area. When the Anglo Americans came, they called the land by the English pronunciation: Texas.

When Navasotans erected a statue of La Salle in the middle of the city's main thoroughfare in 1930, they were celebrating the man whose presence led to the birth of Texas. Through its association with La Salle, Navasota can lay claim to the title "Cradle of Texas."

Navasota can also claim to be the "Crossroads of Texas." The city is on the La Bahia Trail, which the Spanish blazed specifically to establish their Province of *Tejas*. Furthermore, that trail led to the Spanish laying a trail from East Texas back to San Antonio called the San Antonio Road. A mixed army of Anglos, Spanish, and Indian freedom fighters traveled over both the San Antonio and the La Bahia Roads in 1813, en route to proclaiming the First Republic of Texas to the world.

Navasota also rests at the crossroads of trails that traversed the state from east to west and north to south, dating to the Second Republic of Texas. In the mid-19th century, these trails became the paths for stage lines. At one time, four stage lines passed through Navasota. Then, in 1859, the Houston and Texas Central Railway laid track through Navasota, only the first of many, leading Navasota to become the center of a vast network of railroad lines.

In the pages of this book, we seek to build on these themes of cradle and crossroads, innovation and networking. With a robust intellectual climate, there are many illustrious examples in these pages in the fields of education, religion, industry, art, music, architecture, and law enforcement. In all of these fields are Navasotans, with reputations extending to national and international levels. For example, Mance Lipscomb and his cohorts, whose innovative style birthed a unique brand of the blues, earned Navasota the official title of "Blues Capital of Texas." There is the boyhood hero of Mance Lipscomb, Frank Hamer, who, as town marshal, plied his unique style of law enforcement to clean up the seedy side of Navasota. This was the same Hamer who later applied the skills he had developed in the streets of Navasota to bring to an abrupt halt the sordid careers of infamous criminals Bonnie and Clyde.

Even as Hamer was taming the ruffians of the town, in the parlors of fine houses, women were taking the lead, tapping the cultural consciousness of genteel society. For example, a woman's club in Navasota was the only one of its kind in the state to establish a library. And numerous were the cultural events and intellectual programs, ranging from art appreciation to the issue of women's roles in an age of industrialization. Exceptional for a city of its size, Navasota supported two opera houses during this era.

Given such a robust intellectual climate, it should come as no surprise that education has been a priority in Navasota. Dr. W.B. Bizzell, for example, president of both Texas A&M University and the University of Oklahoma, was first superintendent of schools in Navasota, Texas. Likewise, the medical history of Navasota is infused with persons of high repute. And Dr. A.R. Kilpatrick, whose writings and influence reached the highest levels of his profession, wrote the first history of Navasota.

There are examples of Europeans who saw in Navasota the intellectual atmosphere to host innovations of world-class magnitude. Henry Schumacher, native of Germany, was an innovator in the business of cottonseed oil, earning him the position of guest of honor at a private party at the residence of then US president Chester Arthur. Relatives and business partners of Schumacher, the Horlocks, were builders of a fine home that now thrives as a tourist center. Likewise, there are numerous magnificent homes in Navasota. The annual home tour is one of the most anticipated events in our time.

As with fine homes, Navasota also has many churches. Some trace their lineage back to Washington-on-the-Brazos. Some were here when most needed, when terrible epidemics—first of cholera and then of yellow fever—struck the town in the late 1860s. During those trying times, Navasotans showed their mantle of high courage. One shining example was a young man named R.H. Giesel, who assumed the suddenly vacant position of mayor and proceeded to tend to the afflicted wherever he might find them. His life was taken at an early age, yet his memory shines as an example to us all.

Also exemplary in Navasota is the blend of cultures and ethnicities, overcoming, like most cities in the south, a history of conflict in this area. And Navasota is proud of the record of its men and women in the service of their country. Ranging from the War Between the States to the latest conflict of arms in defense of our land, representatives of our city are many and proud.

In the final analysis, this book is about everyday people and everyday happenings. In short, the pictorial history of Navasota is a microcosm of "Hometown America."

Now come with us, read, and enjoy.

One

Cradle of Texas

As noted in the introduction, Frenchman René Robert Cavelier Sieur de La Salle motivated the Spanish to establish and control the province of Texas. Likewise, when Mexico gained its independence from Spain in 1821, it sought to defend Texas. Accordingly, Mexico invited colonists from the United States to come to Texas. Among these, the most significant colonizer was Stephen F. Austin. By 1828, over Austin's territory, Mexico created the Austin Municipality, stretching north to south from the Gulf of Mexico to the San Antonio Road and east to west from the Lavaca River to the San Jacinto River.

In 1835, a large section of the northern part of Austin Municipality became known as Washington Municipality, an area encompassing all, or part, of nine present counties. The capital was at Washington-on-the-Brazos, just across the river from present Navasota. The leader of this municipality was Joshua Hadley, with Jesse Grimes part of the second tier leadership. It was at a convention at Washington that Texas declared its independence from Mexico. Jesse Grimes was there and signed the document.

Navasotans are proud of this heritage. The Navasota chapter of the Daughters of the Republic of Texas (DRT) takes its name, Zuber–Hadley, partially from Joshua Hadley. The county in which Navasota is located is named Grimes, after Jesse Grimes. Furthermore, before it was approved at the Washington Convention, the Declaration of Independence was written just a few miles south of Navasota.

Truly, Navasota is within the Cradle of Texas.

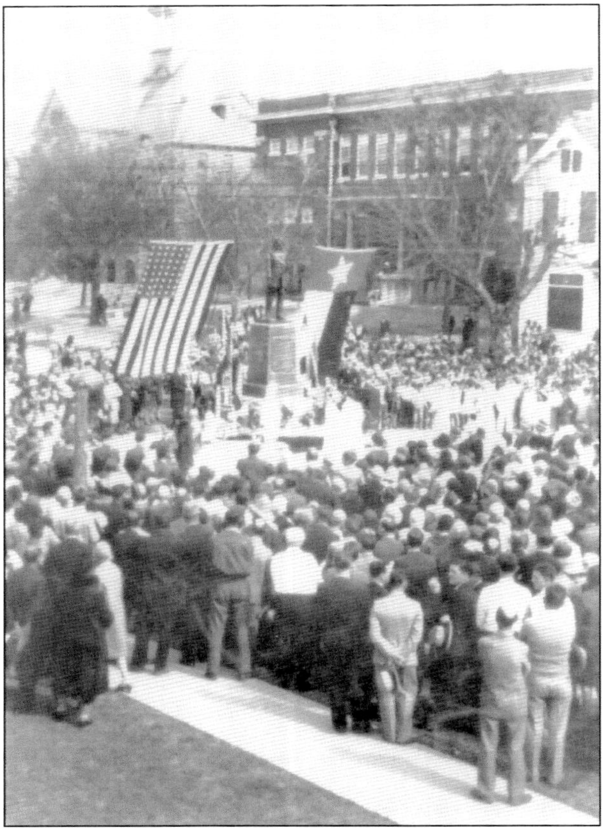

On March 6, 1930, the Robert Baines chapter of the Daughters of the American Revolution (DAR) hosted a ceremony unveiling the La Salle monument on Washington Avenue. The monument is the work of noted sculptor Frank Teich. La Salle was a French explorer, shot by his companions in the area of today's Navasota on March 19, 1687. It was La Salle's presence in the area of New Spain that prompted the Spanish to establish a mission in the land of the Caddo, leading to the birth of the province of Texas under Spain. Across the street are, from left to right, the Atchison Institute school building and the Victoria Felder Manual Training Building, both now razed. (Both, courtesy Navasota Public Library.)

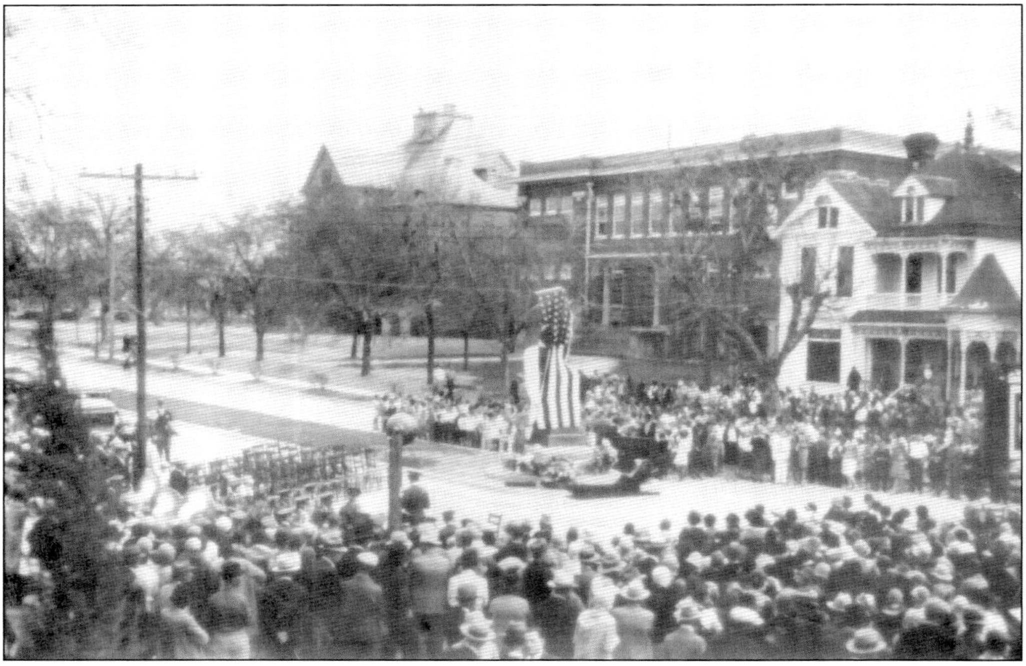

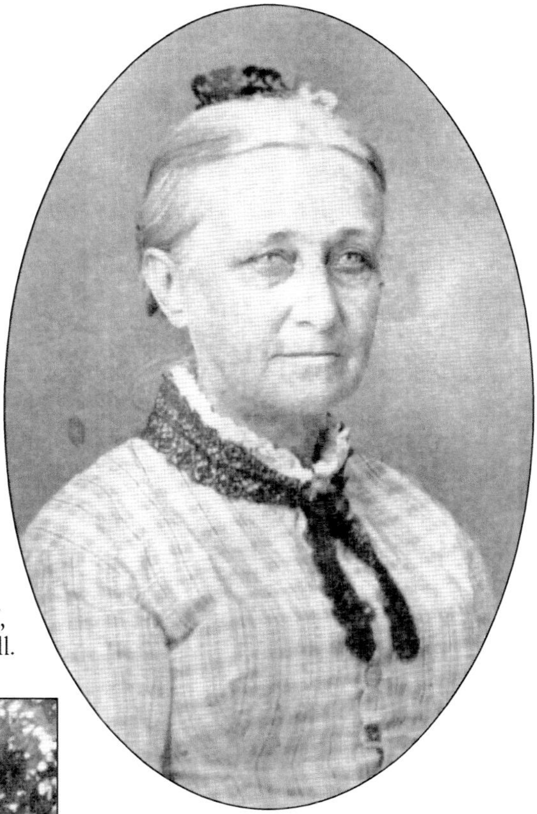

Pictured here are Caroline Hadley and John F. Martin. Caroline, born in 1822, was the daughter of Joshua Hadley. Joshua Hadley was the alcalde of Washington Municipality, which covered, under Mexico, areas included in some nine present counties. He was also one of Stephen F. Austin's 64 original land grantees in what became Grimes County in 1846. Caroline Hadley married John F. Martin in 1836, after he had arrived in Texas about 1830. After John Martin's death on February 15, 1846, the land where he was interred was given to the Odd Fellows Lodge, which marked the beginning of Odd Fellows Cemetery. In 1847, Caroline Hadley Martin married Oliver H.P. Hill. (Courtesy Navasota Public Library.)

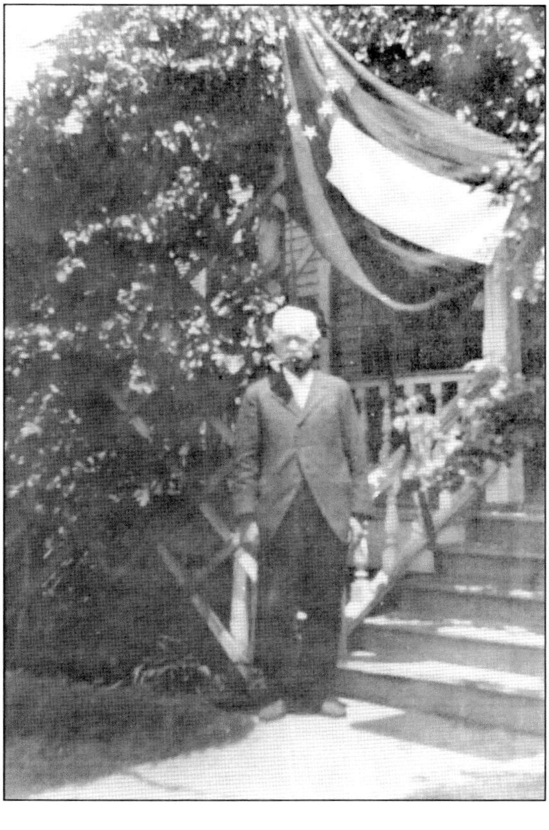

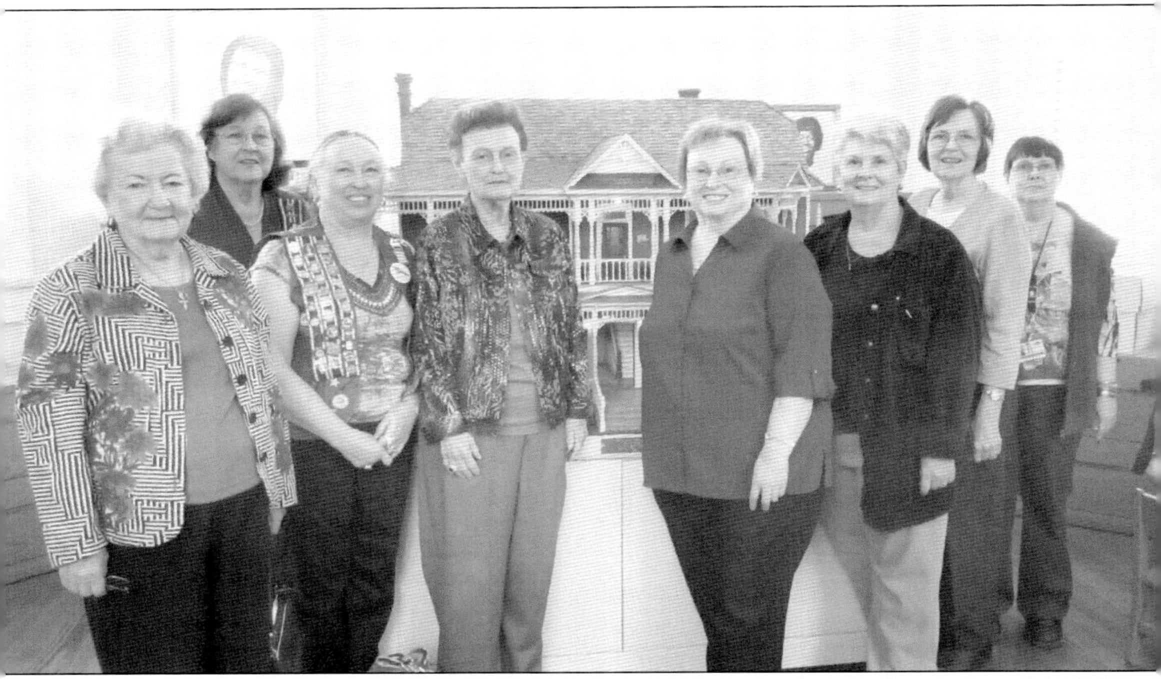

This November 2011 photograph shows members of Navasota's Zuber–Hadley chapter of the DRT at the Carnegie History Center in Bryan. From left to right are Marie Robison, Pres. Winona Kaminskas, Linda Evans, Lillian Fuqua, Marie Fuqua, Judy Mersin, and Ann Fuqua. On the far right is tour guide Nancy Ross. The chapter takes its name from Joshua Hadley; the Zuber name comes from William Zuber. As a lad, Zuber was with Sam Houston's army at San Jacinto. He also wrote the treatise that made famous the story of William Travis, who drew the line in the sand at the Alamo, inviting those who wished to stay to cross. The one who did not cross, Moses Rose, told his story to William Zuber's parents who, in turn, related the story to William. (Courtesy Robin Montgomery.)

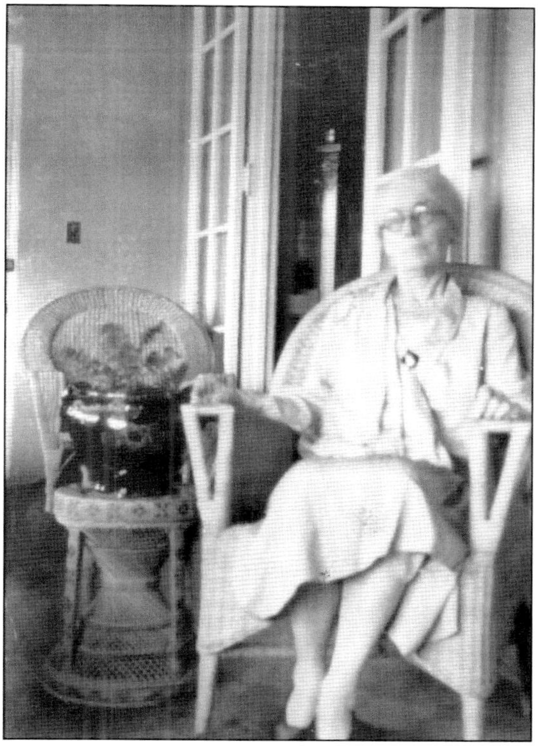

Pictured here around 1927, Lula Davis Jones was a charter member and first president of the Zuber-Hadley chapter of the DRT. The chapter was founded in 1910 in Navasota. Lula Davis was born in Courtney in 1864, the daughter of Col. E.B. Davis and Mary Ellen Lawrence. The photograph below shows Christopher Pegues "Kit P" Jones, husband of Lula Davis Jones. Kit P was born in Alabama in 1859 to Dr. Richard W. and Rebecca Pegues Jones. An attorney, he married Lula Davis in 1886. (Both, courtesy Navasota Public Library.)

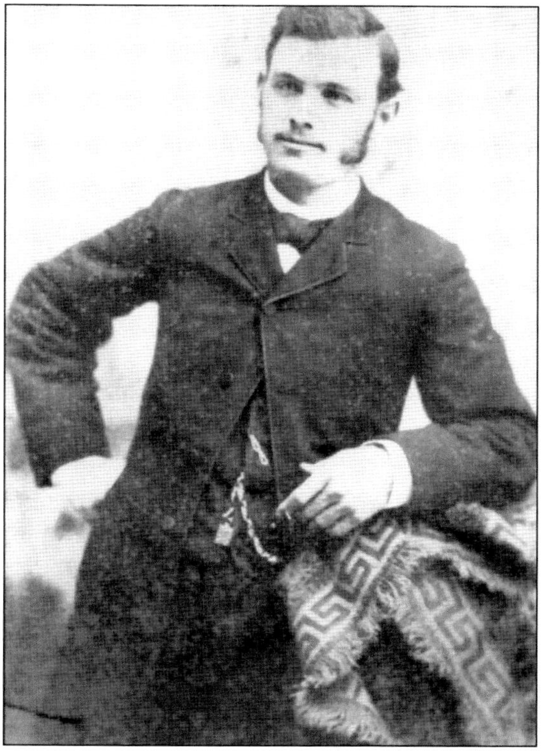

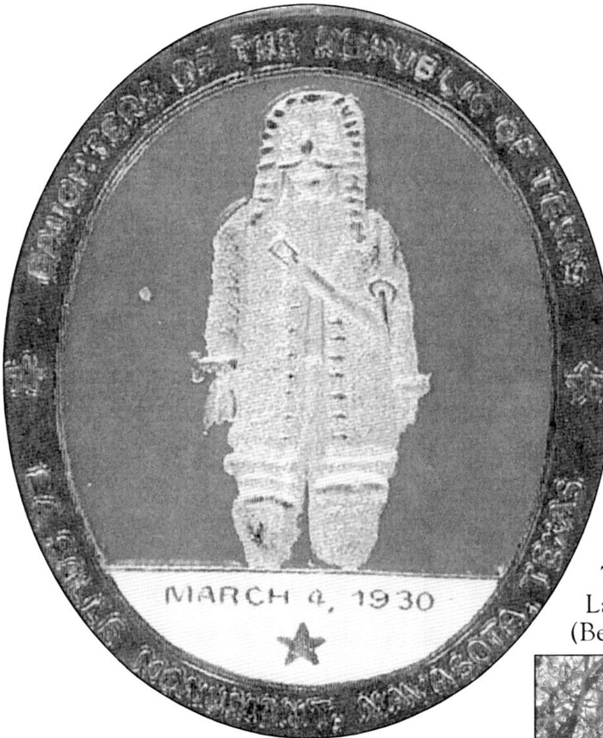

In 1976, the bicentennial celebration of the Declaration of Independence of the United States from Great Britain ignited a spark flashing beyond US shores to France. Accordingly, France donated the La Salle Statue to the city of Navasota, pictured below. Lula Davis Jones's niece Linda Evans designed the La Salle Monument pin, in the photograph at left, when she was president of the Zuber-Hadley chapter of the DRT. The pin was made in 2000, in celebration of the 70th anniversary of the erection of the La Salle Statue on Washington Avenue. (Below, courtesy Joy Montgomery.)

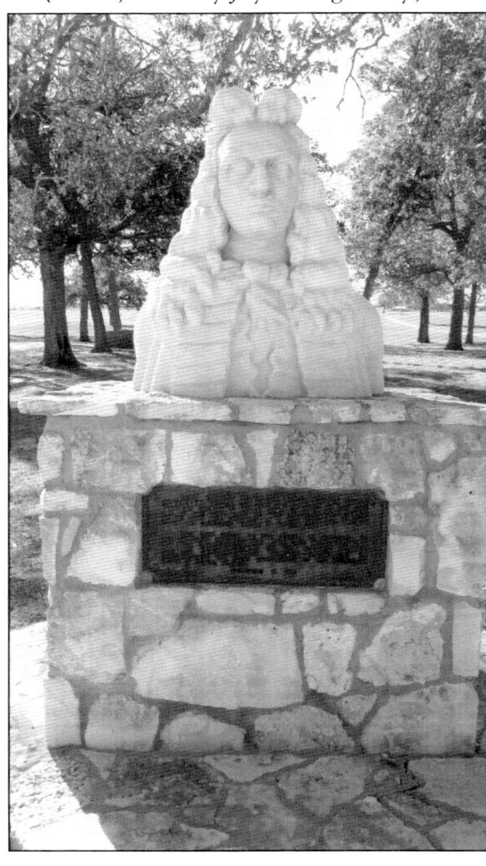

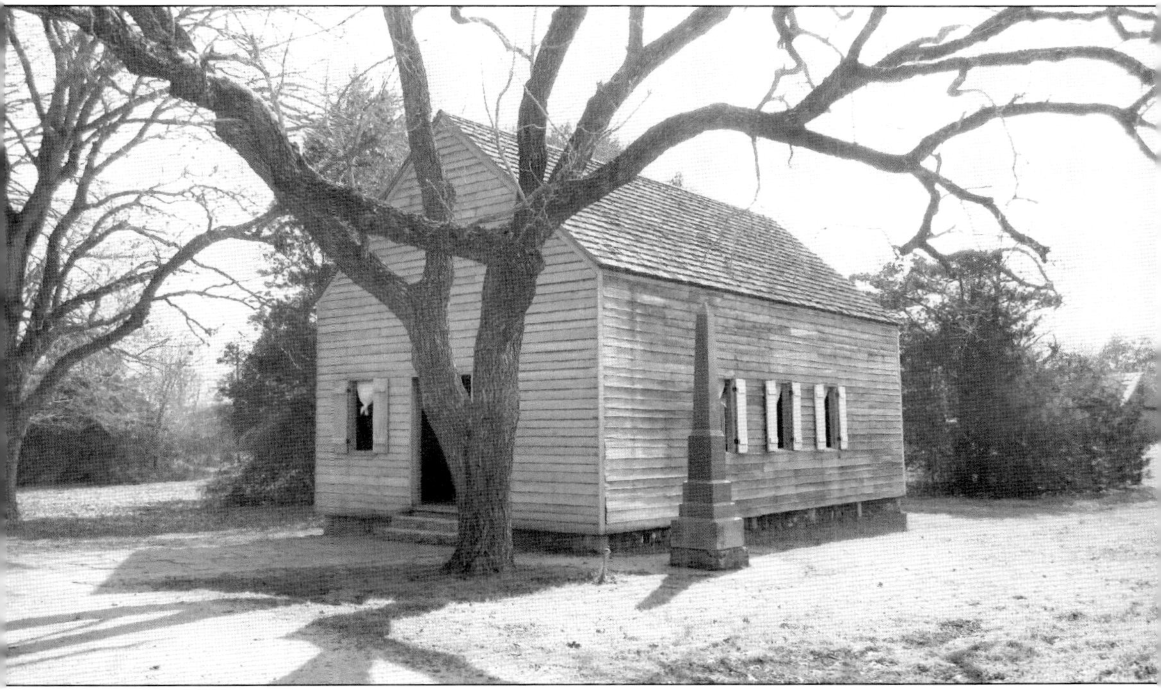

Texans met at this building in Washington-on-the-Brazos on March 1-17, 1836. Here, they signed the Declaration of Independence from Mexico on March 2, the declaration having been written the previous night a few miles below Navasota. On March 17, the 23 municipalities of Mexican Texas became counties. Among those was Washington, forerunner of Montgomery County, which, in turn, was the predecessor of Grimes County. In so many ways, Washington is the parent city of Navasota, adding to Navasota's claim as the Cradle of Texas. Besides the fact that the Declaration of Independence was written in its suburbs, many Washington citizens, businesses, and churches relocated to Navasota, especially after Navasota became a railroad center. Navasotans are proud of this heritage and feel a special link to this spot where heroes dwelled for 17 days, to mark out the destiny of their great state. (Courtesy Joy Montgomery.)

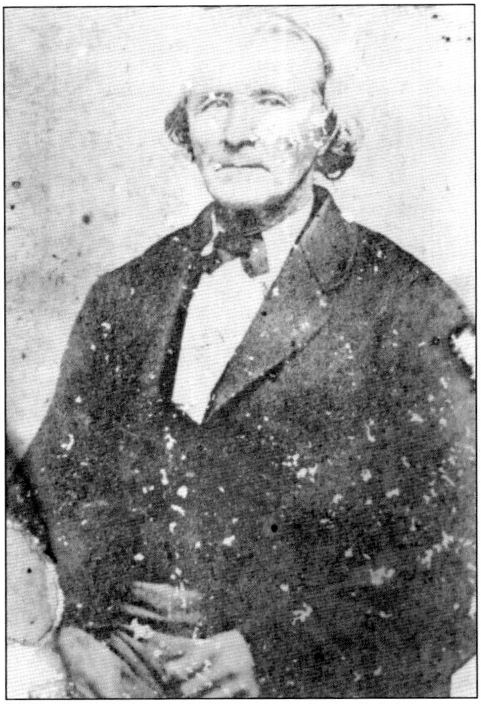

Pictured here are Jesse Grimes and his daughter Martha. A signatory of the Texas Declaration of Independence at Washington-on-the-Brazos in 1836, Jesse Grimes was the man for whom Grimes County was named in 1846. He served in the War of 1812 and arrived in what would become Grimes County in 1827. In 1830, the Mexican government created the district of Viesca, stretching from the Brazos to beyond the San Jacinto River. Over this area, Jesse served as lieutenant of militia, *sindico procurador*, *regidor*, and treasurer. During the Republic of Texas (1836–1845), he served as the first chief justice of Montgomery County and also represented Washington, Montgomery, and Brazos Counties in the legislature. With statehood in 1846, he served four terms as state senator for Grimes County, rising to senate pro tempore. His son Charles was martyred at the Alamo in 1836. (Both, courtesy Navasota Public Library.)

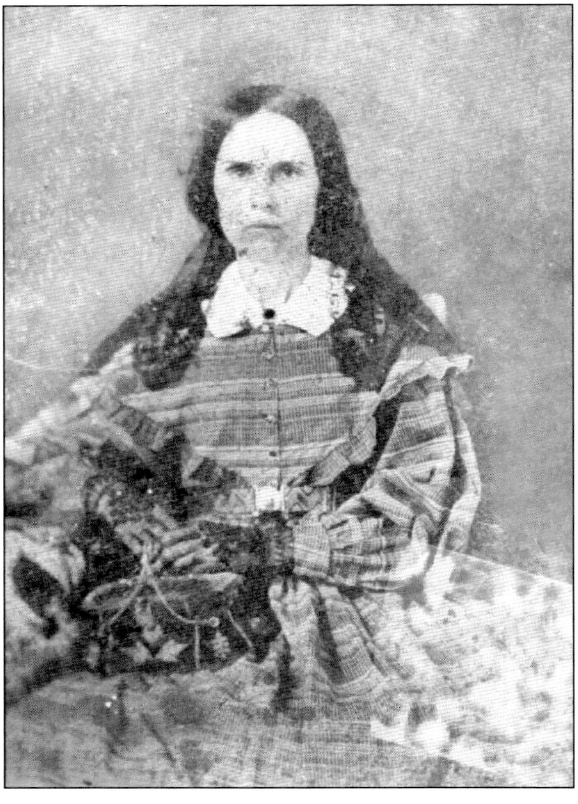

Two

Crossroads and Transportation

In 1822, members of the Francis Holland family settled on a creek—now Holland Creek—between Anderson and present Navasota. By the early 1850s, James Nolan had settled some six miles to the west, closer to the junction of the Brazos and the Navasota Rivers. And this was on the route of the old Bahia Trail. Cognizant of his surroundings, Nolan, and others who followed, had, by 1854, named the location Navasota for the nearby river. In 1866, the community would receive incorporation under that name.

Before the close of the 1850s, four stage routes were carved through Navasota. Then, in 1859, the Houston and Texas Central Railway made its presence felt. Neighboring Washington-on-the Brazos, having failed to accommodate a railroad, began its downward climb leaving Navasota a major economic player on the eve of the Civil War. Though those war years and the postwar Depression brought hard times to Navasota, it soon recouped its momentum. By the 1880s, a Navasota-Montgomery rail line had been established, followed by a vastly extended line under the management of the Gulf, Colorado, and Santa Fe Railway. By the turn of the century, the International and Great Northern Railroad had made its debut, and Navasota was ready to entertain the arrival of the first automobiles. With trucks taking the place of wagons to bring produce to market, such as watermelons and cotton, Navasota regained its momentum.

At the crossroads of first-class highways and with an air presence and an entrepreneurial spirit born of a robust past, Navasota is on the march.

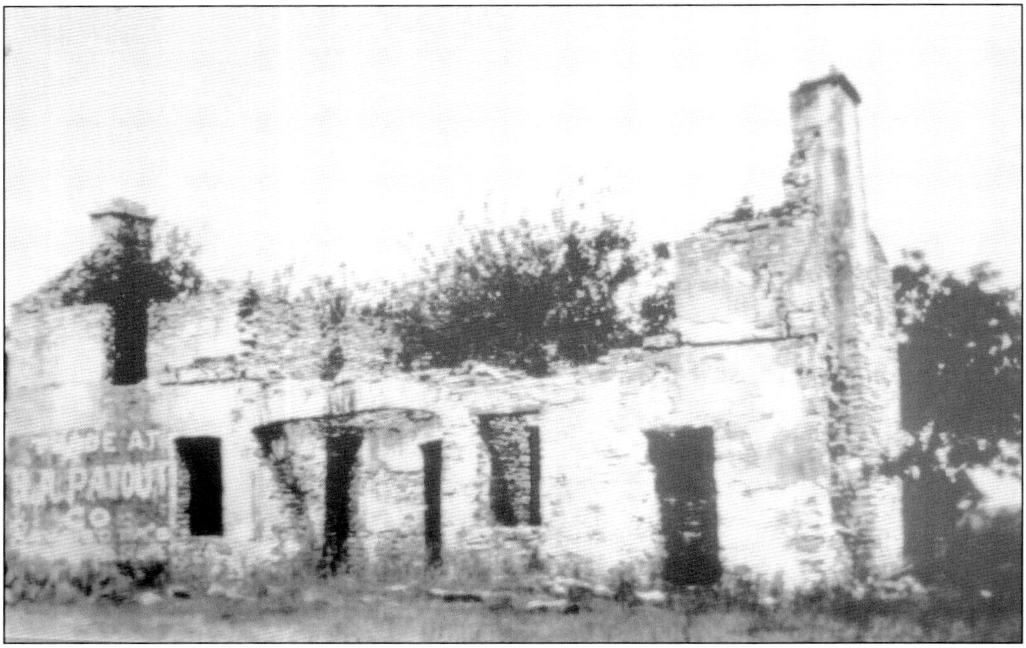

The original Camp Hotel and Stagecoach Inn are pictured here. Ira Malcolm Camp bought a league of land in 1852, just northeast of the main part of present Navasota. From rocks in his fields, he built this imposing structure, cementing it together with lime burned from the limestone on the place. The structure was of two and one-half stories. The below parts were for the business, while the half story was a haven for bees imported from Italy. There also was a cellar, the entrance to which was kept covered by a rug. It is said that Sam Houston, a friend of Camp, stayed there while in town to make a speech promoting the Union on the eve of the Civil War. (Both, courtesy Navasota Public Library.)

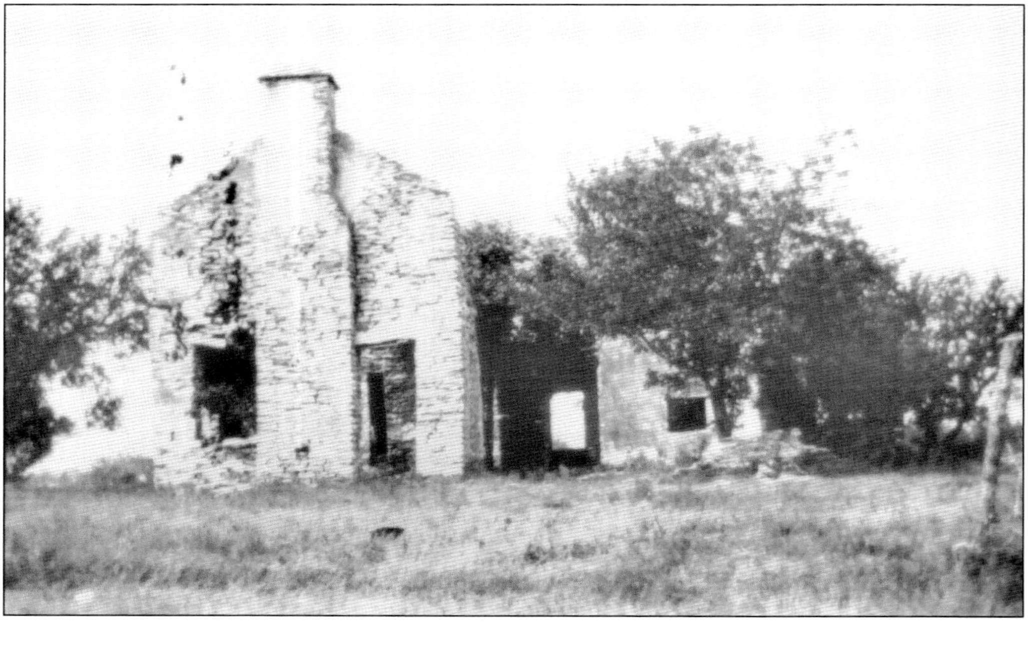

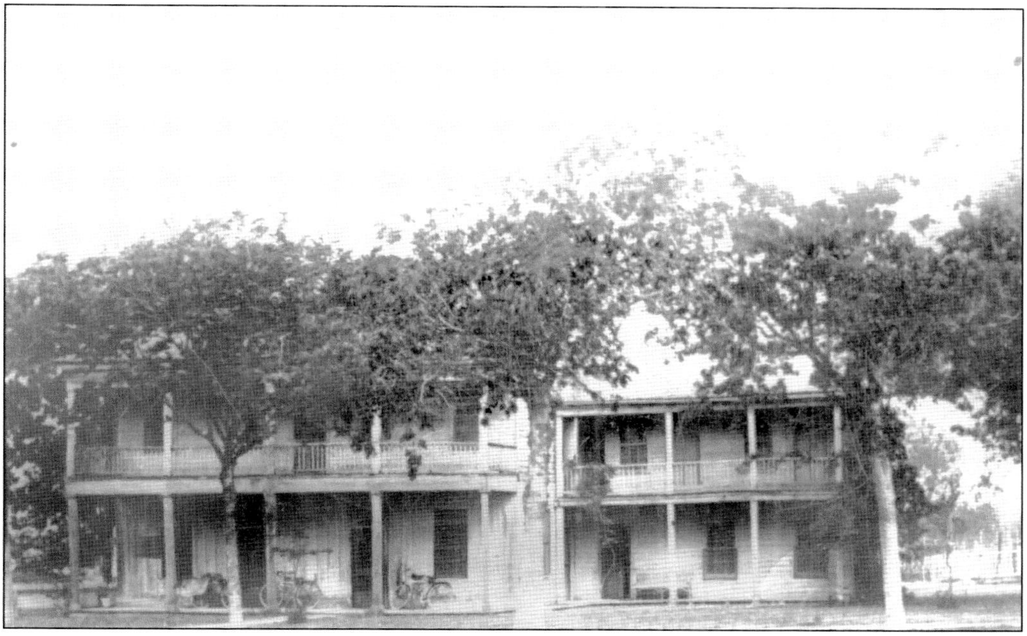

An indication that Navasota was a thriving crossroads in the middle of the 19th century lies in its two first-class inns, the Camp Inn (see previous page) and the Freeman Inn, pictured here. This two-story pine building was built by Ira M. Freeman in 1856. Coaches and teams for the stagecoaches were kept in Freeman's barns. (Courtesy *Navasota Examiner.*)

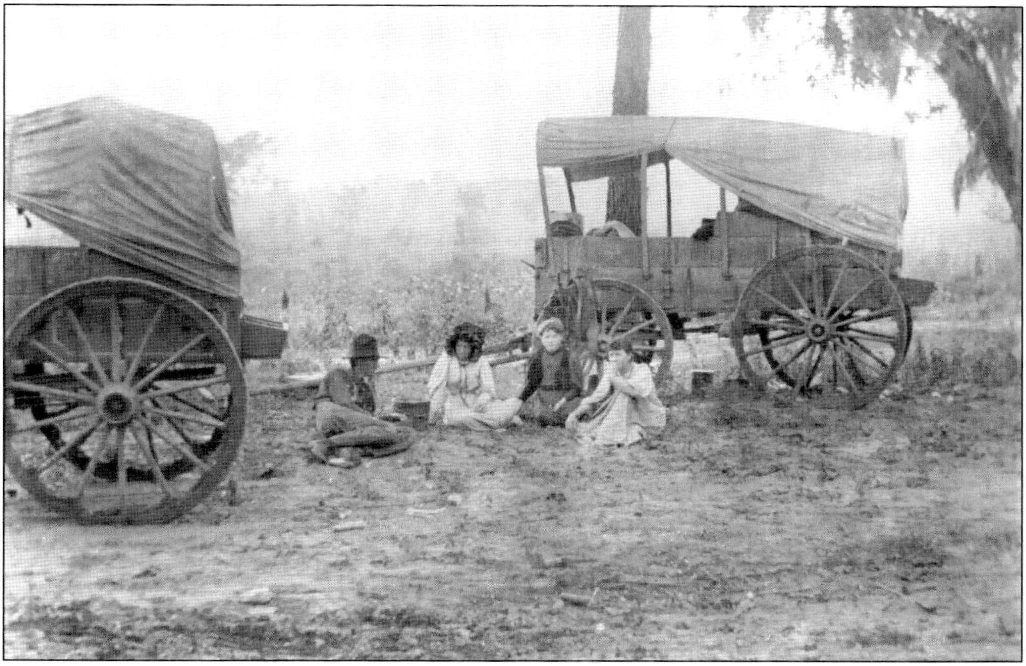

While Navasotans have advanced far in their methods of travel, memories yet remain of families driving their wagons through the town and camping, having meals, and sleeping in or near those wagons. Pictured here in 1890, a family travels through the area. (Courtesy Marcus Mallard.)

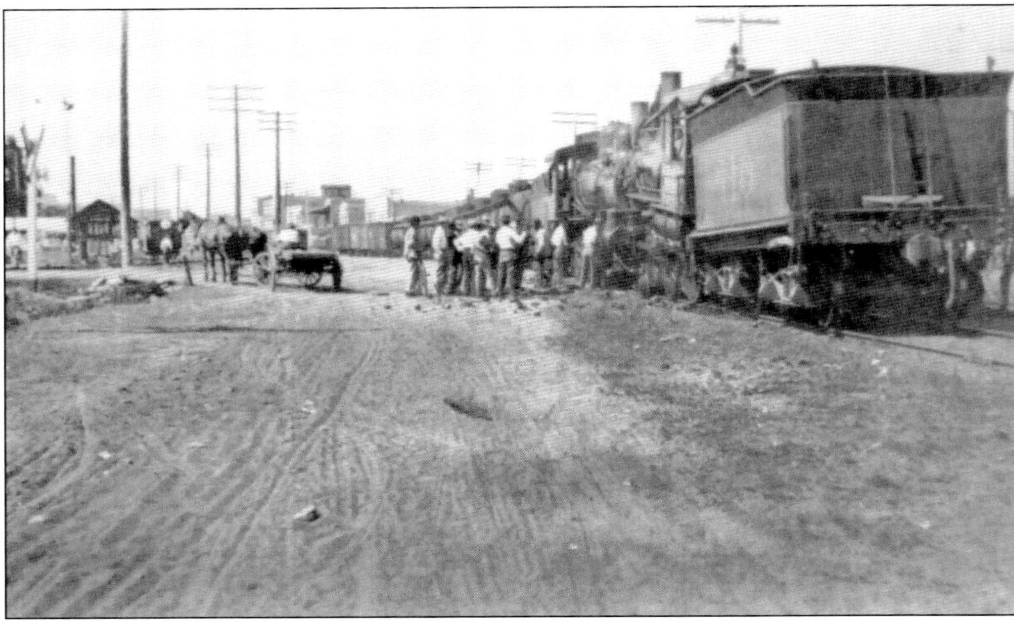

As the number of rail lines increased through Navasota, the communication process became progressively more precarious. Pictured here is the aftermath of a head-on collision on the main line on September 19, 1910. Note the unpaved streets alongside the track and the horse and wagon. (Courtesy Navasota Public Library.)

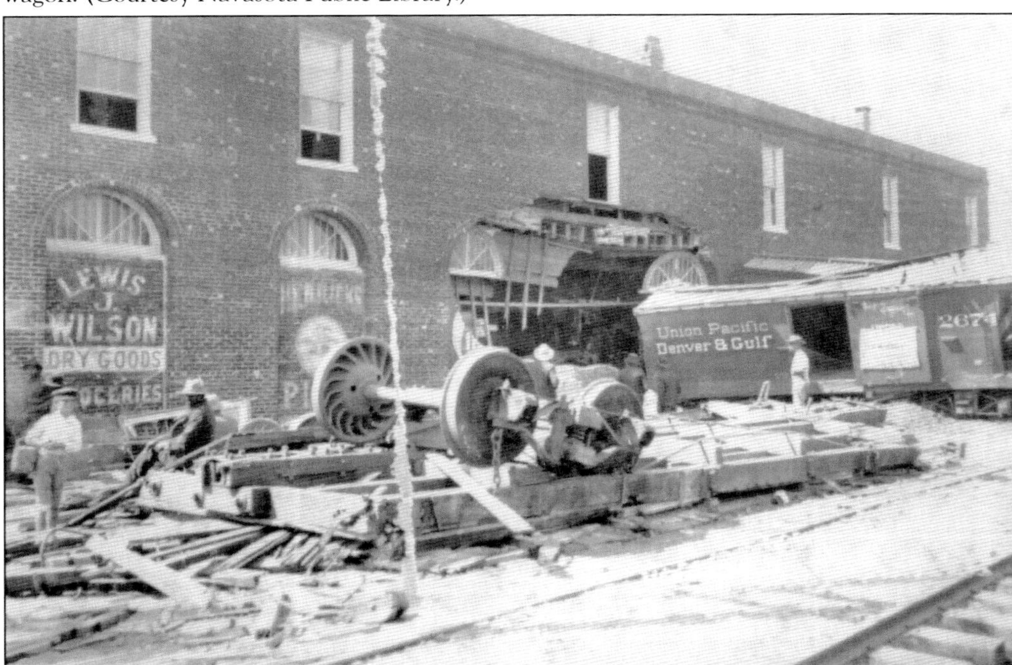

This is another photograph of the results of a wreck in the adventurous days of early rail travel through Navasota. Note the Lewis J. Wilson Dry Goods/Groceries sign in the background. Even brick buildings were precarious targets, it seems. (Courtesy Navasota Public Library.)

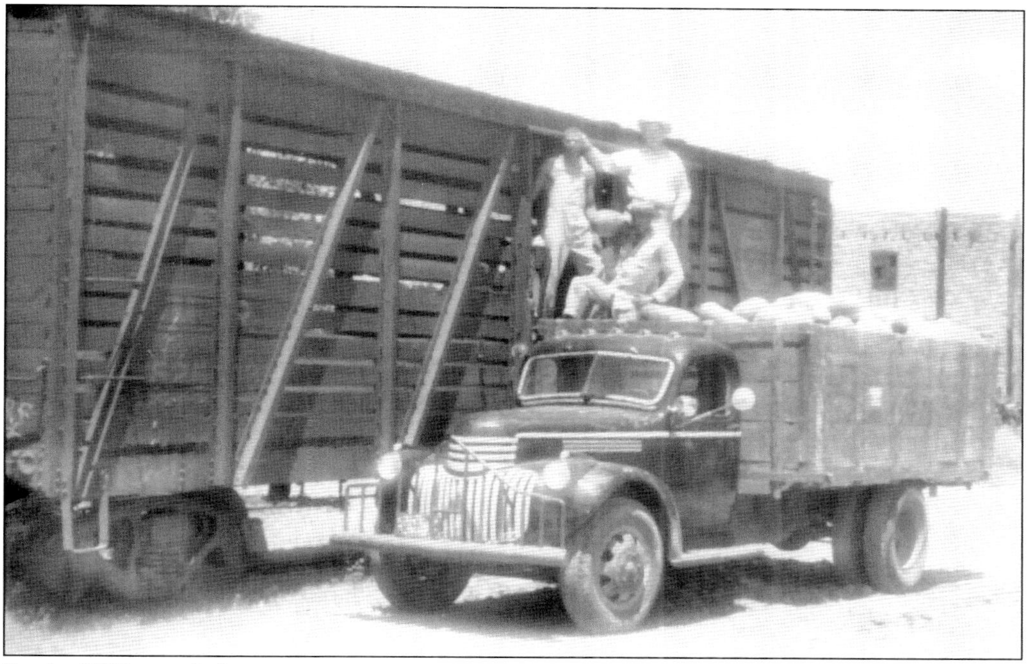

By the 1930s, truck farming was making great headway in the Navasota region. One of the main products was watermelon. The photograph above shows men bringing in a huge load of the fruit in their truck, ready to load onto boxcars. The photograph at right exemplifies the great mass of melons hauled over the country, making Navasota a key source of such produce. This photograph features Navasotan Levi Steptoe standing at the door, expressing awe at the sight of so many melons. Both photographs are dated 1938. (Both photographs courtesy Navasota Public Library.)

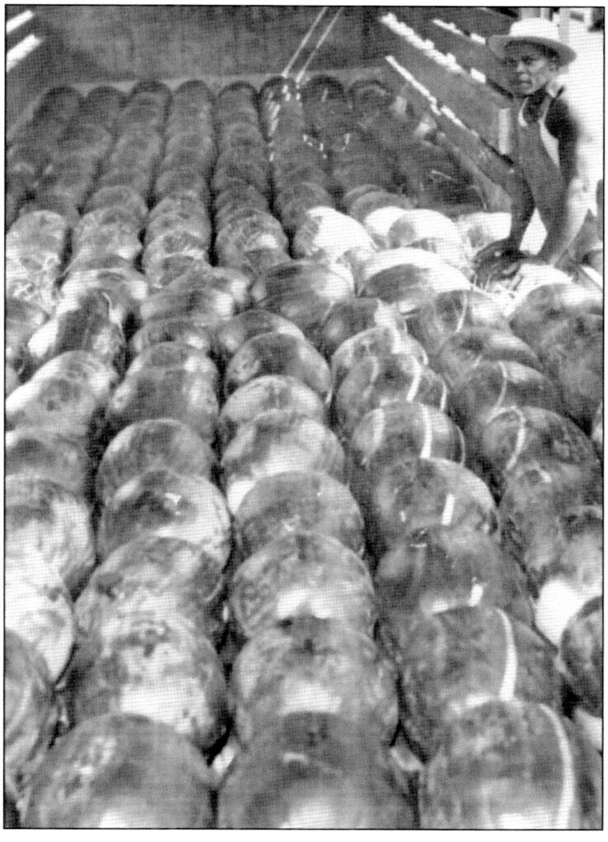

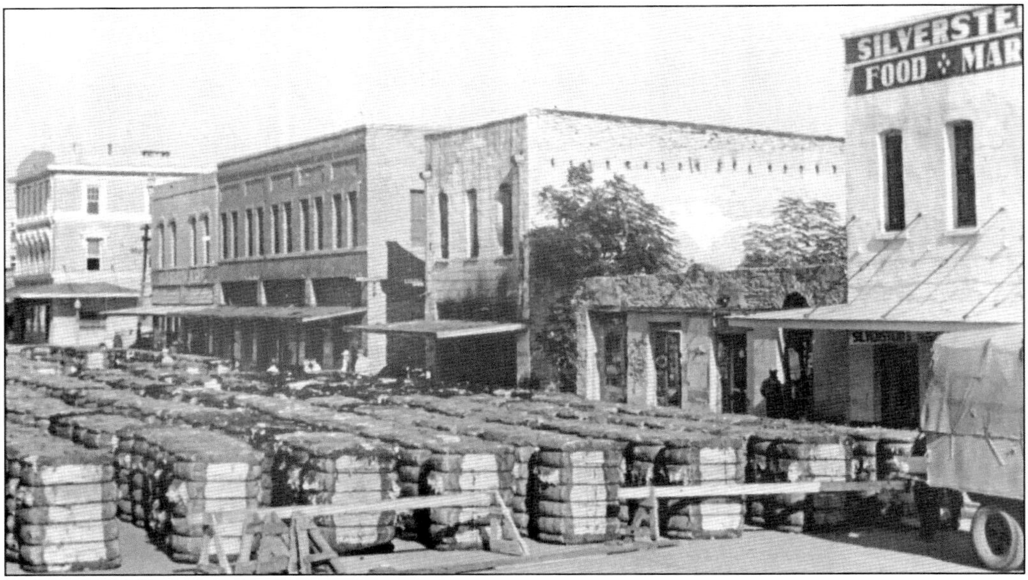

Spurred by the development of rail travel, Navasota became a center of the cotton trade. Here is a wonderful example of the main drag of Washington Avenue filled with baled cotton, ready for shipping. (Courtesy Russell Cushman Collection.)

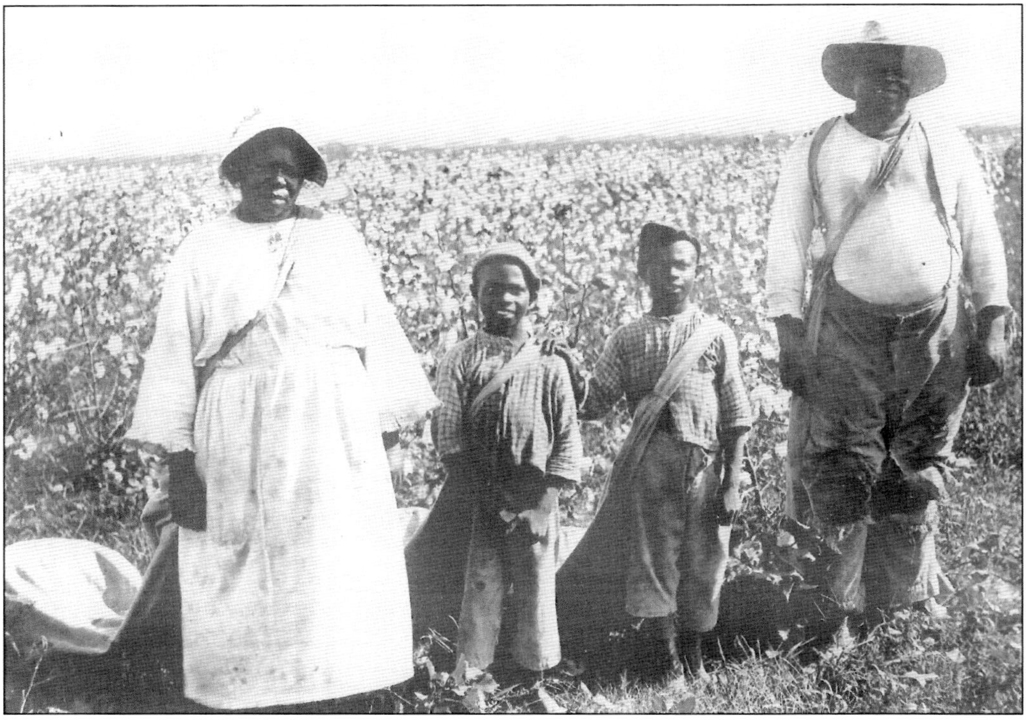

The cotton industry has had a cyclical existence. It was grand until the Civil War, declining after that tragedy, and even more so with epidemics of cholera and yellow fever. Over the succeeding years, it rose again until about 1940, when mechanized farming was in vogue. This affected the livelihood of workers, such as those seen here, who handpicked cotton. (Courtesy Marcus Mallard.)

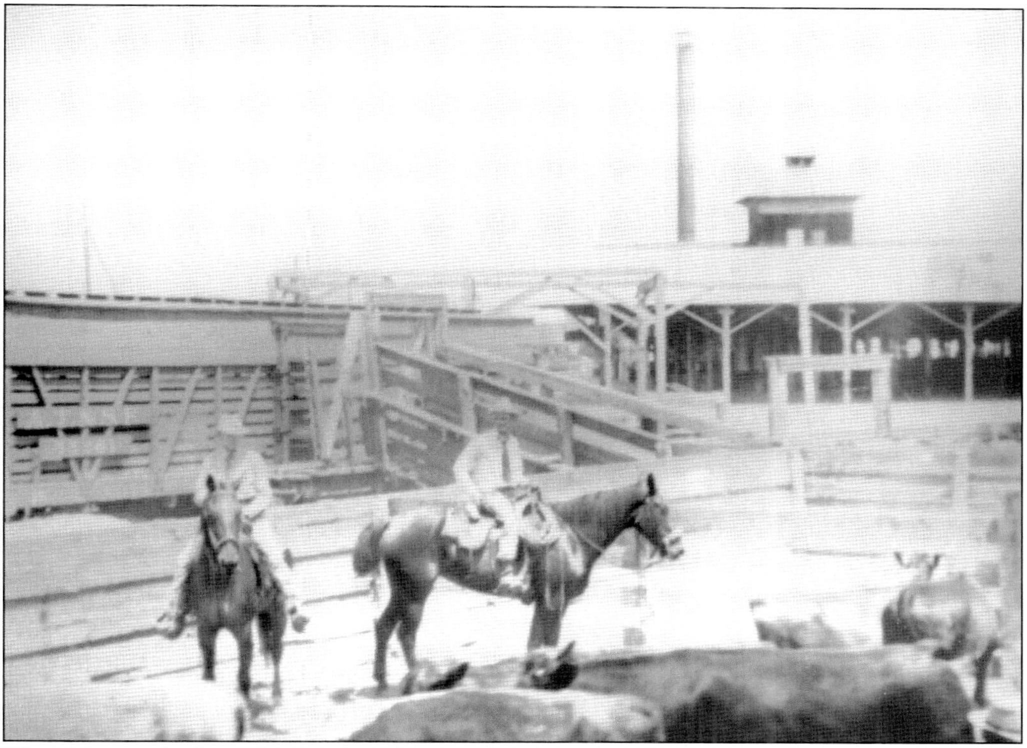

The photograph above depicts the advancement of Navasota's rail system to the point that men would drive their cattle into the city, where they would be processed through the Missouri Pacific Stockyard on Railroad Street. From there, cattle would be shipped by rail to meat packing plants in faraway places. Note the cotton compress in the background. The below photograph features the J.W. Smith Cattle Auction held in 1930. (Above, courtesy Navasota Public Library; below, courtesy Russell Cushman Collection.)

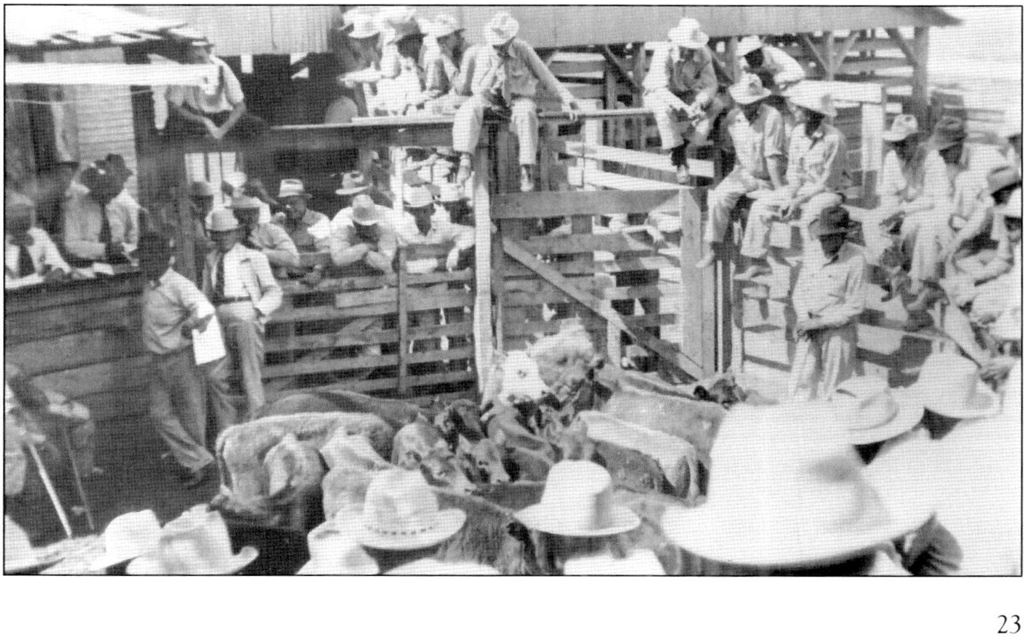

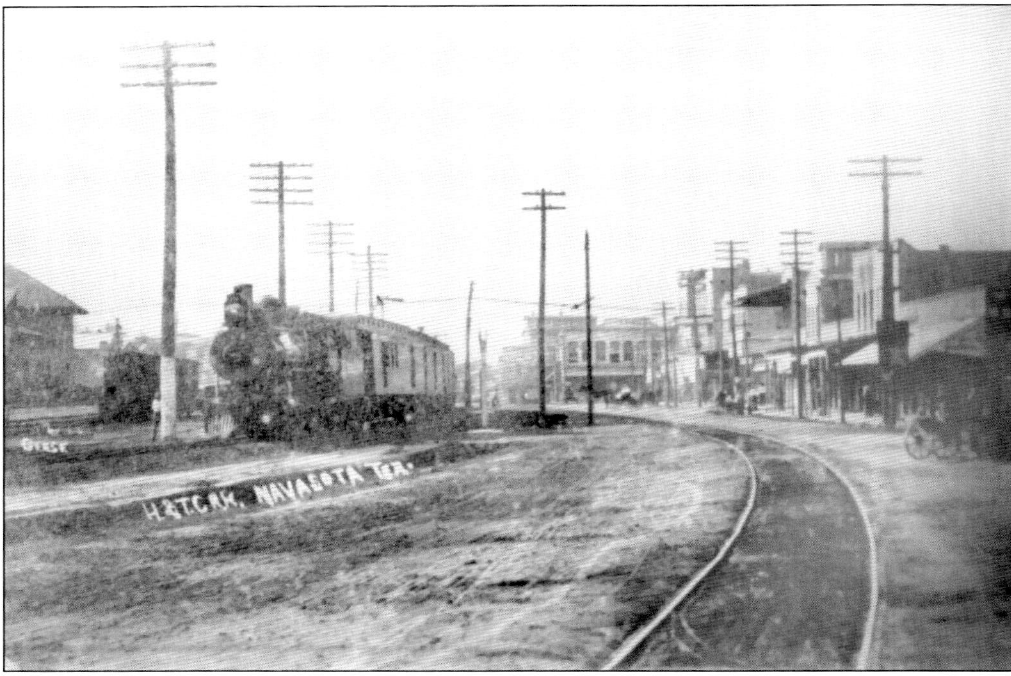

These photographs may be labeled "Horse and Buggy Days on Railroad Street," contrasting growing dependence on mechanized travel with tradition. In the photograph above, a train rolls in on the Houston and Texas Central line. A slice of the railroad station is visible on the left. On the right, one can discern W.W. Kennard Bottling Works. The photograph below features another view of Railroad Street in the horse-and-buggy days. (Above, courtesy Navasota Public Library; below, courtesy Russell Cushman Collection).

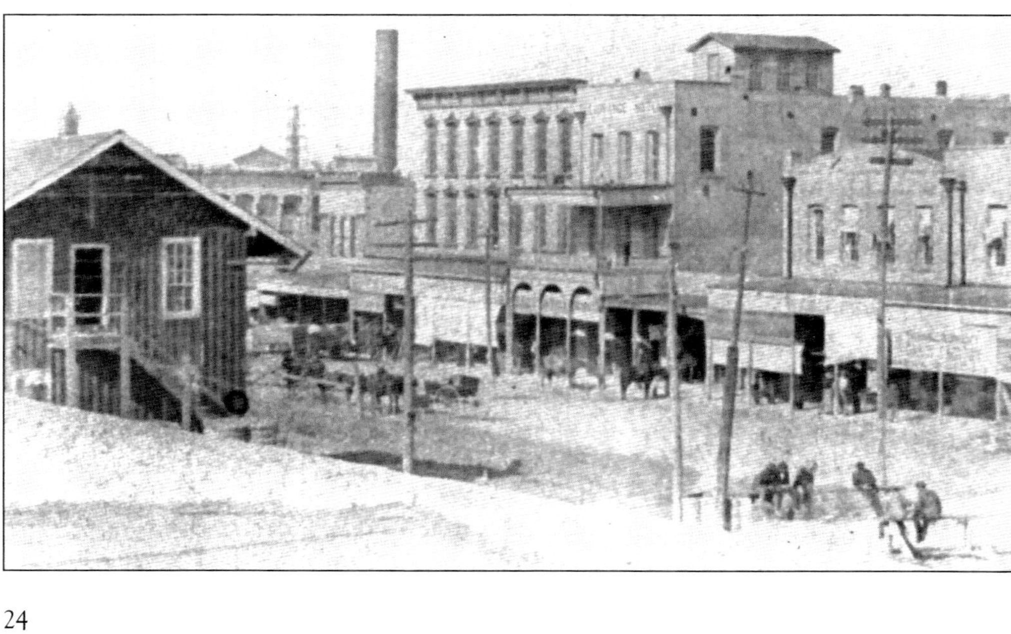

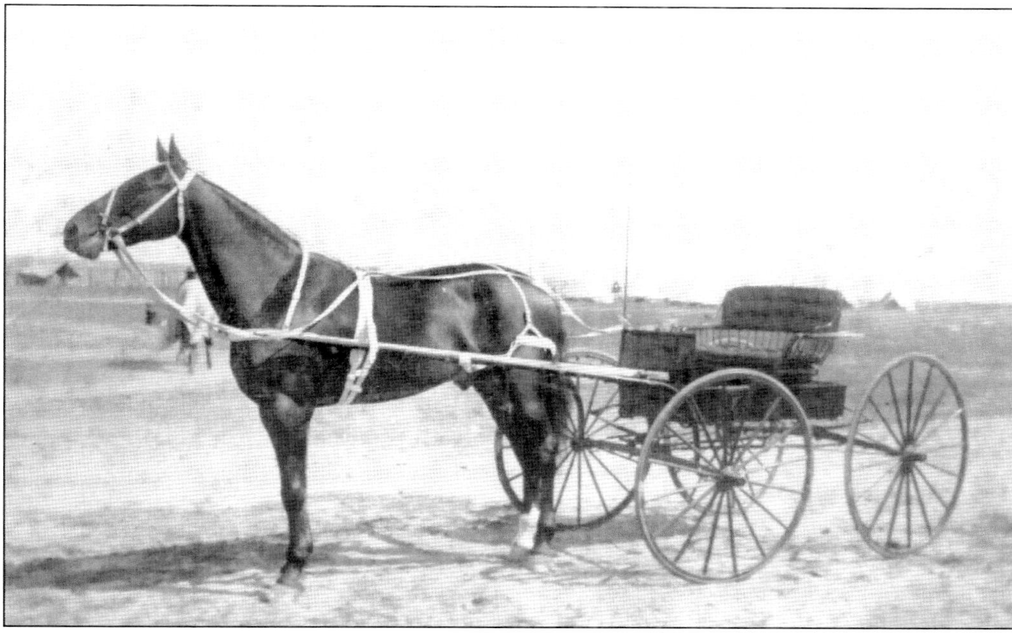

A Navasota horse stands proud in this photograph, seeming to defy the trend toward the "Iron Horse." In 1902, R.A. Patout, a leading citizen of Navasota known as "Robert I," entered a horse and carriage in a horse show in Houston. A special premium was won for the best roadster. (Courtesy Navasota Public Library.)

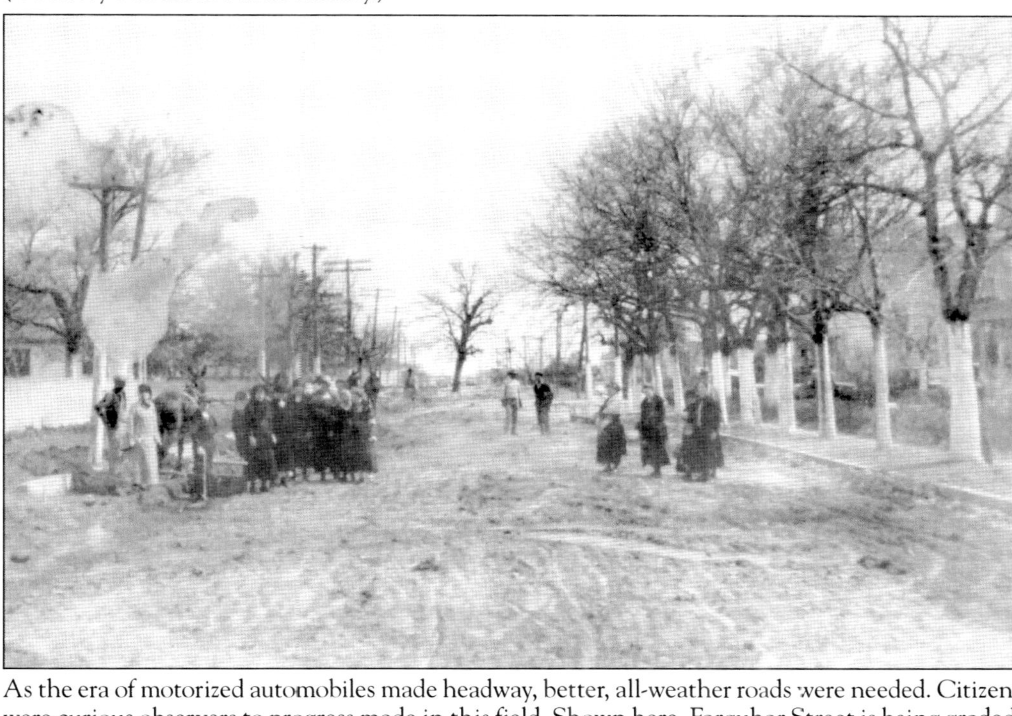

As the era of motorized automobiles made headway, better, all-weather roads were needed. Citizens were curious observers to progress made in this field. Shown here, Farquhar Street is being graded. Note the wooden curbs on the sides. (Courtesy Navasota Public Library.)

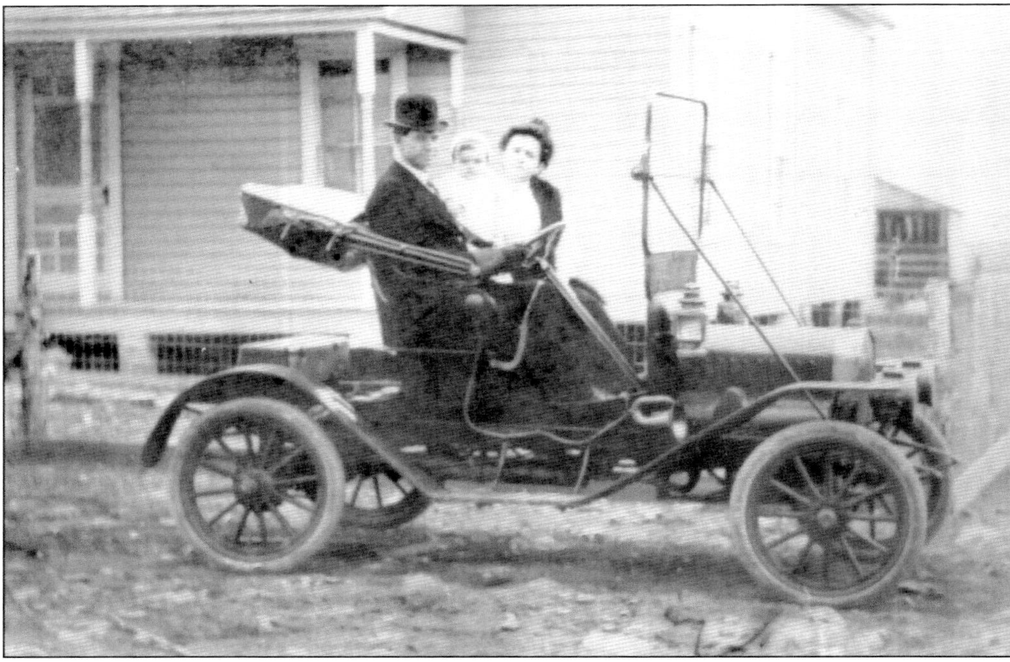

Though roads were being graded, not all were finished as the first cars began to make an appearance on Navasota's streets. Those first cars were simple but sturdy, ready-made for adventurous souls. Three of those adventurous souls are Dr. J.I. Collier, his wife, Susie Saunders Collier, and their son Ivan. (Courtesy Navasota Public Library.)

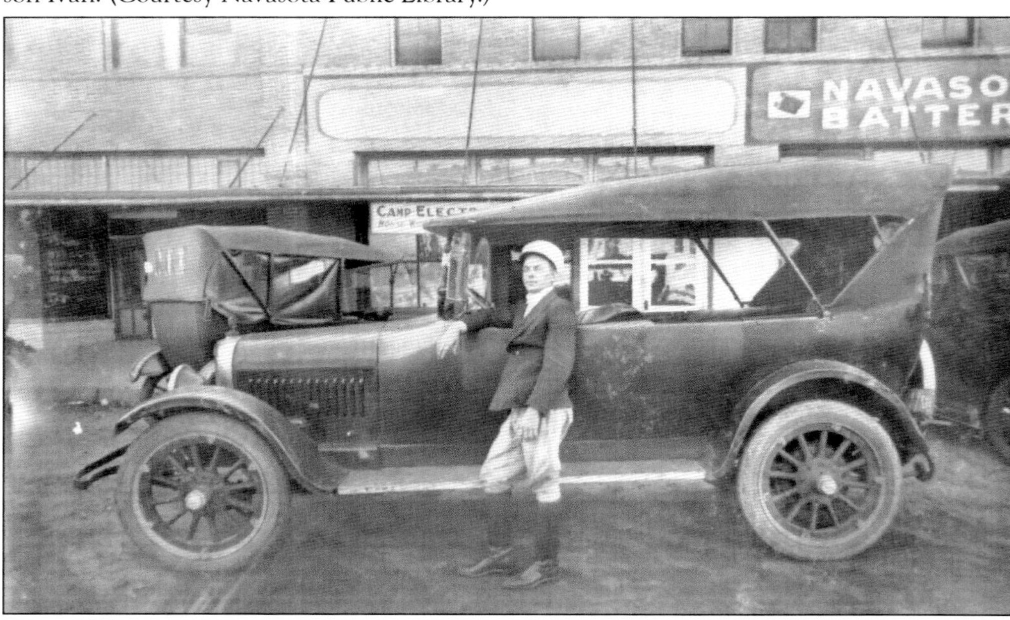

Some of those early Navasota automobiles were long and elaborate, with plenty of ventilation through open windows. Shown here, a driver is dressed for duty on Farquhar Street, parked in front of Navasota Battery and Camp Electric. The inscription on the back of the photograph asks, "Is it Father's touring car?" (Courtesy Navasota Public Library.)

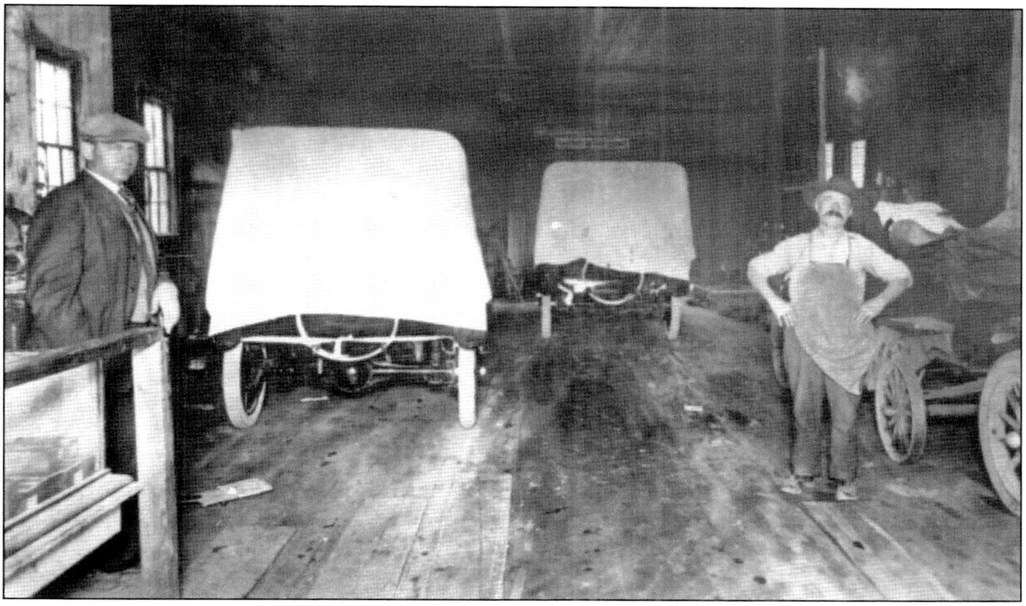

As automobiles became plentiful, the need arose for automobile repair shops. This c. 1915 photograph shows a garage in Navasota. C.W. Becker is on the left. Shoe repairman Carl Wink stands with his hands on his hips, wearing the apron. The building was known as the "Old Cheap John Place." Signs in the back read, "Not Responsible for Autos in Case of Fire" and "Positively No Tools Loaned." (Courtesy Navasota Public Library.)

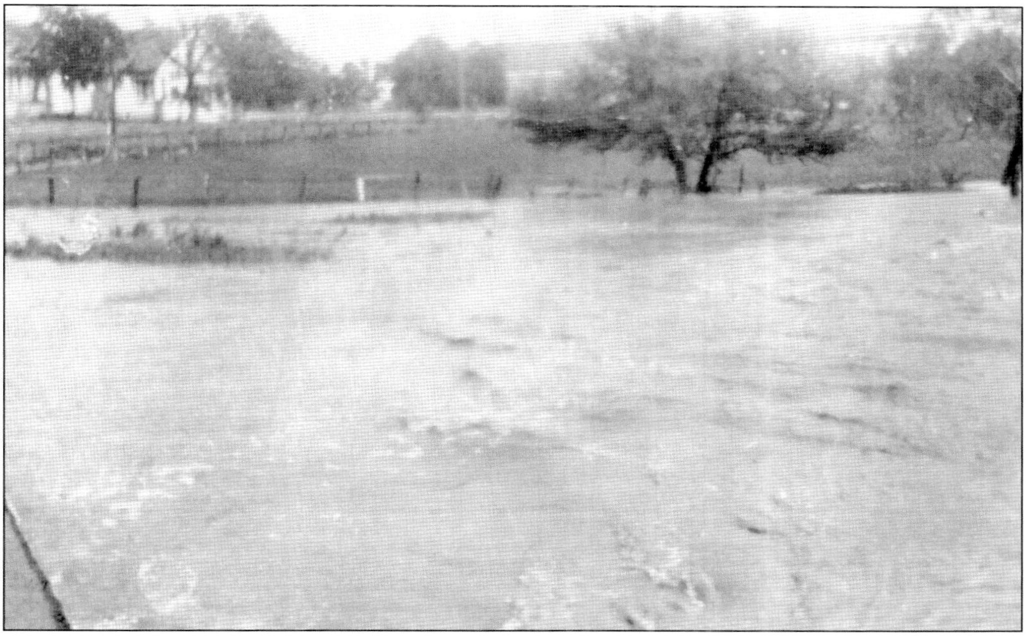

With the early automobiles traveling on largely unpaved roads, it was imperative that the weather cooperated. When the rains came, times were rough for automobile travelers. Navasota appears here in the 1920s, when rain fell in overabundance. This is a part of Navasota's Town Creek, overflowing its banks at that time. (Courtesy Navasota Public Library.)

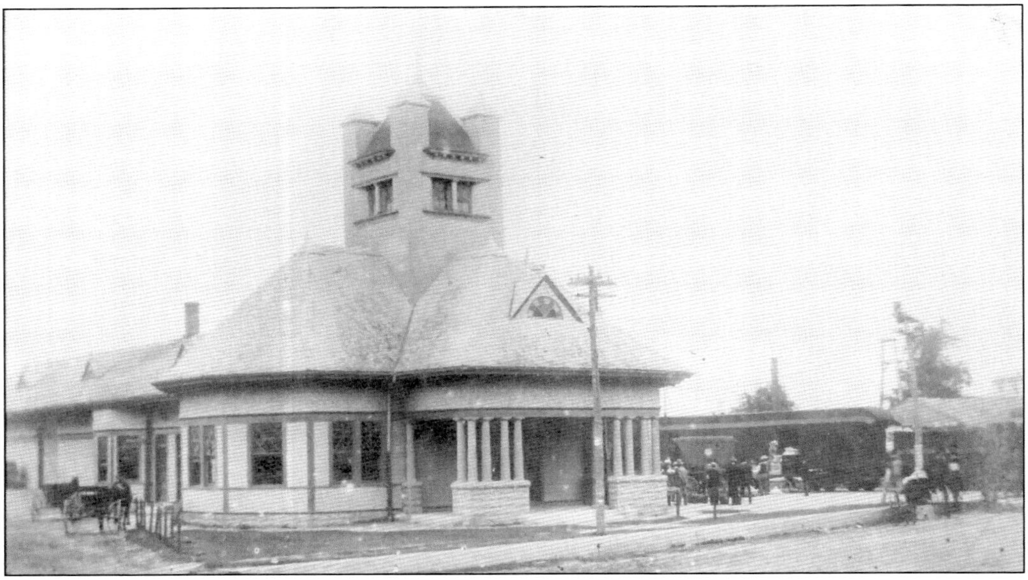

Navasota was once a town that could brag of two depots. The depot in the photograph above stood at the corner of Holland and Railroad Streets, while the depot below sat between the Santa Fe and Southern Pacific tracks, just south of the business district. The Houston and Texas Central Railroad came to Navasota in 1859. In 1883, the Gulf, Colorado, and Santa Fe Railway made its debut. This was followed in 1900 by the International and Great Northern Railroad, which established a line starting in Spring, extending to Fort Worth. Three years later, the same company extended its Navasota-Madisonville branch through Anderson, the line lasting until 1944. (Both, courtesy Marcus Mallard.)

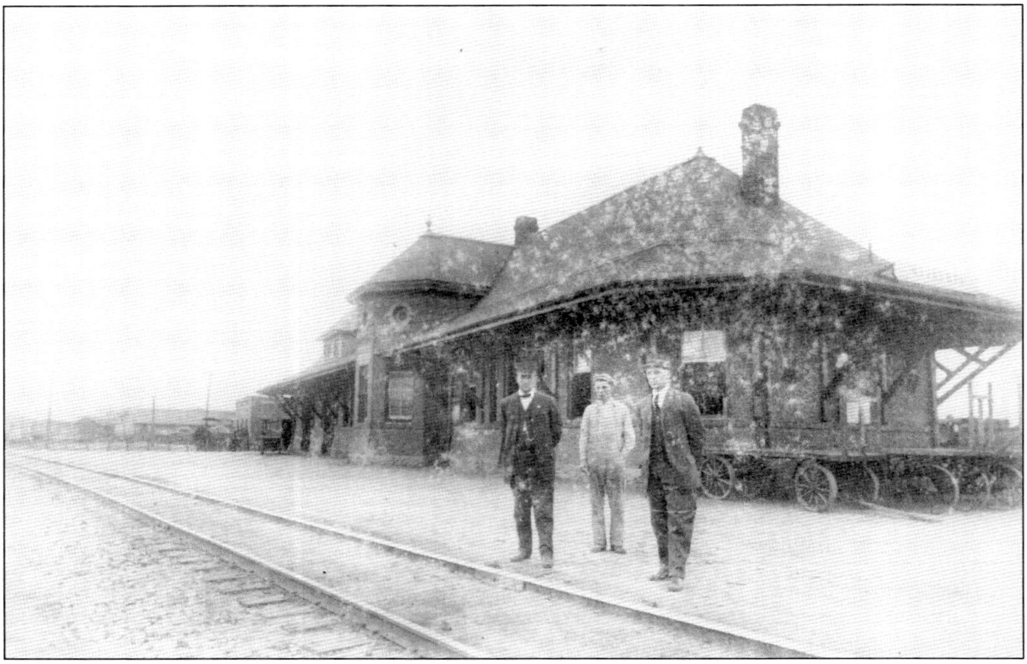

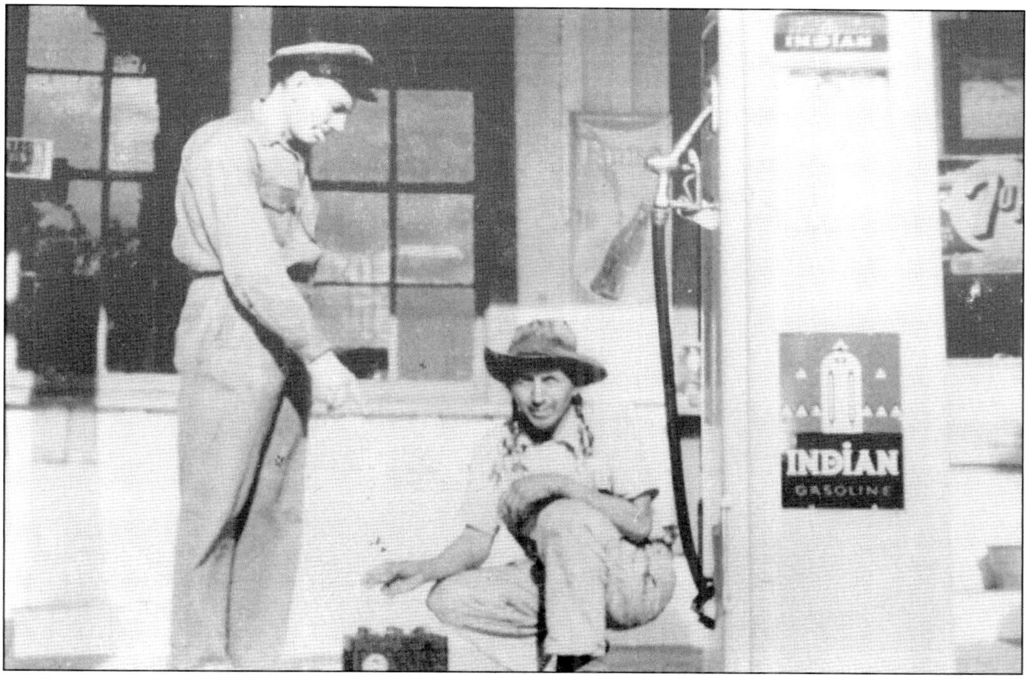

"Indian Gasoline" was in vogue in early Navasota; gasoline advertisements were numerous. A sample of the particular design, shown here, was sold on the Internet for $170 on March 14, 2010. Pictured here are Otto Druckhammer (standing) and Sky Eagle (kneeling). (Courtesy Marcus Mallard.)

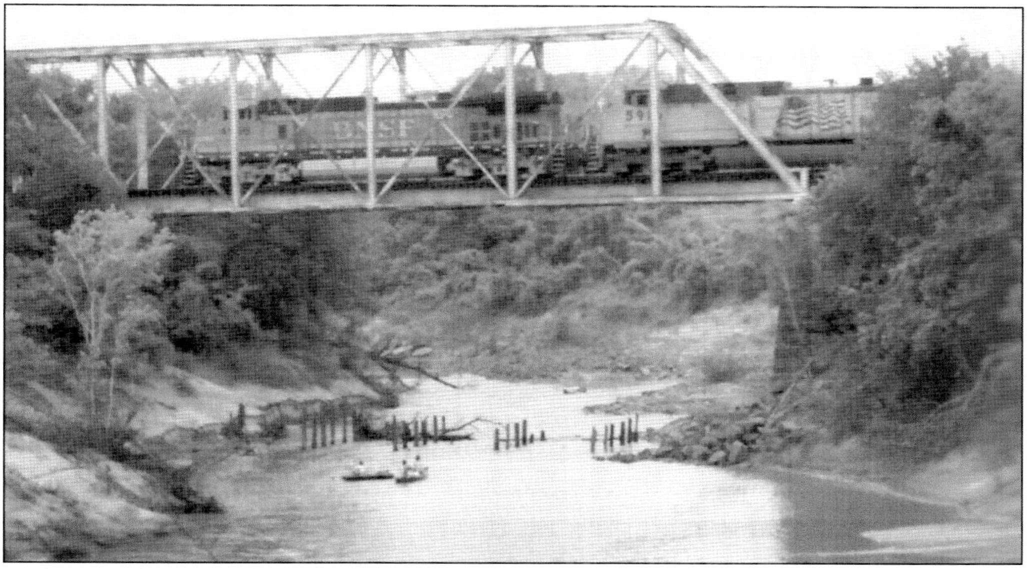

Highway and air travel have made great strides in Navasota; however, trains continue to thrive. Though passenger trains are currently out, freight is still a big business. Here is a photograph of a modern locomotive near Navasota. Several times a day, citizens of Navasota downtown are reminded of their history as a crossroads community as train whistles signal their arrival. (Courtesy Nancy Perry.)

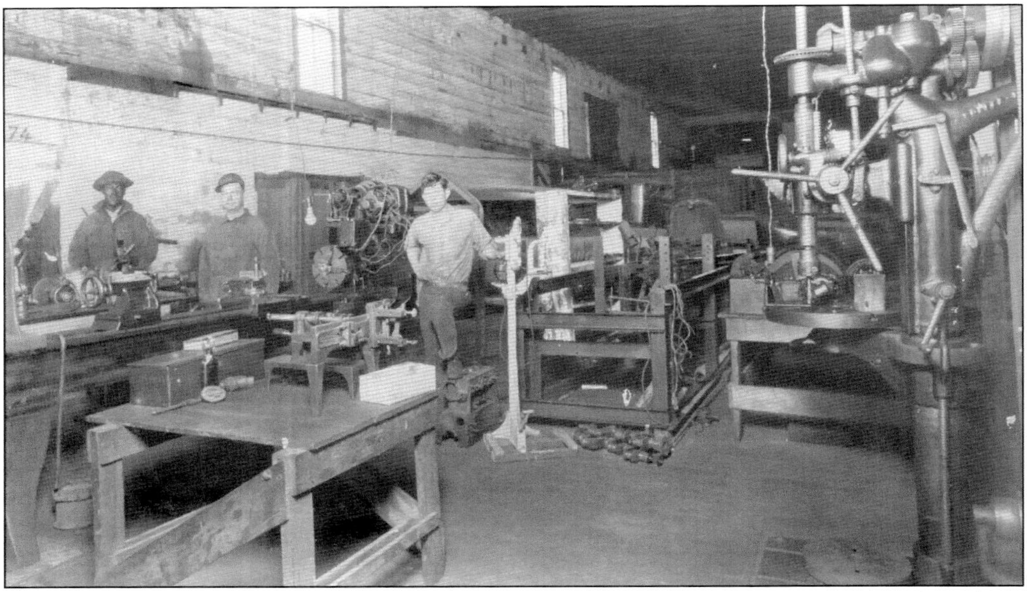

In the 1920s, Navasota was into an era of enhanced mechanization. Short's Garage and Machine Works in the Ahren Beck Building on West Washington Avenue testifies to the changing times. Owner Curtis C. Short appears in the middle, while the others are unidentified. (Courtesy Navasota Public Library.)

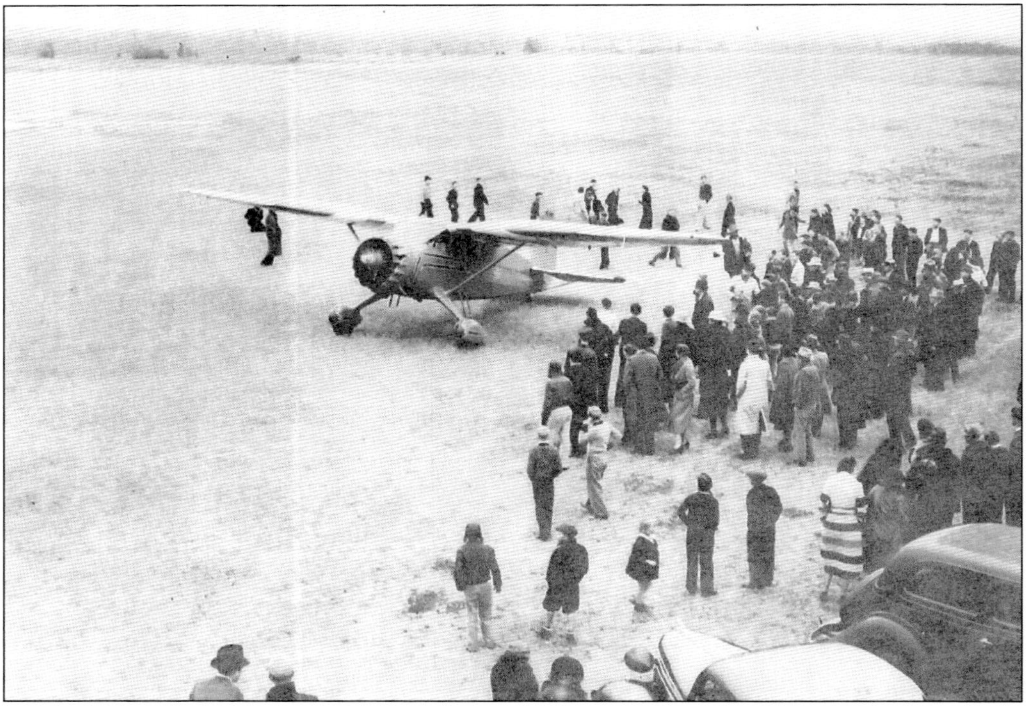

The first airplane lands in Navasota on what appears to be a cold day. With this event, Navasota was truly into the modern age, with all the modes of travel extant represented in its environs. (Courtesy Russell Cushman Collection.)

Three

PARADES AND EXHIBITIONS

Situated between the historic towns of Washington-on-the-Brazos and Anderson, the area that became Navasota is heir to events that brought Texas independence from Mexico. The spirit of freedom has been alive and well throughout Navasota's history as evidenced in its penchant for parades and in the nature of those parades.

The photographs in this chapter illustrate that Navasotans have embraced parades celebrating the pivotal Battle of San Jacinto, for example. Similarly, the Civil War era resonates with the citizenry of Navasota. Memories of the famous "Hood's Brigade" are especially significant. Company H of that legendary unit was formed in Grimes County.

Then there are the parades celebrating those who have served in later wars and a Labor Day parade. Furthermore, a love of Texas symbols is celebrated in the various versions of the Bluebonnet Parade over the years. The area surrounding Navasota is blessed with some of the loveliest bluebonnet fields in Texas.

Finally, just for fun, even May Fest has been a cause for celebration. The people of Navasota have a bent for festivals.

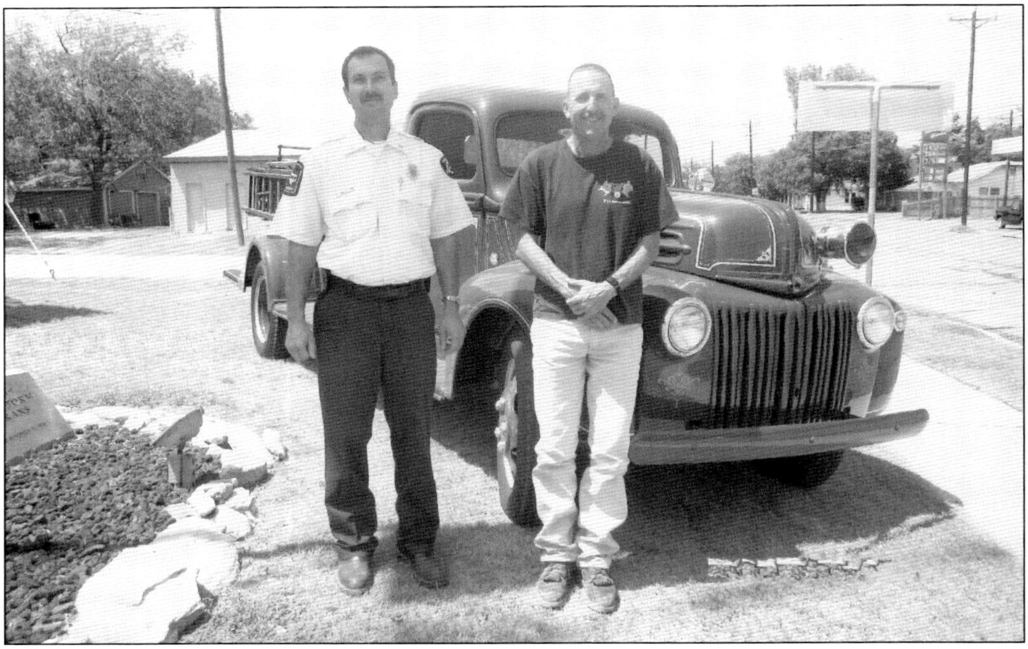

The fire department has been the initiator and supporter of many of the parades over the years. Fire chief Jason Katkosky and assistant Mitch Kroll are pictured here in 2011, standing by a remodeled vehicle dating to 1942. The fire department was organized formally in 1886 and has been housed in three different buildings. The present building was completed in 1993. The fire department has saved many ledgers and other artifacts for posterity. Within them are invaluable data for historians of the town, as they give information relating to events both of the history of the department itself, as well as of the broader history of the town. Another view of the 1942 vehicle is below. (Above, courtesy Joy Montgomery; below, courtesy Russell Cushman Collection.)

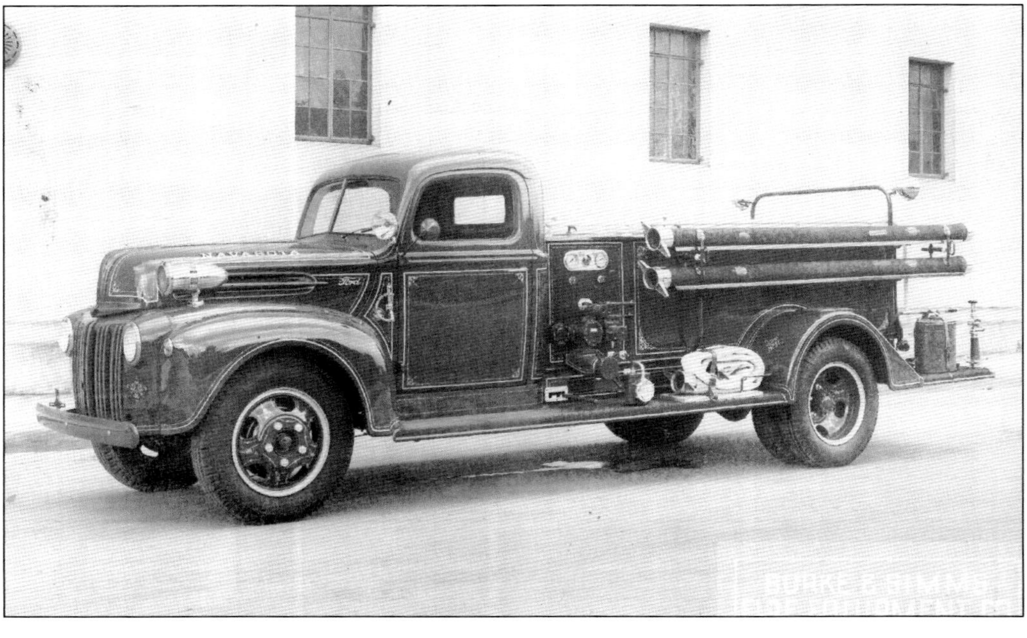

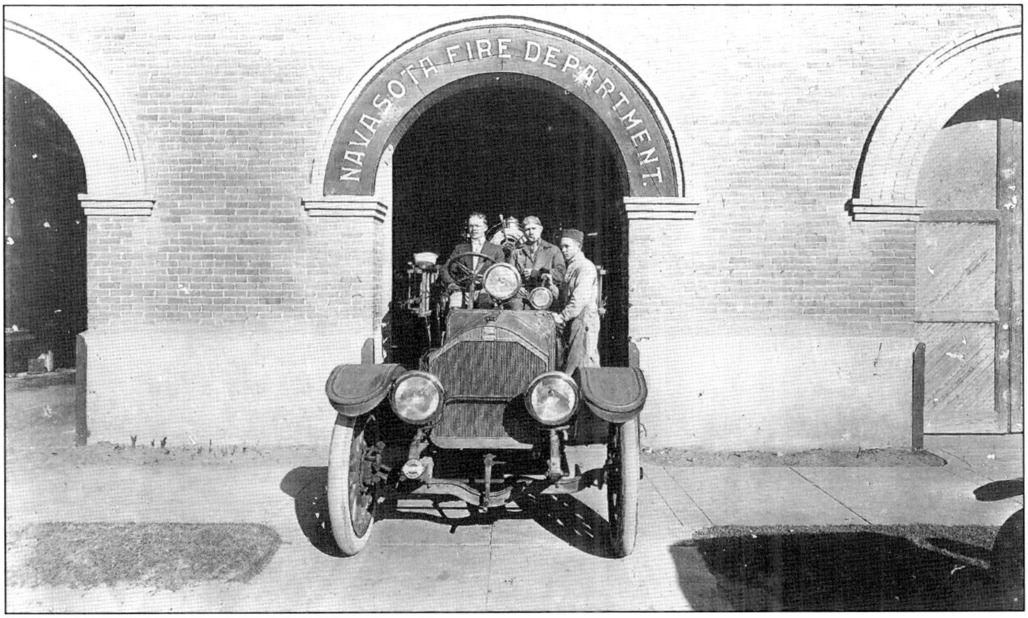

The Navasota Fire Department, then housed in the city hall dating to 1903, gathers in the 1920s. Pictured here are driver C.C. Short and George Clark, who lived with his wife, Lillian Floyd Clark. The other person is unidentified. (Courtesy Navasota Public Library.)

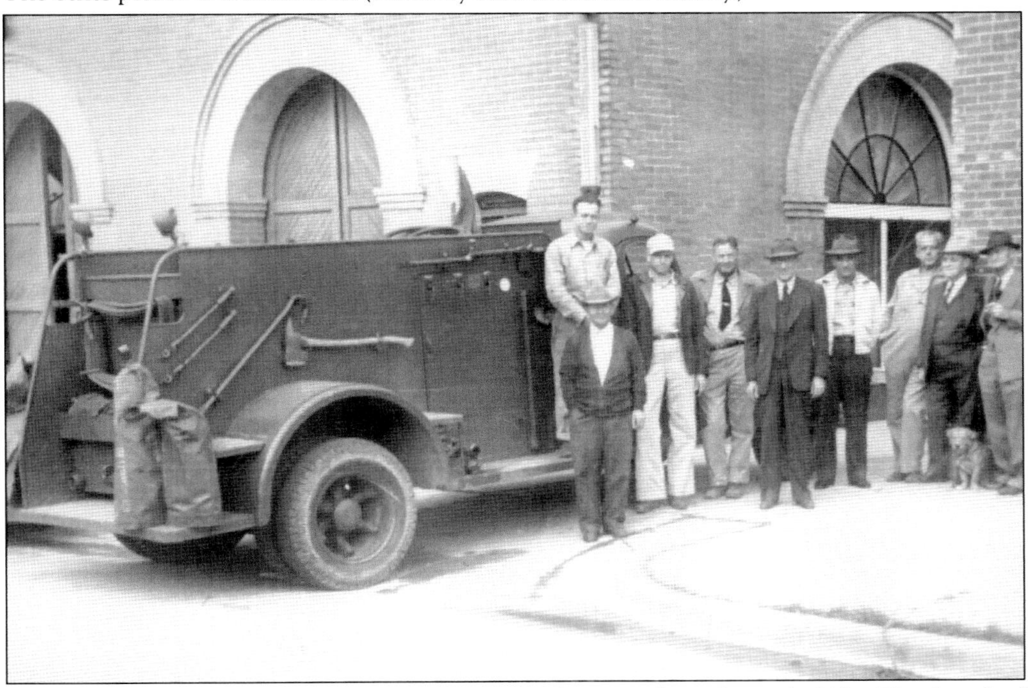

The volunteer fire department is pictured here with its truck in the mid-1940s. The fire chief at the time was E.P. Ayres. City hall was demolished in 1957, but a fire station continued on the site. That station was in use until the present station was built in 1993. (Courtesy Navasota Public Library.)

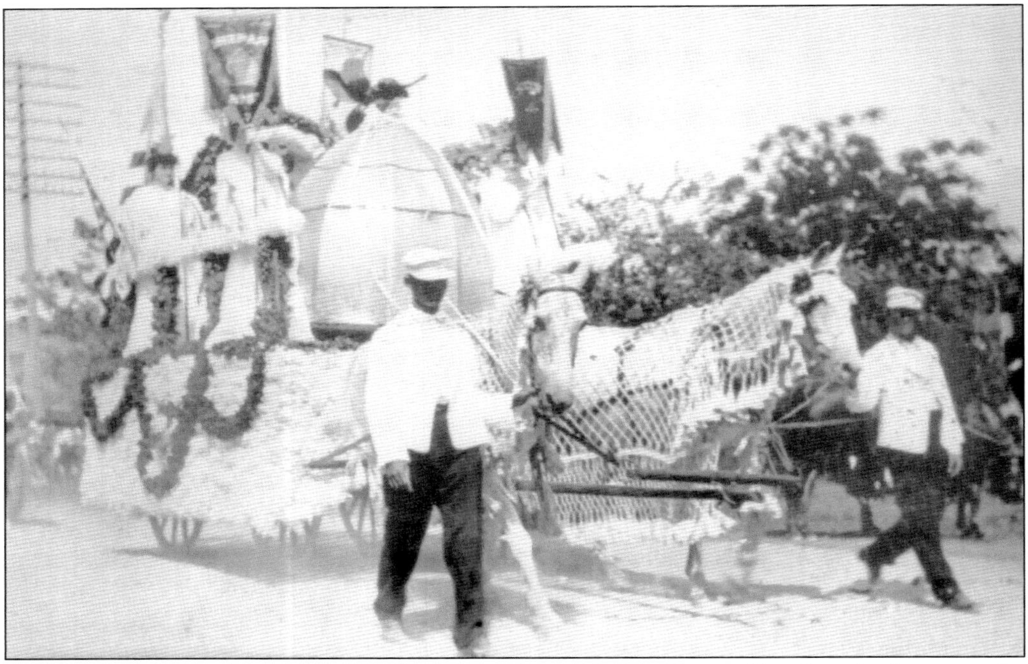

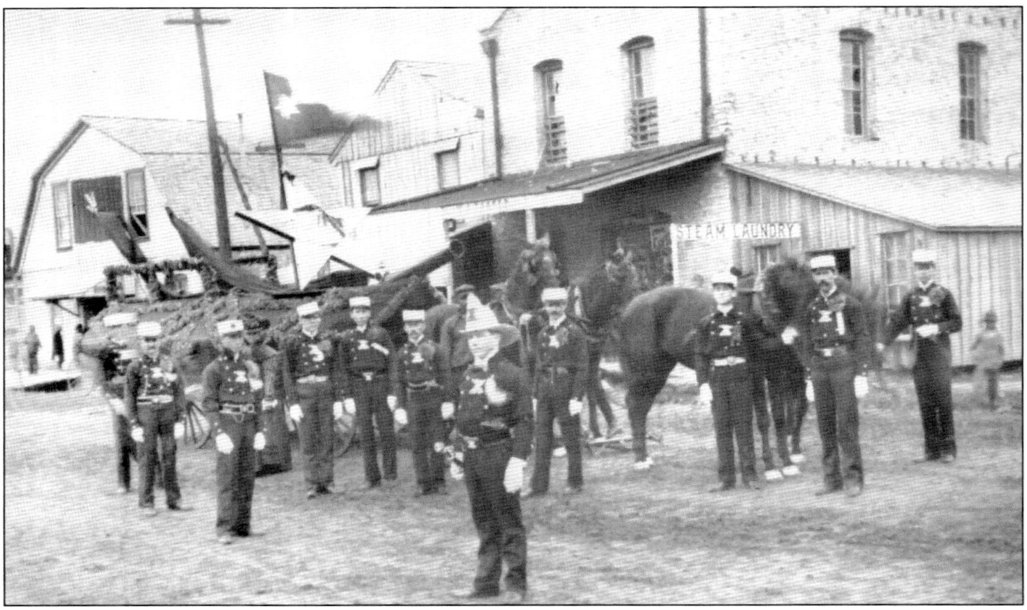

Seen in the above photograph is a float from the 1899 San Jacinto Day Parade. It was at the Battle of San Jacinto on April 21, 1836, that Texas gained its independence from Mexican troops fighting under president and general Santa Anna, who had just inflicted the massacre at the Alamo. A good number of citizens from the area surrounding what would become Navasota participated in the battle. Among them was Andrew Montgomery, a direct ancestor of the authors of this book. The photograph below is titled "Navasota Hook and Ladder Co., No. 1." This was taken after the parade on April 21, 1909. Capt. R.A. Patout is in the foreground. (Both, courtesy Navasota Public Library.)

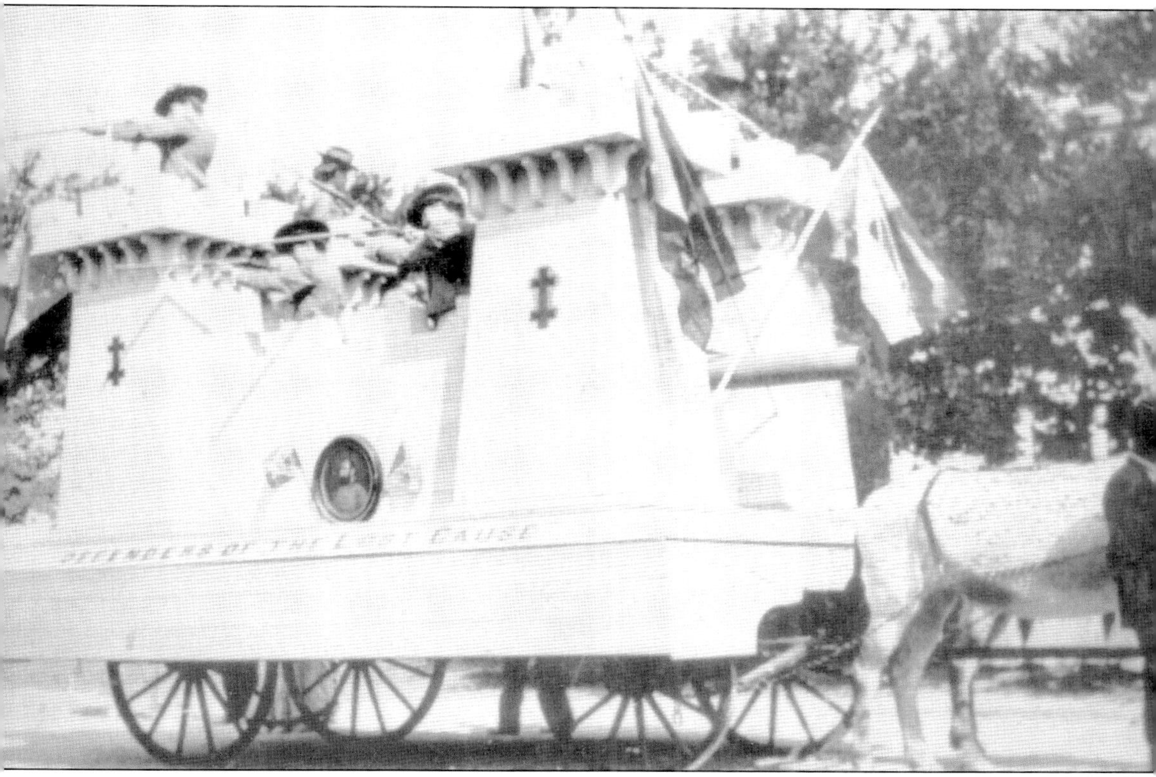

A parade was held honoring veterans of the famous Texas Hood's brigade in 1907, shown here. Gracing the side of the "fort" is a portrait of Gen. Stonewall Jackson. Under the portrait, the caption reads, "Defenders of the Lost Cause." Company H of the Fourth Texas Regiment of Hood's Brigade was a tri-county company. Formed at Red Top just east of Shiro, Grimes County, the captain of the company was Proctor P. Porter of Montgomery County, while the first lieutenant was James T. Hunter of Walker County. The second lieutenant of Company H was Thomas M. Owens of Grimes County. The brigade was named for Gen. John Bell Hood. For a while, however, Gen. Jerome B. Robertson of Independence, Texas, just northwest of Navasota, led the brigade. (Courtesy Russell Cushman Collection.)

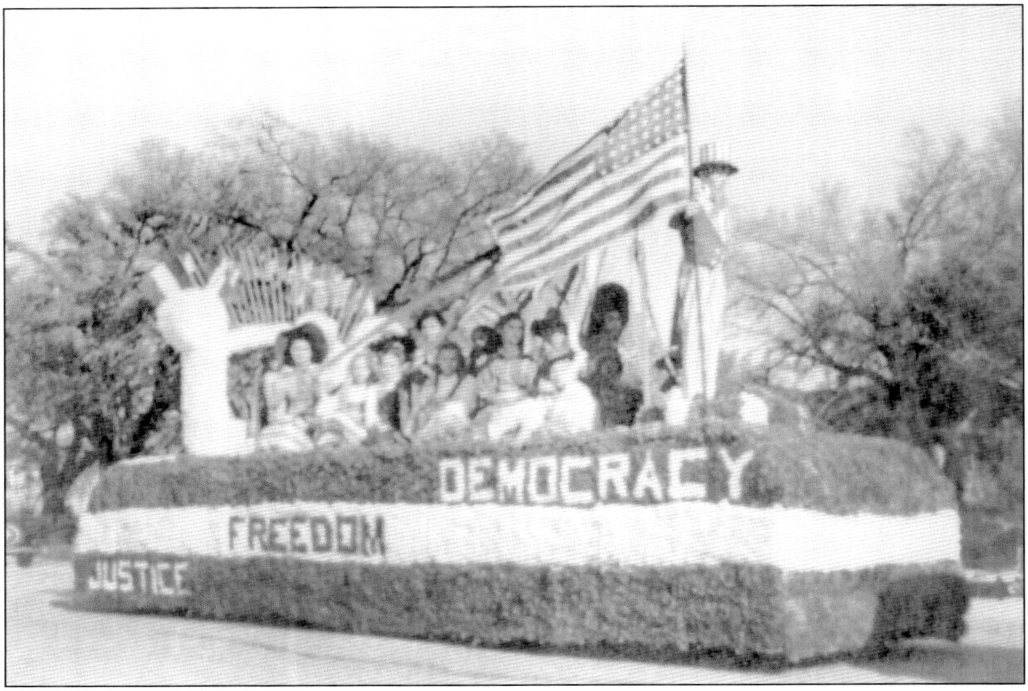

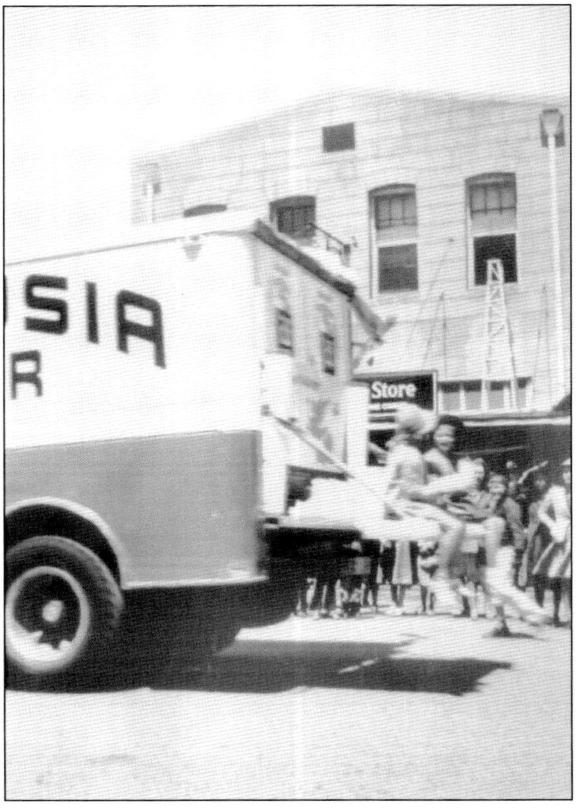

The area around Navasota features some of the most beautiful fields of bluebonnets in the Bluebonnet State, one of the area's foremost attractions. Navasota's Bluebonnet parades are also popular. Pictured in April 1941, this parade featured the patriotic temper of the times. Note the words "Justice, Freedom, Democracy" printed under an American flag. (Courtesy Navasota Public Library.)

Here is another photograph of the 1941 Bluebonnet Parade. Mary Lou Houston and Louise Pearson dangle their legs off the Sol Meyer's Flour truck. (Courtesy Navasota Public Library.)

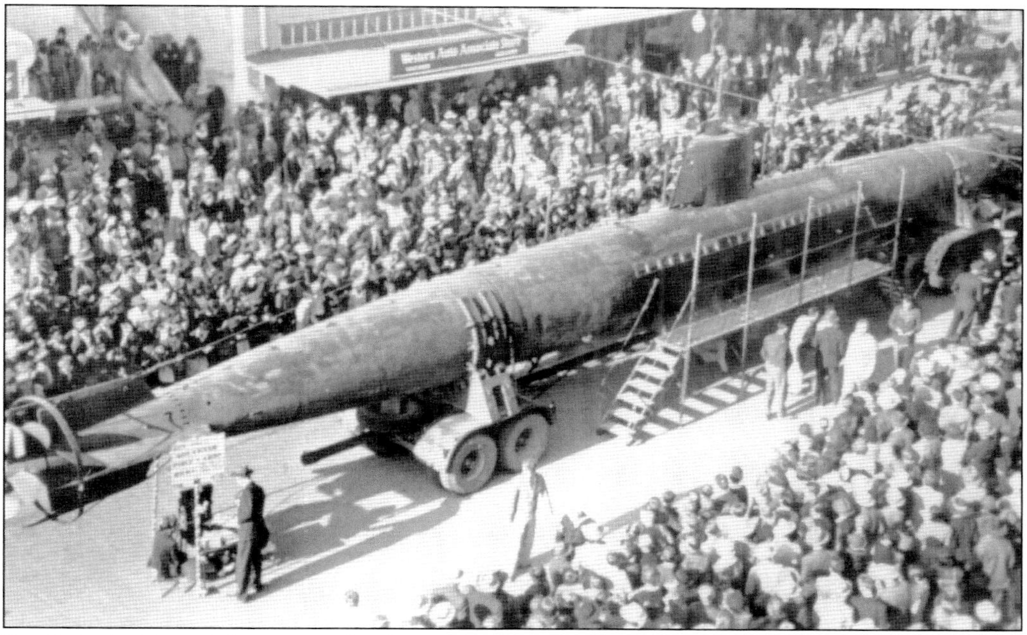

By 1943, the United States was deeply involved in World War II. On February 15, 1943, primary focus was on Japan, with memories still fresh of the infamous attack at Pearl Harbor. Shown here, multitudes turned out for a World War II bond drive on Washington Avenue, which featured a Japanese missile. Pictured below is the exotic Perian Club float in a Fireman's Parade, date unknown. From left to right in the float are Mrs. Blackshear holding Bess Roan, later Bess E.K. Rowe; Pearl Garvin, later Pearl J.T. Swanson, holding Lillian Graig; unidentified holding Myrtle Evans, later Myrtle Henry Baker; and Cora Froelich, later Cora F. Winter, holding Irma, later Irma Chas Lincoln. (Both, courtesy Navasota Public Library.)

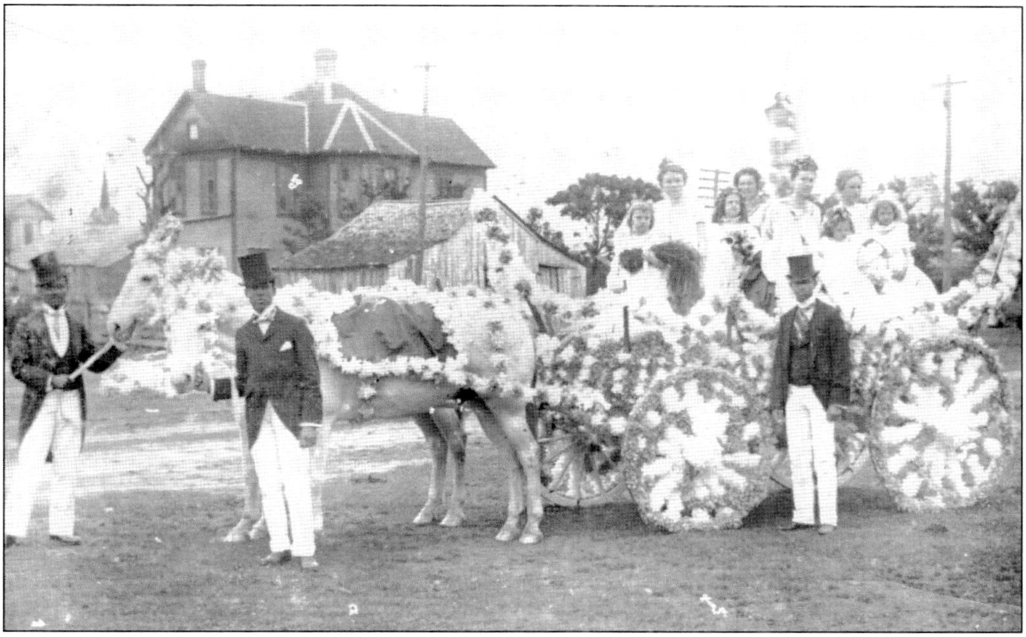

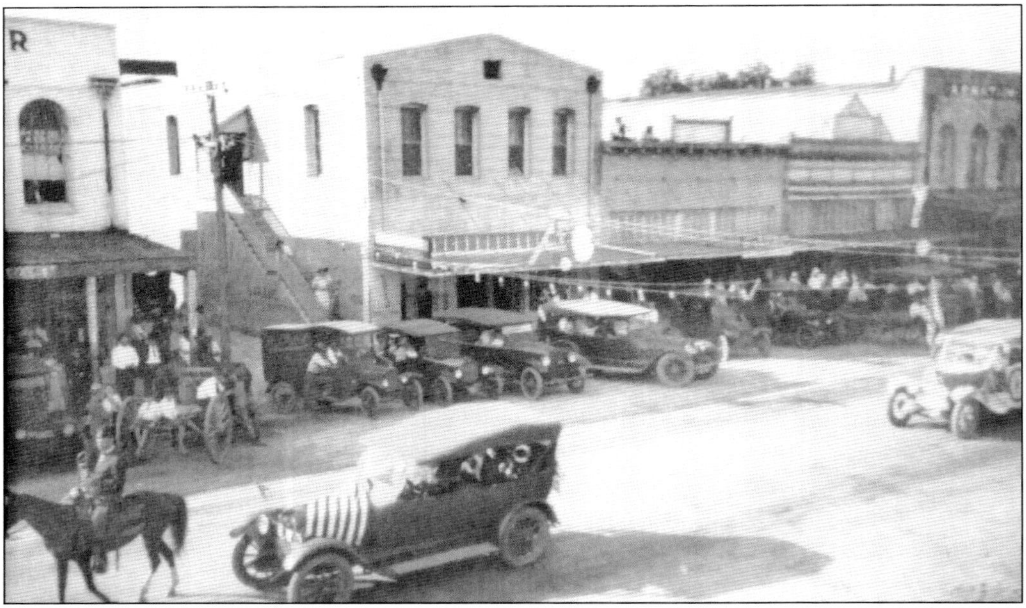

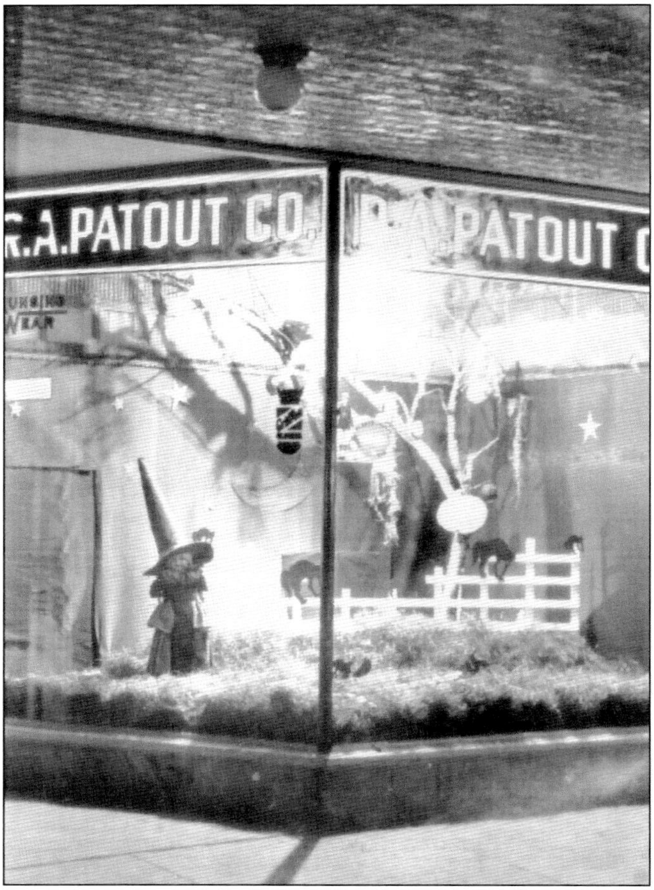

The 1921 photograph above shows a Labor Day Parade down Washington Avenue. Navasotans were proud of the strides made in labor and were ready to celebrate in a fashion first marked out in New York City on Tuesday, September 5, 1882. By 1884, Monday had become the designated day of the festival. Speculation centers on either Peter J. McGuire or Matthew Maguire as founders of the day. The photograph at left is further evidence that Navasota has ever been a city of public celebration; in 1928, the R.A. Patout Store window is ready to welcome the spirits of Halloween. (Both, courtesy Navasota Public Library.)

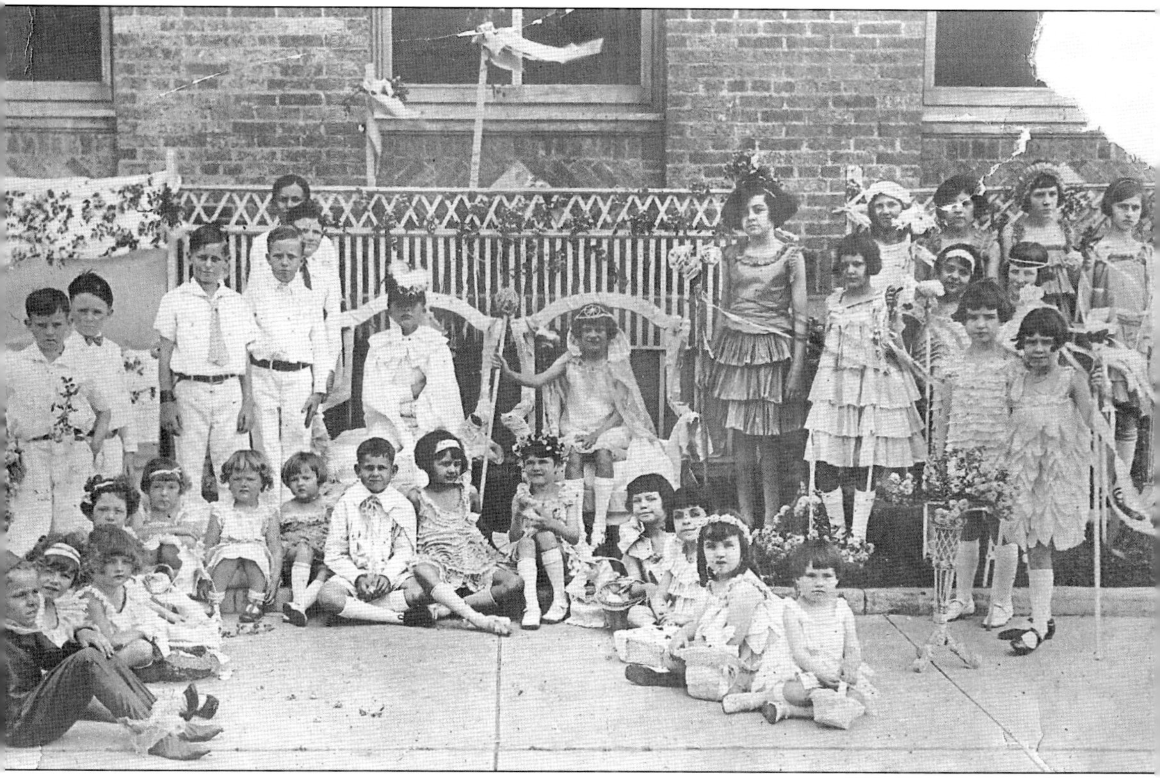

Yet another celebration in Navasota was the May Fete, the first of its kind. From left to right (seated) are Billy Williams, Madie Givinity, Gwendolyn Guess, ? Smith, Joyce Ann Moore, Edna Swanson, Eugenia Davison, Max Crittenden, Mary Ellen Brule, Mary Grace Spann, Mary Virginia Bledsoe, Ruth Nemir, Margaret Johnson, and Lillian Alley; (left, standing) W.C. Alley, Osborne Johnson, Kenneth Bowen Jr., James S. Harrison III, Robert Lord, Dan Swanson; the king is Erwin Ney, the queen is Daisy Love Harrison; (right, standing, first row) ? Bryan, Mary Terrell; (right, standing, second row) Katherine Ewing, Clara Maudella Brule, and Ruth Neal Todd; (right, standing, third row) Doris Coe, Olga Crittenden, Lucille Nemir, ? Lindsay, and Laura D. Gibson. (Courtesy Navasota Public Library.)

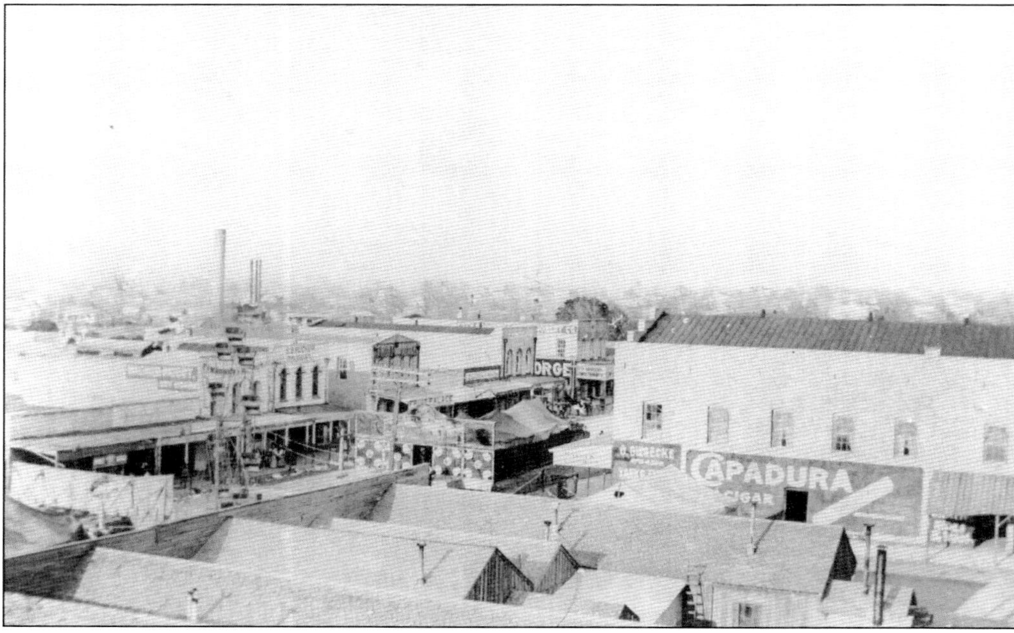

A carnival is held on Washington Avenue in 1890. As seen here, the carnival is set up in the middle of the street in the main part of town. (Courtesy Russell Cushman Collection.)

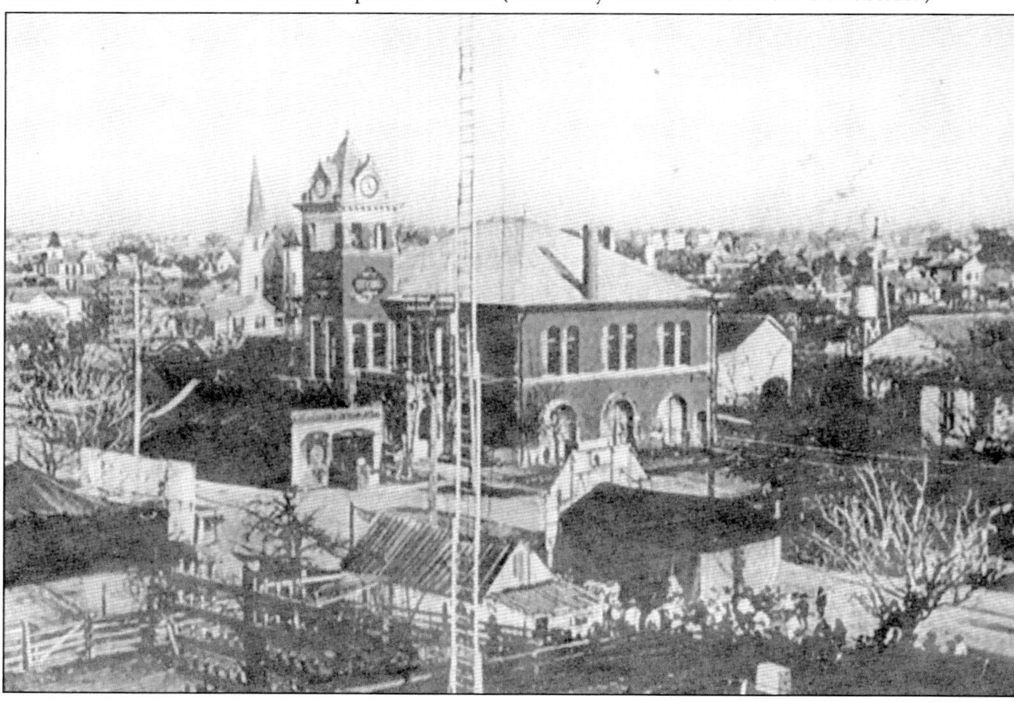

Sometime after the carnival on Washington Avenue in 1890, a circus came to town. Note several tents around city hall. One is directly in front of city hall, another crowds the site of the present-day post office, and another is at the location of the present-day Corner Café. (Courtesy Russell Cushman Collection.)

Four

Innovation and Imagination

While Navasotans pay homage to the past and its heroes, they are also a forward-looking people, prone to innovation in various fields and with the imagination to bring their ideas to fruition.

For example, the citizens took to the idea of canning their meats to better preserve their food. Navasotans quickly warmed to the practice. And it came naturally to the people of this city to engage the cotton industry and build fine gins. After all, the first cotton crop and first gin in Anglo-Texas was just a few miles below the later town of Navasota, courtesy of the intrepid Jared Groce. Furthermore, it was a Navasotan who played a giant role in developing new avenues for cotton with a world-class plant centered on cottonseed.

Navasota has been blessed with a long list of superbly gifted and energetic medical doctors who have served their city and country magnificently. Among their contributions were pioneering efforts toward addressing the dreaded yellow fever epidemics of the 1860s.

Imagination was rife in several works of history over the years, recording for posterity the times in which the authors' lived. Supplementing efforts to preserve history is a fine array of artists. And then there is music. The Trans-Brazos Blues is a phenomenon that can rightly be called "the Navasota sound." Continuing the plethora of excellence in the fine arts, Navasota has a history of high-quality theatrical productions.

Dating from the 19th century, a key role in plying the mind to address pivotal issues of politics and social issues has been played by the women of Navasota. It was, for example, a women's club that started the first library.

Navasota: a city by two rivers, blessed with imagination and a penchant for innovation.

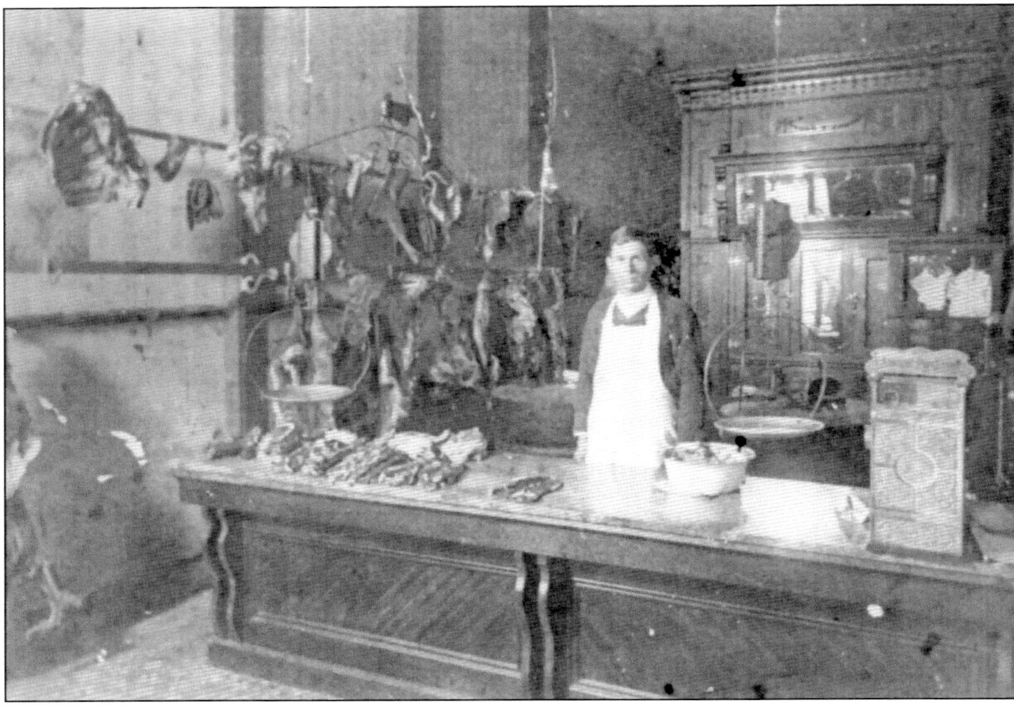

The butcher shop of Ed K. Woodward of Navasota is pictured here in the mid-1890s. A.J. Keith worked here as a teenager for his aunt and uncle. Typically, meat was cut to a uniform shape, permitting gradual and consistent drying. (Courtesy Navasota Public Library.)

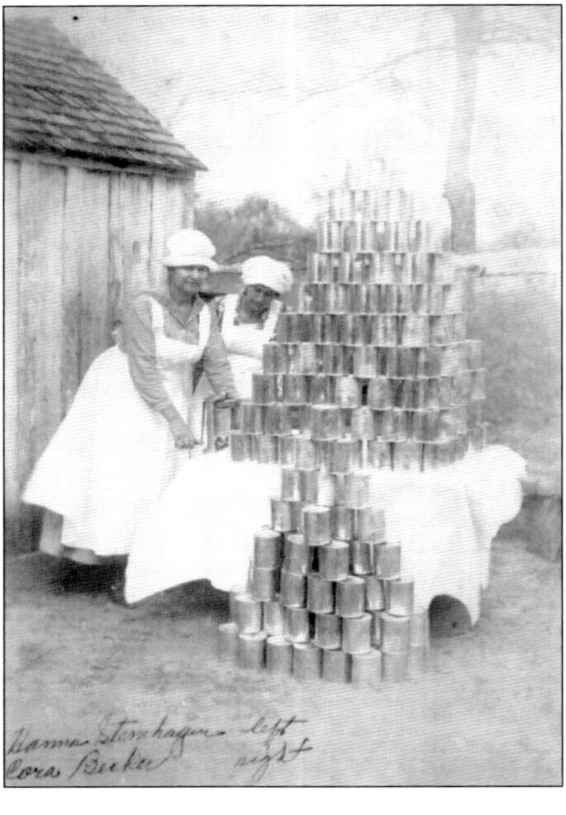

During the Depression of the 1930s, county agents were instrumental in teaching citizens to preserve food by canning in tins. From left to right, Hannah Becker Steinhagen and Cora Becker seal tins at the Christian Becker homestead. During the World War II years, about 5,000 canning centers were established in communities across the country. (Courtesy Navasota Public Library.)

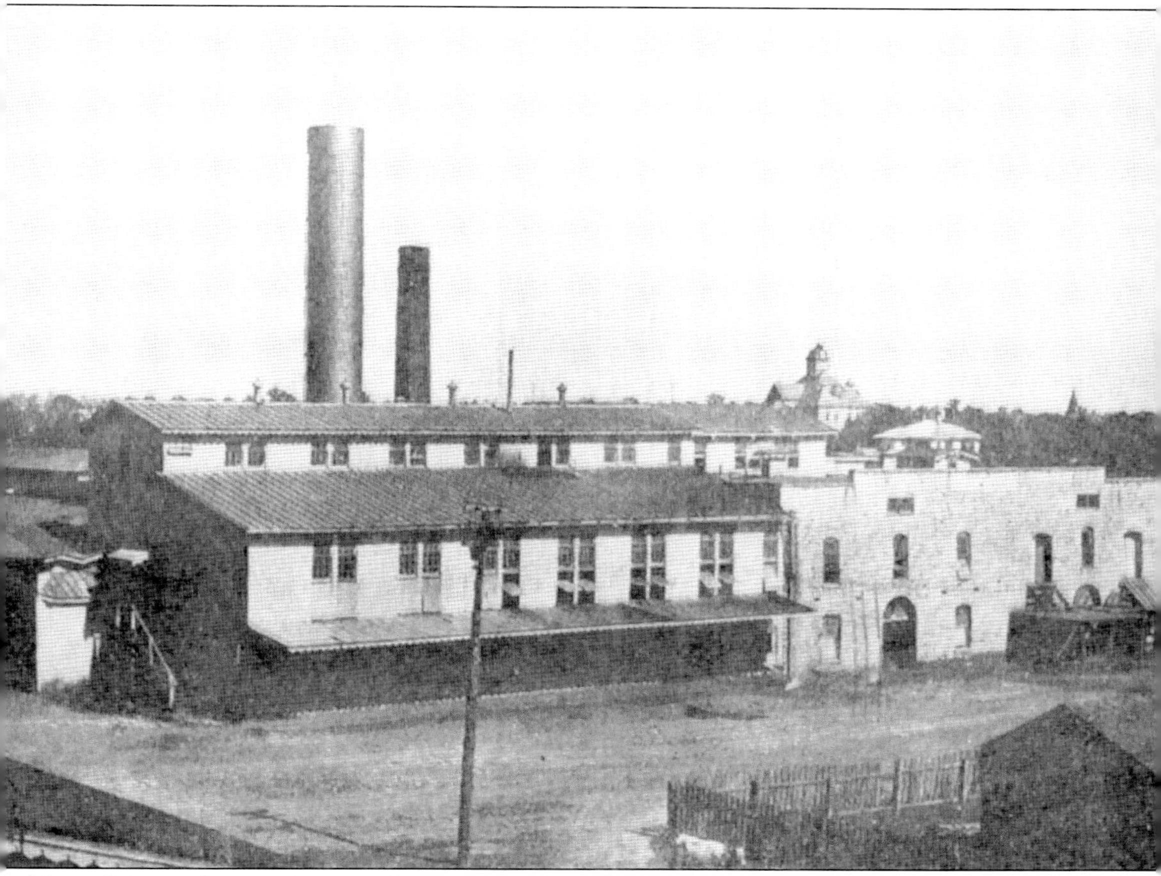

Henry Schumacher was born in Germany on November 25, 1832. In 1873, he established this cottonseed oil mill in Navasota. Processing approximately 1,500 tons of cottonseed each year, the oil mill was known to run 24 hours a day during the early years. These were the times when Schumacher and his brother-in-law R.A. Horlock were learning to market various by-products of cotton. Little was wasted from a boll of cotton, so profits were sizeable. In 1884, Pres. Chester A. Arthur recognized Henry Schumacher for his part in developing the cottonseed oil industry in the South. Soap, vegetable oil, seed cake for cattle, cellulose for gunpowder, and linter's cotton for upholstery were just some of the products derived from cottonseed. (Courtesy Russell Cushman Museum, Horlock House.)

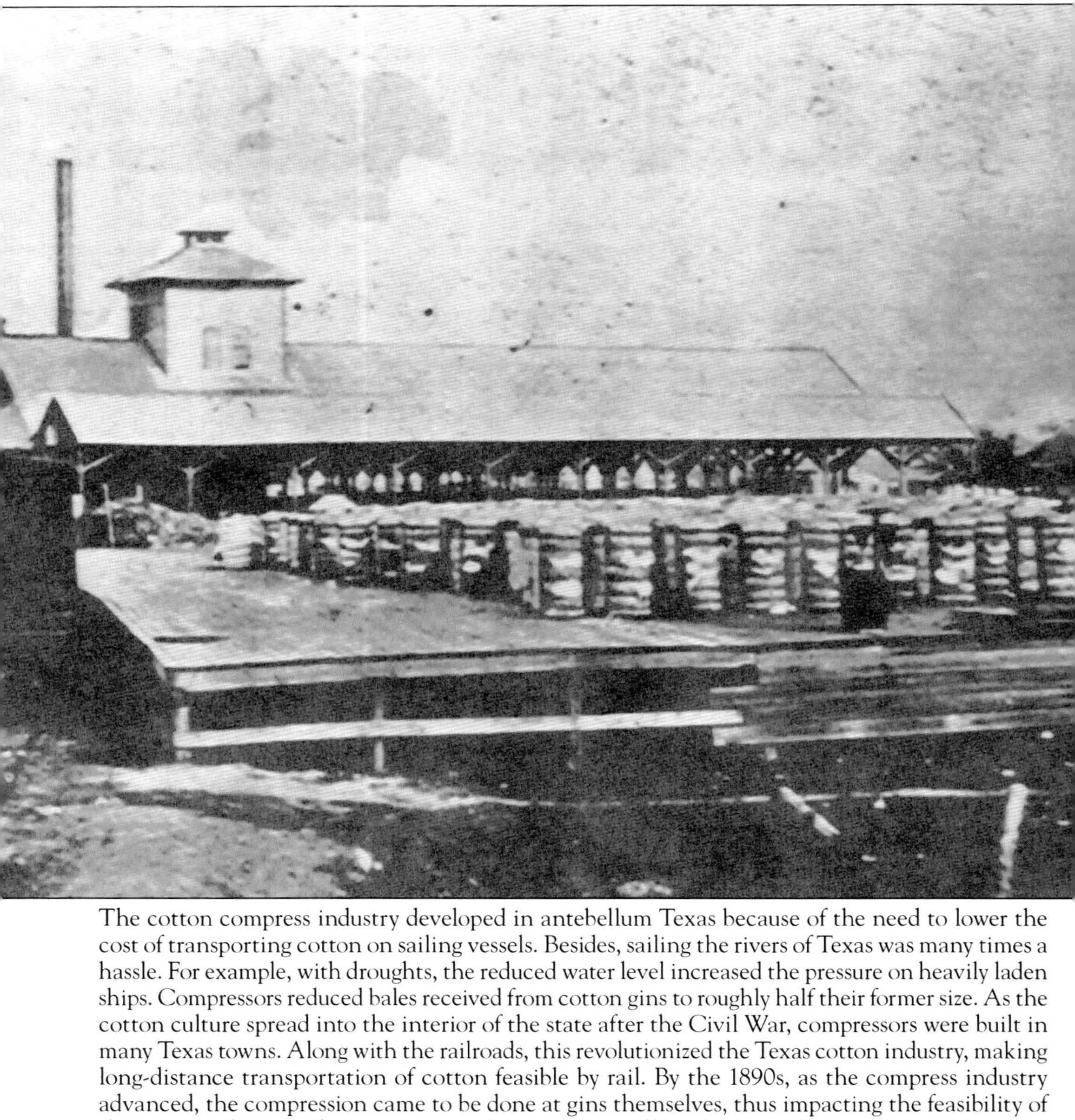

The cotton compress industry developed in antebellum Texas because of the need to lower the cost of transporting cotton on sailing vessels. Besides, sailing the rivers of Texas was many times a hassle. For example, with droughts, the reduced water level increased the pressure on heavily laden ships. Compressors reduced bales received from cotton gins to roughly half their former size. As the cotton culture spread into the interior of the state after the Civil War, compressors were built in many Texas towns. Along with the railroads, this revolutionized the Texas cotton industry, making long-distance transportation of cotton feasible by rail. By the 1890s, as the compress industry advanced, the compression came to be done at gins themselves, thus impacting the feasibility of the separate factories for compression. (Courtesy Russell Cushman Collection.)

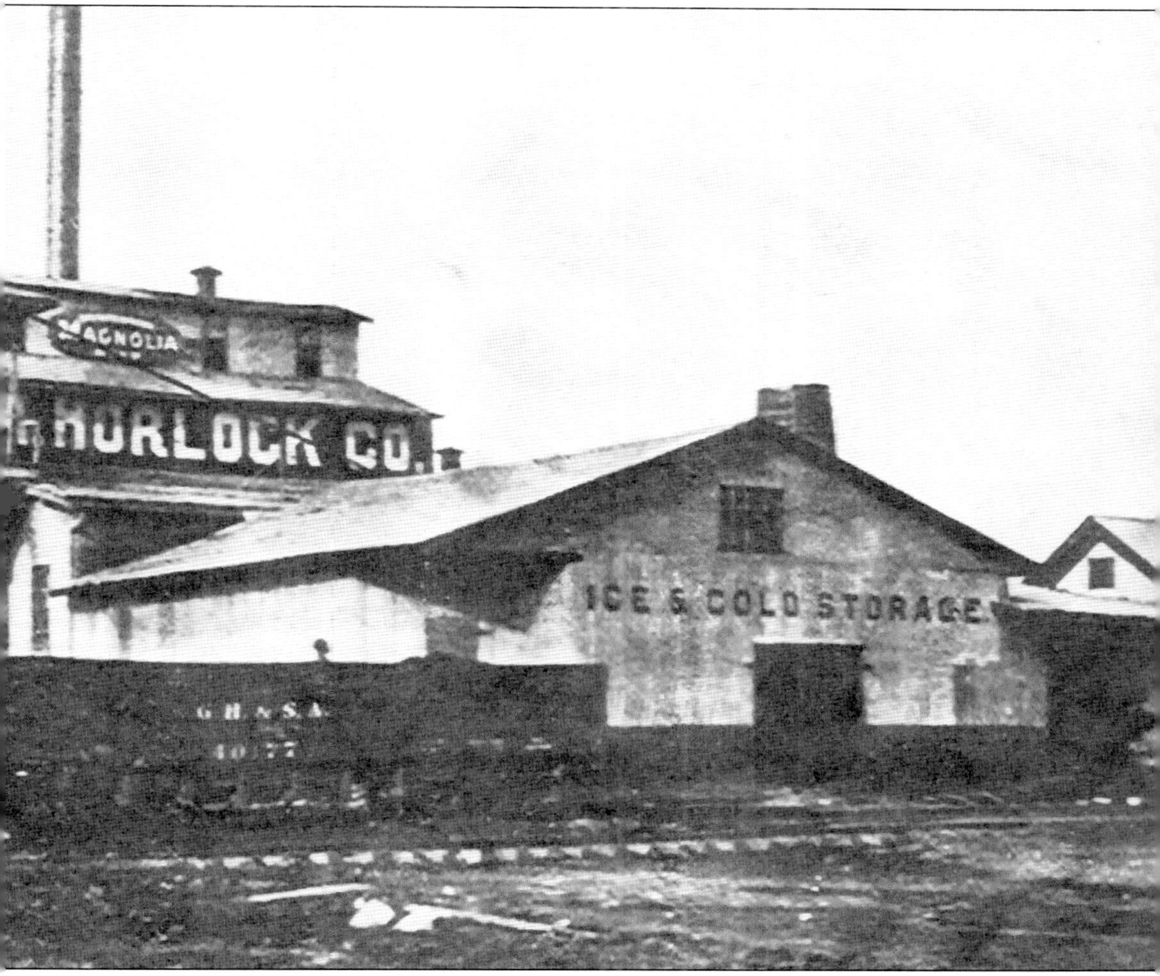

Pictured here is an icehouse, one of the many businesses of the highly influential Horlock family. Robert Augustus Horlock came to Navasota in 1871 and married Ella Lyon. They had two children. About the time Henry Schumacher began his cottonseed oil plant, he employed his brother-in-law R.A. Horlock. When Schumacher died in 1901, Horlock became the manager of the cottonseed oil mill. During the 1880s, in addition to the icehouse pictured here, Horlock bought into a local telephone company, an electric powerhouse, a cotton gin, a gristmill and Navasota Water Works. Along the way, in 1877, upon the death of Ella Lyon, he married Agnes Mason White. It was with her that he moved into what became known as the Horlock House in 1892. She bore him eight children before she died in 1936, about 10 years after her husband died. (Courtesy Russell Cushman Collection.)

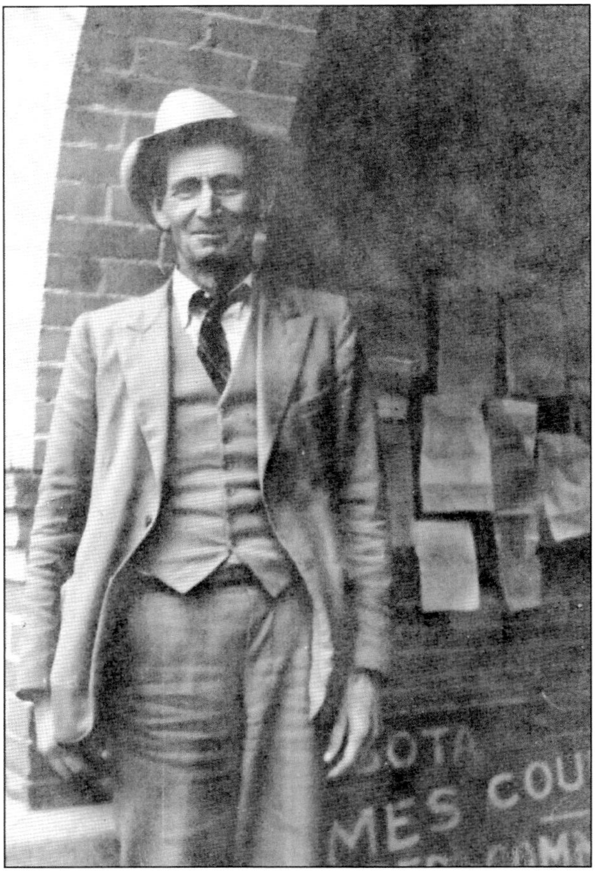

Marshall Newman is pictured at left in civilian dress and pictured below in police uniform. He is believed to be the first Navasota policeman to wear a uniform. On the police seal, it is noted that the police have existed as a unit since 1866. Since then, they have kept order through some critical times, beginning with the rugged days of Reconstruction, then the insecurities in the wake of the big shootout at Anderson at the turn of the century, followed closely by the problems which called for the assistance of Marshal Frank Hamer. Through it all, Navasota's police force stood tall. (Both, courtesy Russell Cushman Collection.)

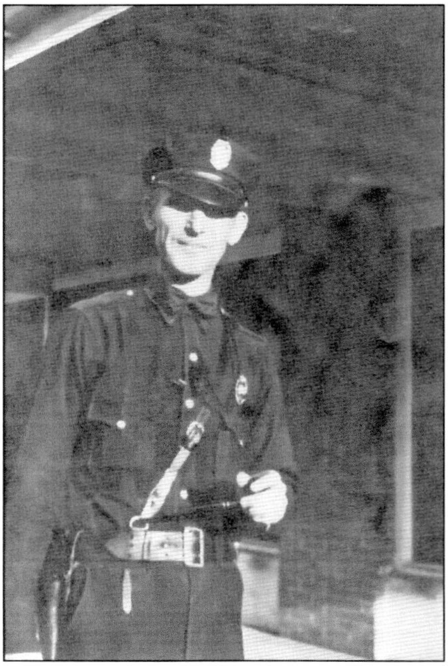

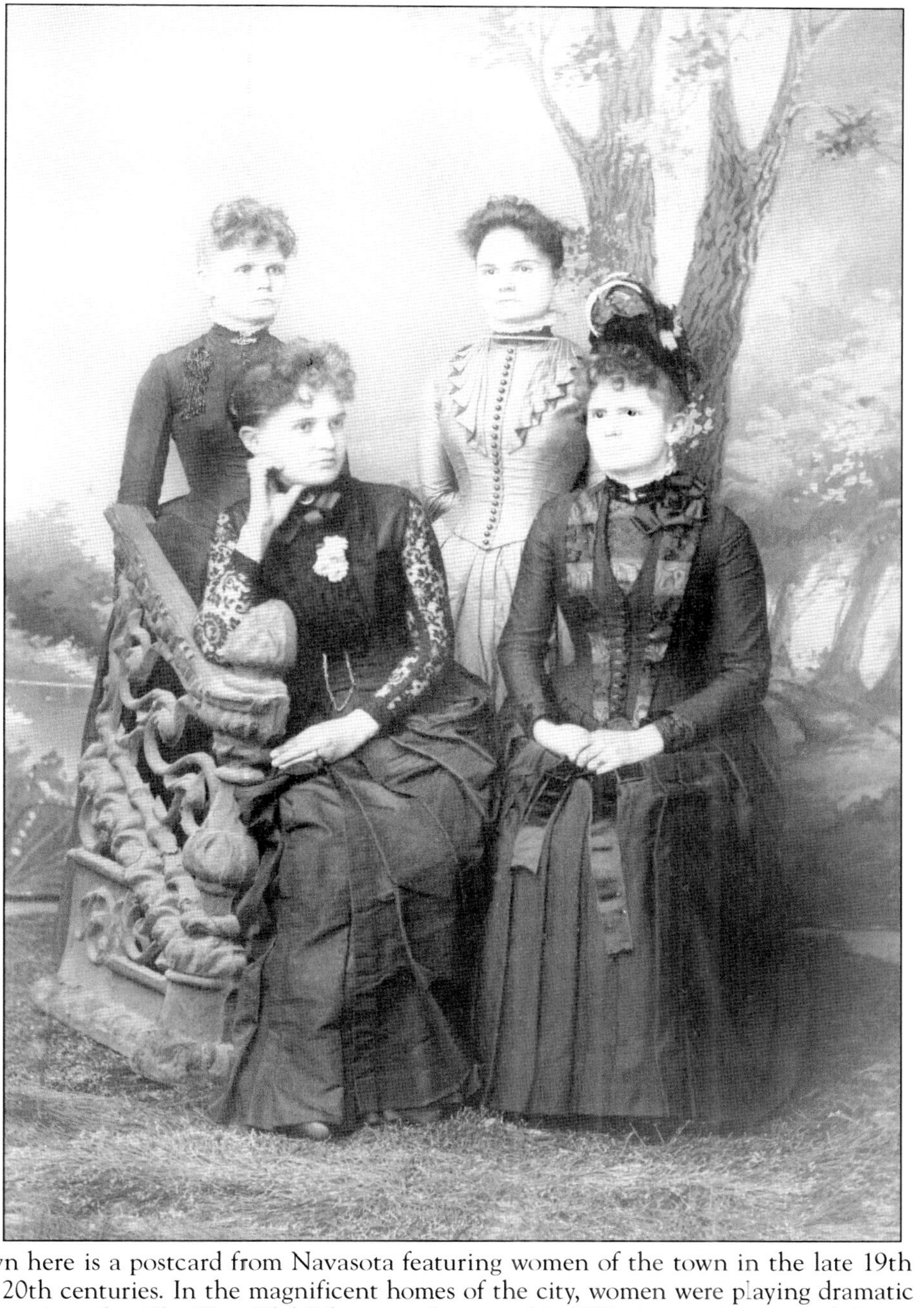

Shown here is a postcard from Navasota featuring women of the town in the late 19th and early 20th centuries. In the magnificent homes of the city, women were playing dramatic and constructive roles. The "Fun Club," for example, started in 1891. Among its accomplishments, it started the Navasota Public Library, the only library in Texas to be started by a women's club at the time. It also is credited with introducing the game of tennis to the city. Then there was the Pyrean Club (PYW), the lovely young women society, and the Perian Club, a society centering on young debutantes. The Navasota Reading Club was especially sophisticated, featuring programs on current social and political issues, including debates on the merits of voting rights for women. (Courtesy Navasota Public Library.)

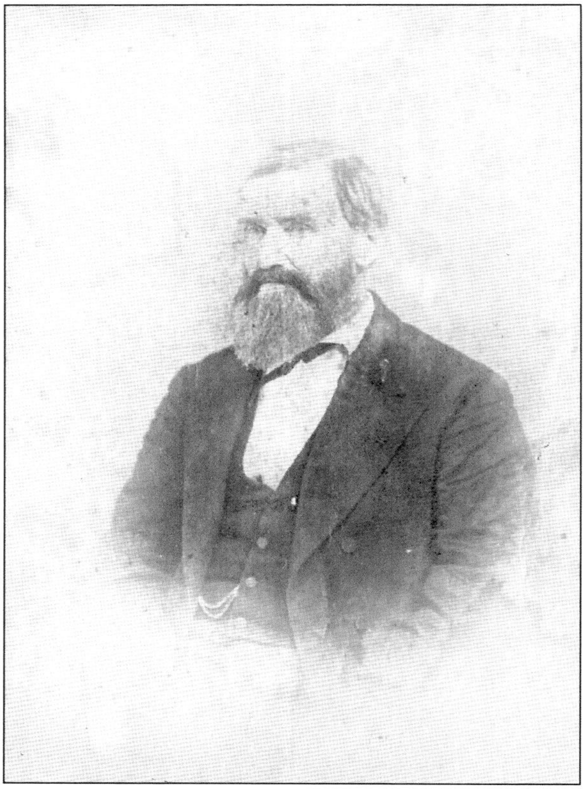

Pictured at left is Andrew Robert Kilpatrick, MD, a significant personality in Navasota. Among his accomplishments, Kilpatrick wrote the first-known comprehensive history of the city. It was titled *Brief Historical Sketch of Navasota, Texas.* It was introduced to the public by the newspaper of the time, the *Navasota Weekly Tablet*, on July 4, 1876. Doctor Kilpatrick also played a key role in tending for victims of Navasota's yellow fever epidemic and published key technical data of the tragedy. The below photograph is of Doctor Kilpatrick's wife, Jeannie Brigance Kilpatrick. (Both, courtesy Russell Cushman Collection.)

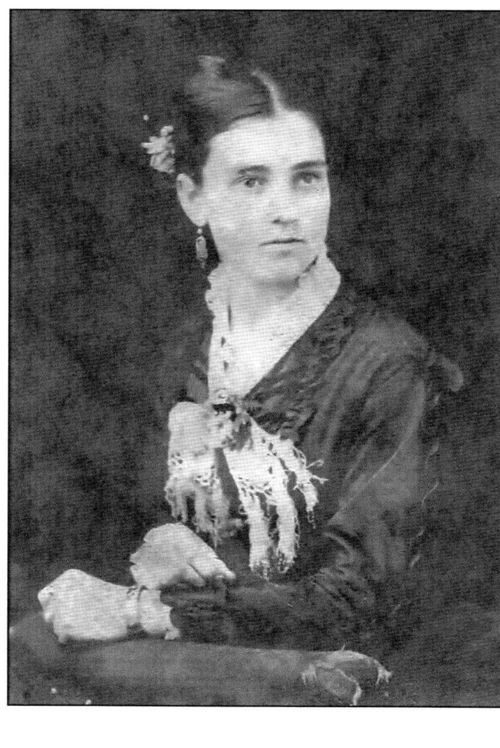

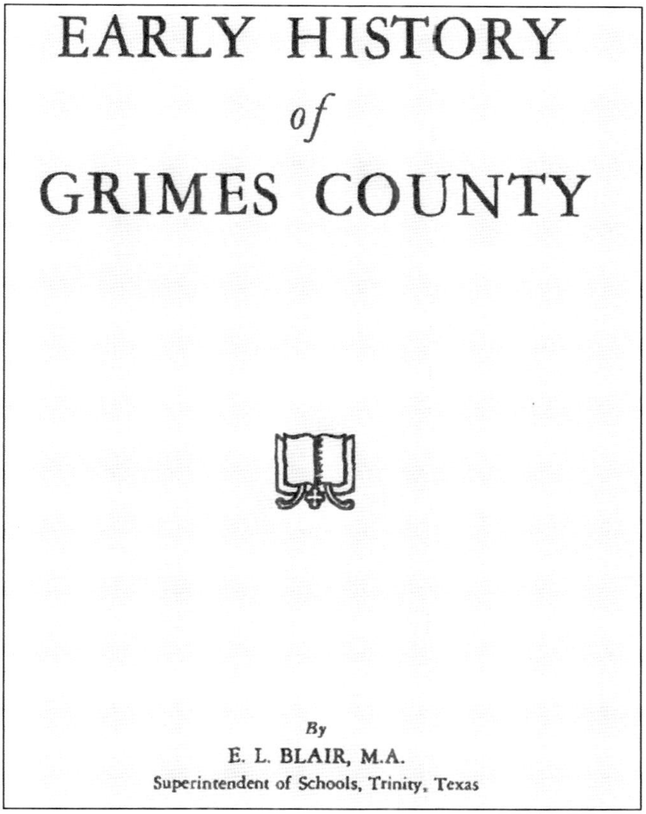

EARLY HISTORY
of
GRIMES COUNTY

By
E. L. BLAIR, M.A.
Superintendent of Schools, Trinity, Texas

E.L. Blair published this book, the first history of Grimes County, in 1930. Now a classic, it examined the foundational stage of Grimes County and engaged a study of the county's Native American groups. The rest of the book focused on biographical sketches of 64 original grantees of land in Stephen F. Austin's first and second colonies. (Courtesy Texas Center for Regional Studies.)

In the 1990s, the US Army Corps of Engineers built locks and dams on the Brazos River near Navasota. Pictured here is an example of their work. This marked the culmination of work begun earlier in the days of the Works Progress Administration. Even further back, similar work was attempted in the days of the steamboat. (Courtesy Marcus Mallard.)

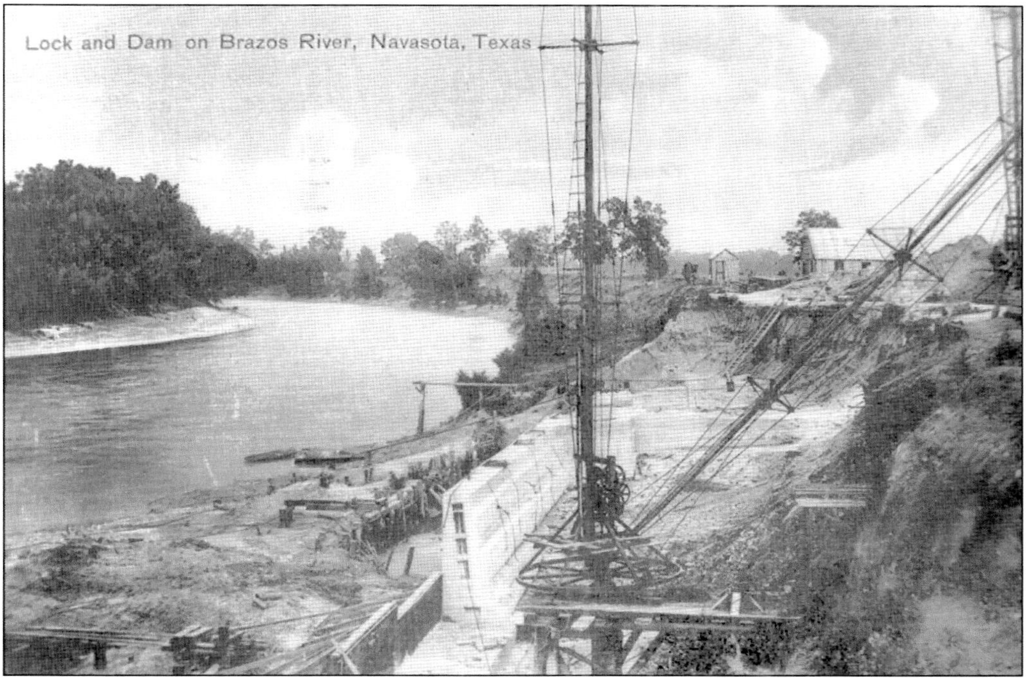

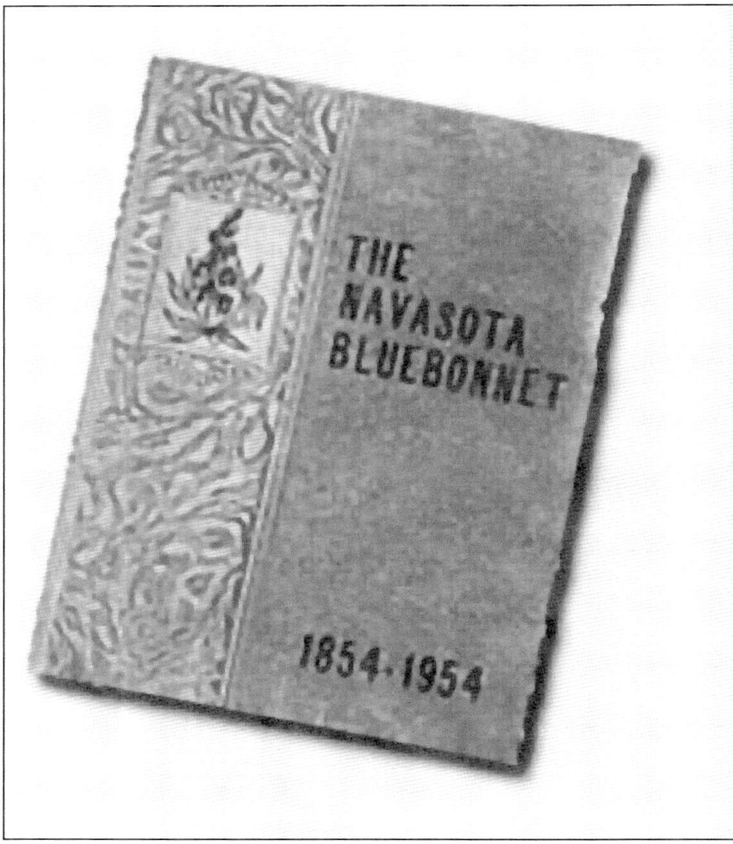

The Navasota Bluebonnet was the dream of a three-person committee including Maurine Chinski, Mayor Ralph Barry, and Sellers Rogers. Chinski was the featured writer. Unfortunately, both Mayor Barry and Chinski died before the projected time to finish the manuscript. Hence, the manuscript never saw its anticipated goal of a comprehensive history of the city. But it is, yet, a magnificent piece of work fitted together by a number of people under rather trying conditions, most notably Dr. Loyal V. Norman and Sellers Rogers. Also instrumental was the editorial board, with Mrs. Stratton Baker, Mrs. Jim Mabrey, Mrs. W.S. Welch, and Gerald C. Fahey. The Grimes County Chamber of Commerce of Navasota underpinned these workers. The book draws on the earlier work by Doctor Kilpatrick, while expanding the story of the city to the 1950s. (Courtesy Texas Center for Regional Studies.)

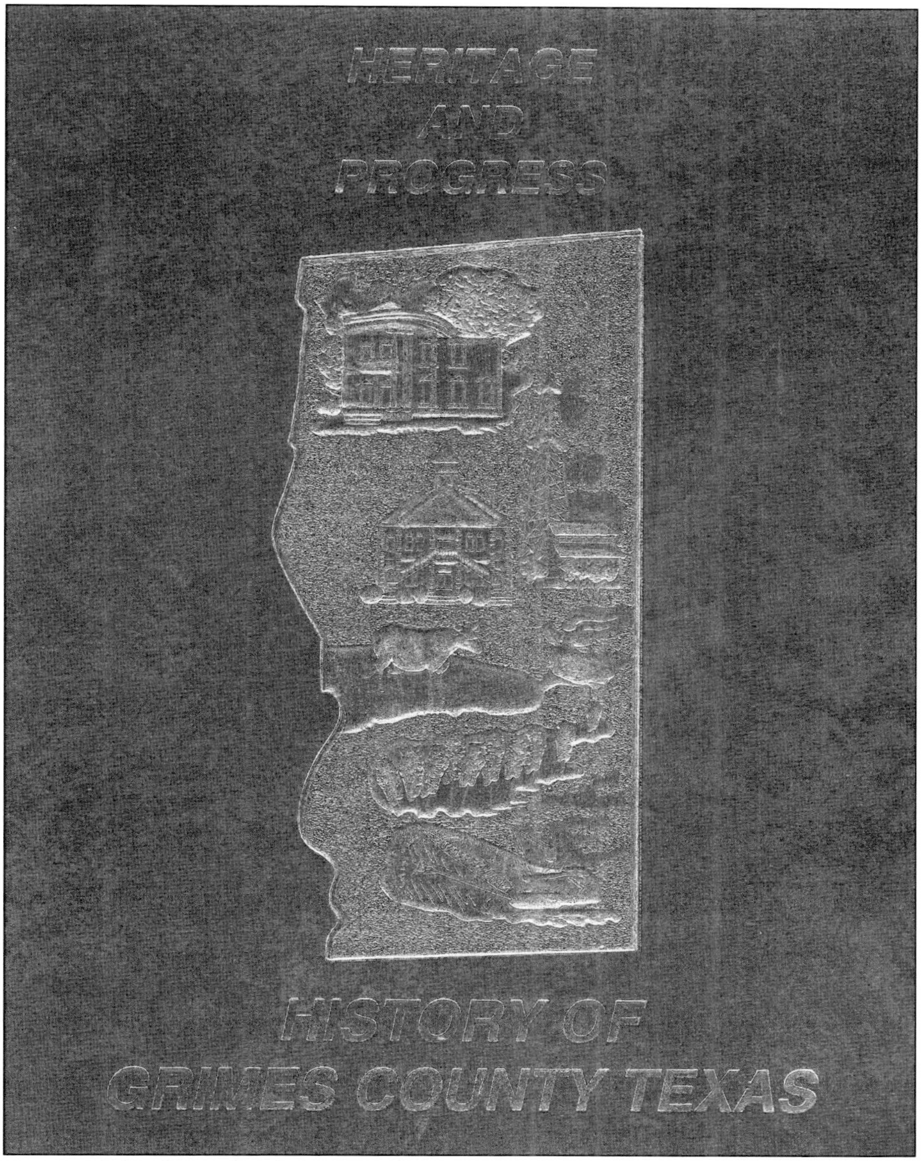

This reprint of the classic family history of Grimes County, *Heritage and Progress*, was originally published by the Grimes County Historical Commission in 1982. The Central History Book Committee consisted of chair Georgia B. Best, Alixe Taylor, Bonnie Armstrong, C.Y. Best, Duane Prestwood, Alene Arrington, Margaret Hertenberger, Katherine Neal, Louise Keelan, Melba Camp Byerly, Chellie P. Raymond, Lovett T. Boggess, and Clark Whitten. In 2007, chair of the Grimes County Historical Commission Jim Westmoreland and president of the River of Culture (ROC) Nancy Perry worked out an agreement. The agreement provided for the *River of Culture* to republish the book, unchanged and unedited. Thanks to the official sanction of county judge Betty Shiftlet and the commissioner's court of Grimes County, the reprint found success. (Courtesy Nancy Perry, River of Culture.)

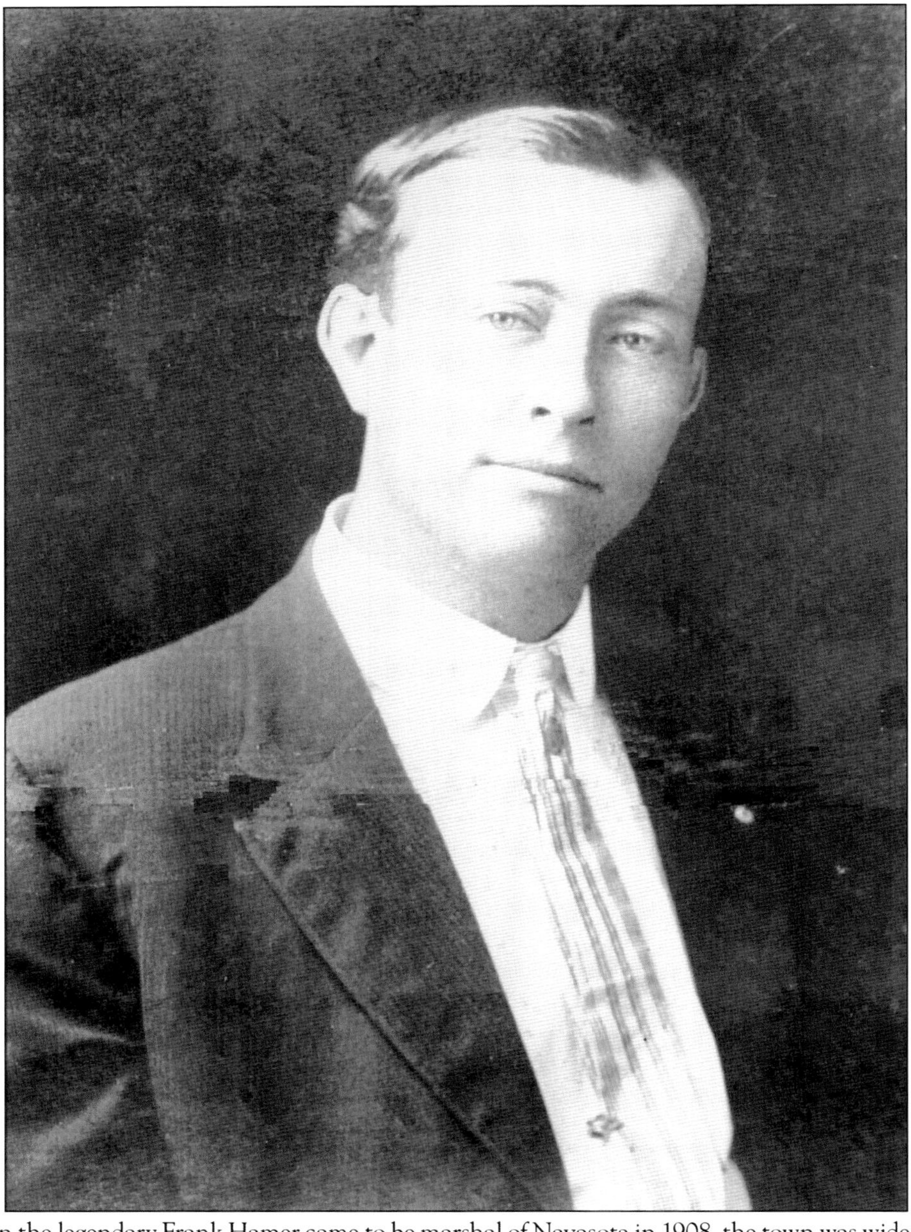

When the legendary Frank Hamer came to be marshal of Navasota in 1908, the town was wide open and out of control. Guns settled hostile situations. Women and children were not safe downtown, even in the middle of the day. Vagabonds, outlaws, and con men ran the streets. Young Hamer, who later became a famous Texas Ranger, cut his teeth on this rawboned boomtown. He stood up to the town's strong men who had muscled in during the lawless Reconstruction years. After several years of his law enforcement, criminals were often known to rush to jail at his command, rather than face his wrath. Everyone agreed that Marshal Hamer left Navasota a much tamer and safer place when he departed in 1911. In 1934, he tracked down and ended the careers of the notorious criminals Bonnie and Clyde. (Courtesy Russell Cushman Collection.)

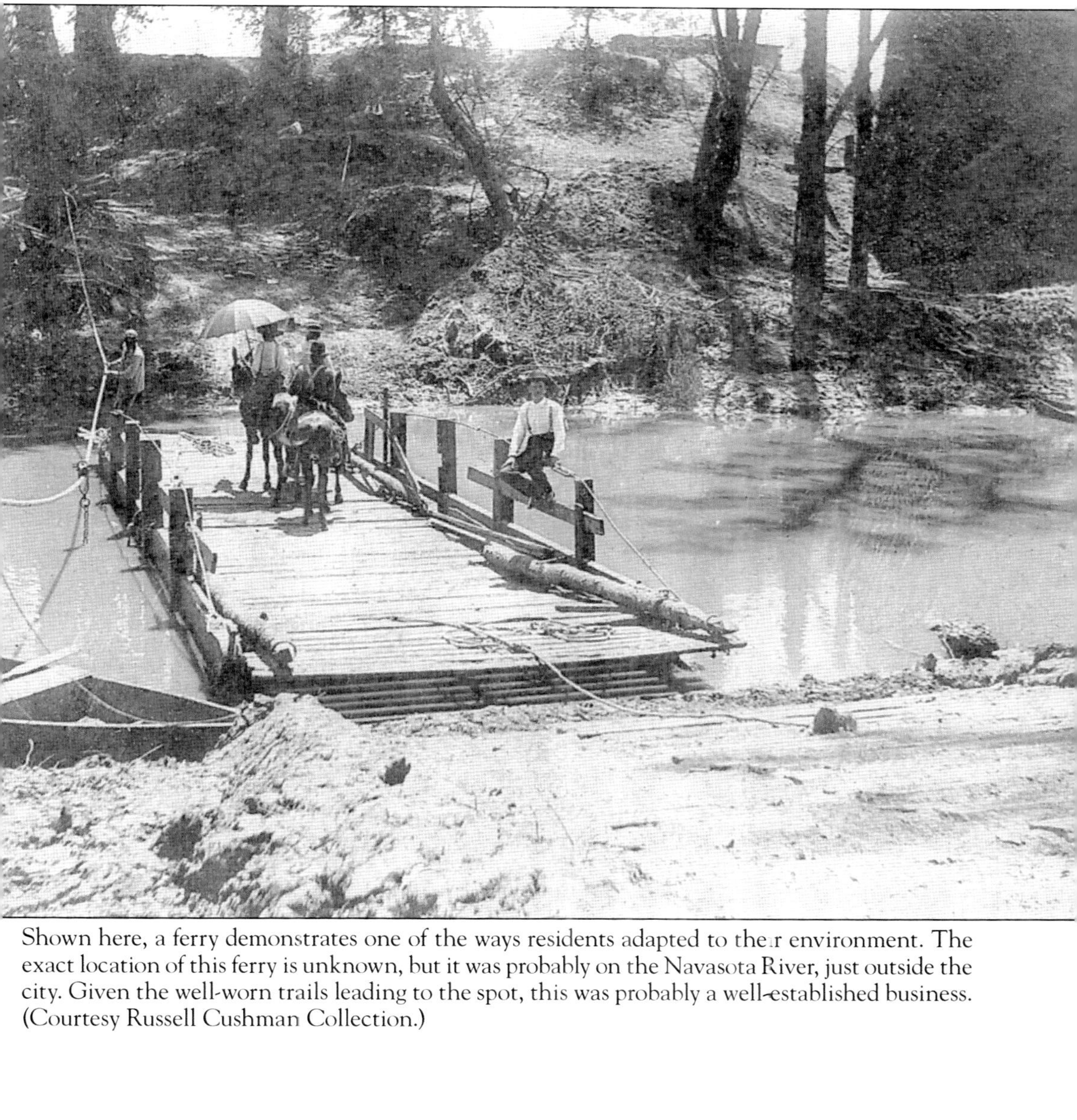

Shown here, a ferry demonstrates one of the ways residents adapted to their environment. The exact location of this ferry is unknown, but it was probably on the Navasota River, just outside the city. Given the well-worn trails leading to the spot, this was probably a well-established business. (Courtesy Russell Cushman Collection.)

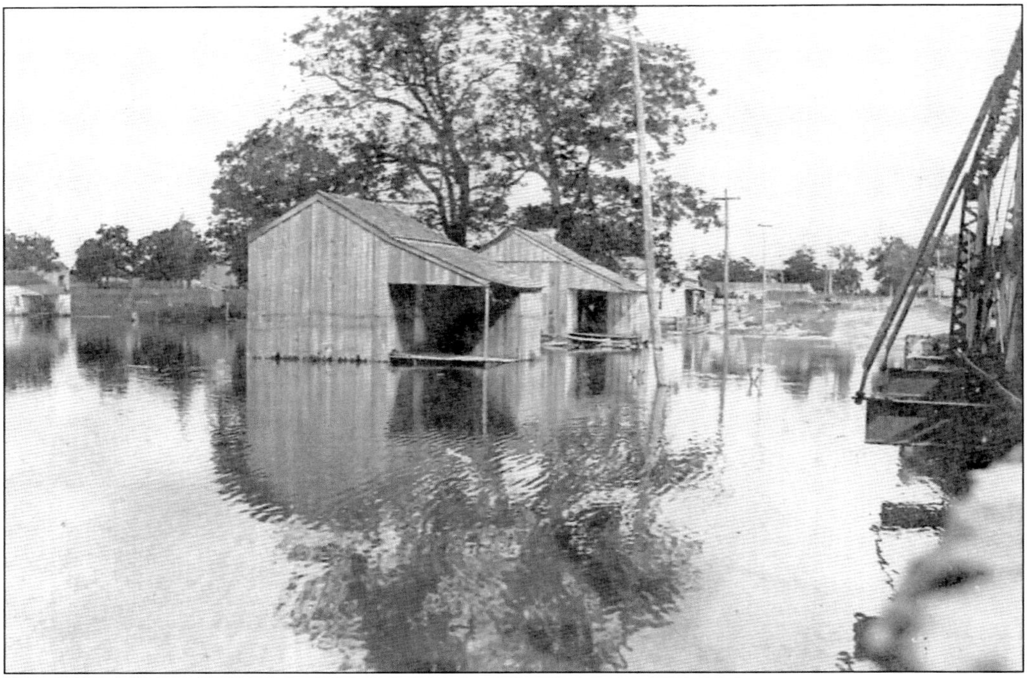

These photographs feature the notorious flood of 1898. Above, buildings are under siege from the swirling waters. And note the portion of a trestle for flood control, innovative for its time. Below is another glimpse of the trestle technology at work. Note that the people are well dressed, most likely on a Sunday outing. (Both, courtesy Russell Cushman Collection.)

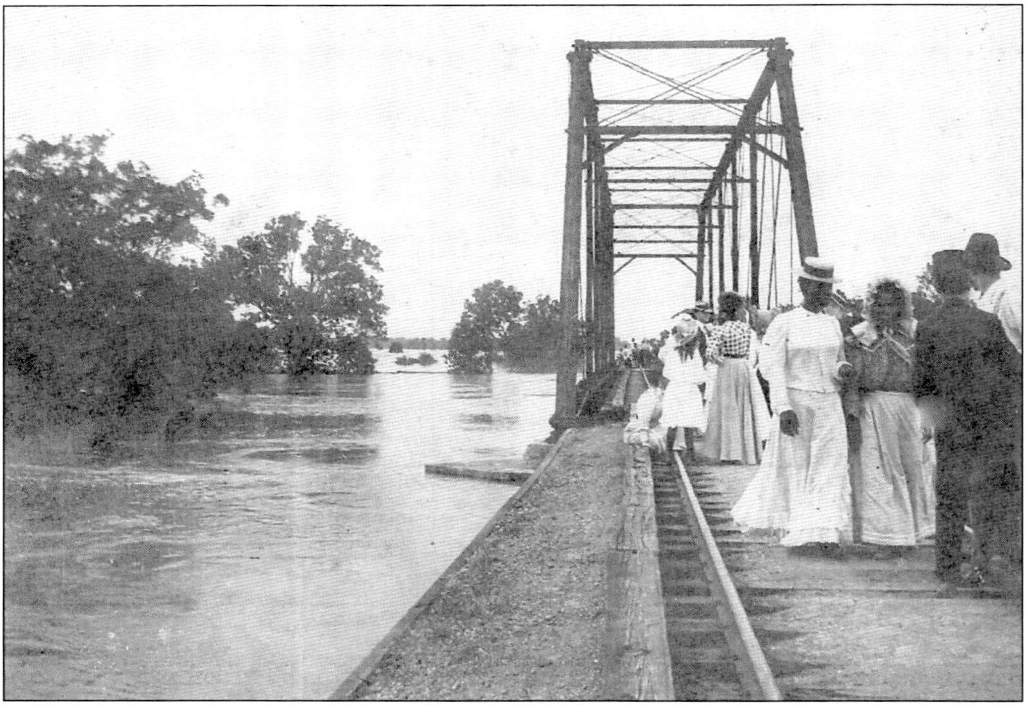

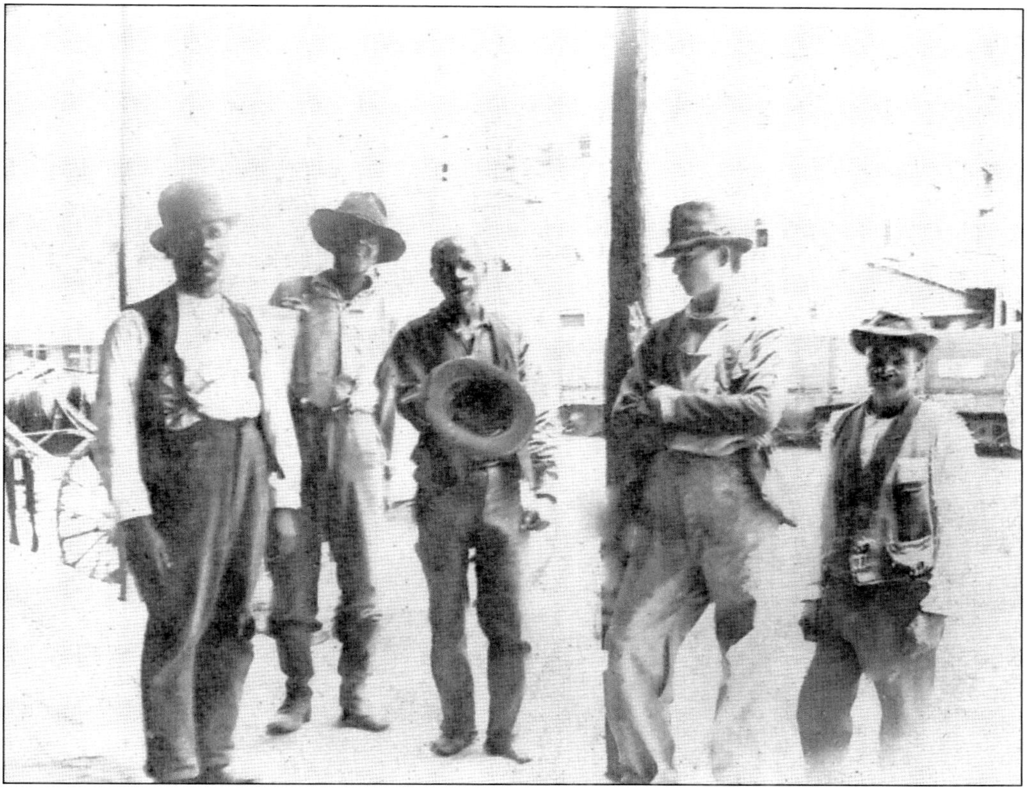

Here are five fortunate survivors of the great flood of 1898, just after they were rescued. The photograph at right shows R.J. Brule. Making his mark in Navasota at a critical time, in the 1930s, Brule was an engineer as well as the city manager. A man of solid accomplishments and reputation, the national government was not hesitant to entrust much work to his guidance in the days of the federal Works Project Administration. Due largely to the impact of R.J. Brule, Navasota received backing to build a fine swimming pool, a viable sewer system, and a football field and stadium, among others. (Both, courtesy Russell Cushman Collection.)

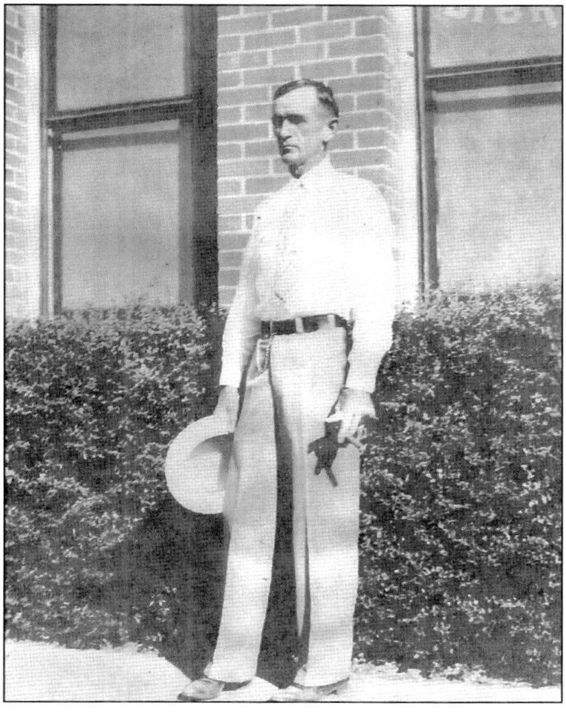

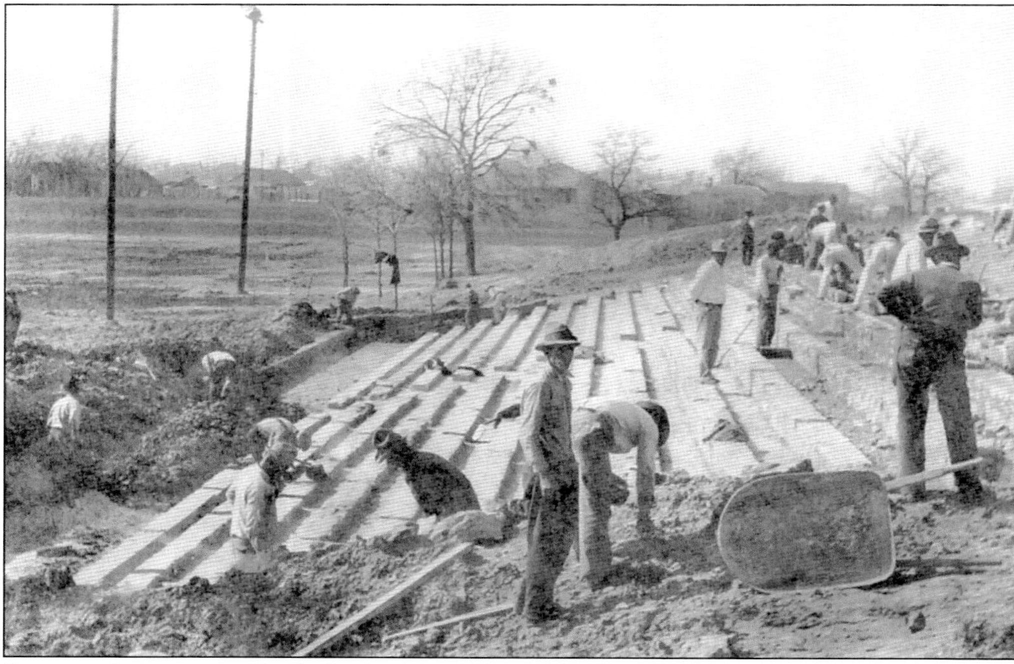

Degrees of progress on Brule Stadium are pictured here in the early 1930s. In the photograph above, men work to develop the seats of the stadium. They work in a field and move up a natural slope in the topography. In the photograph below, the stadium is ready for its first game. Lights are there and the seats are set, but note that the field itself is yet unleveled. Taking its name from the great R.J. Brule, the stadium, when fully functional, was first rate for its time. (Both, courtesy Russell Cushman Collection.)

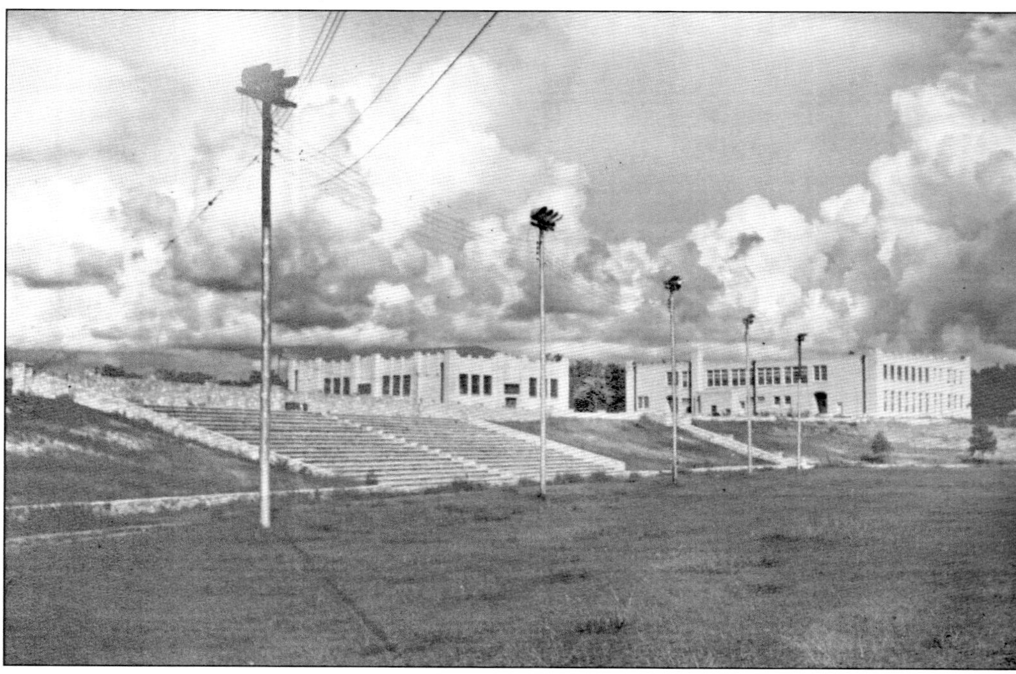

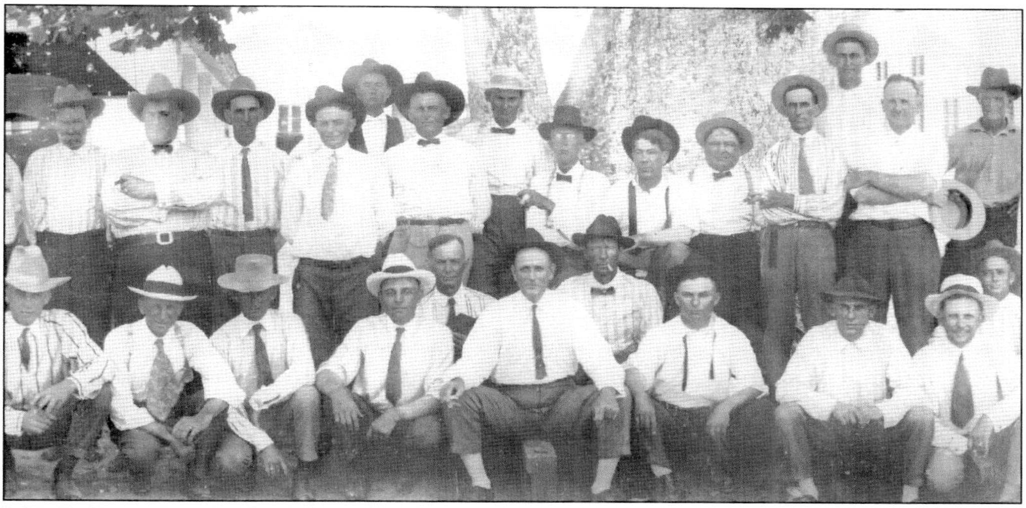

John D. Rogers I was a first-class adventurer. In 1850, by way of Panama, he went to California to pan for gold. Later, he became captain of Company E of the famous 5th Texas in the Civil War. Along the way, he also became a medical doctor. He is known in Navasota as the owner of Allen Farm. His grandson and namesake John D. Rogers II inherited his sense of adventure. Rogers II assumed ownership of Allen Farm and served for a time as mayor of Navasota and president of the East Texas Chamber of Commerce. In the photograph above, people gather at Allen Farm; local lore has it that the famous country singer Jimmy Rogers is visible in the photograph. The photograph below features lawmen on guard on the premises of Allen Farm. (Both, courtesy Russell Cushman Collection.)

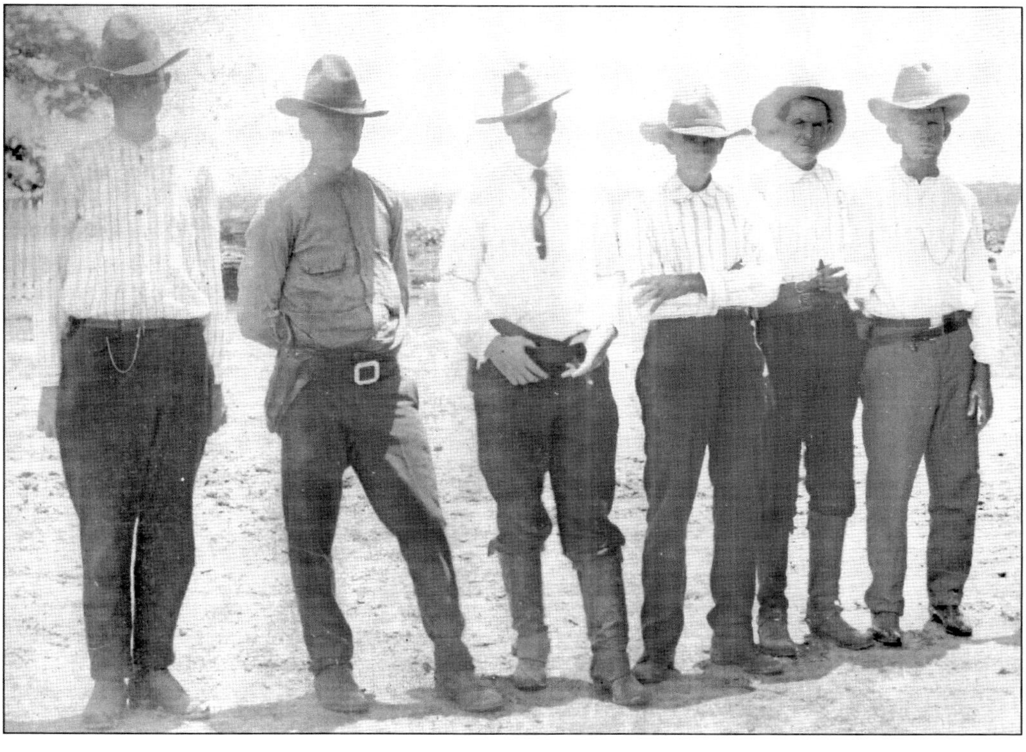

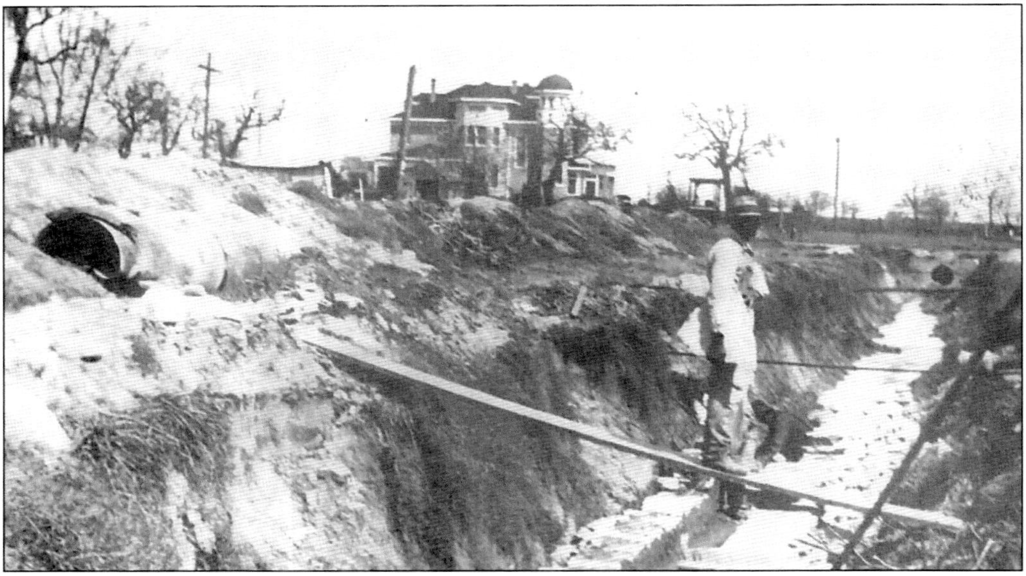

These photographs reflect the impact of the WPA in Navasota. In the photograph above, workmen dig ditches where a modern sewer line will be laid. Even with WPA support, the work was extremely tedious as well as time-consuming. Note the splendor of the Templeman House in the background, known to this day as "the Castle." In the photograph below, work on a bridge over Cedar Creek is underway, making Navasota more accessible to further reaches of its neighborhoods. (Both, courtesy Russell Cushman Collection.)

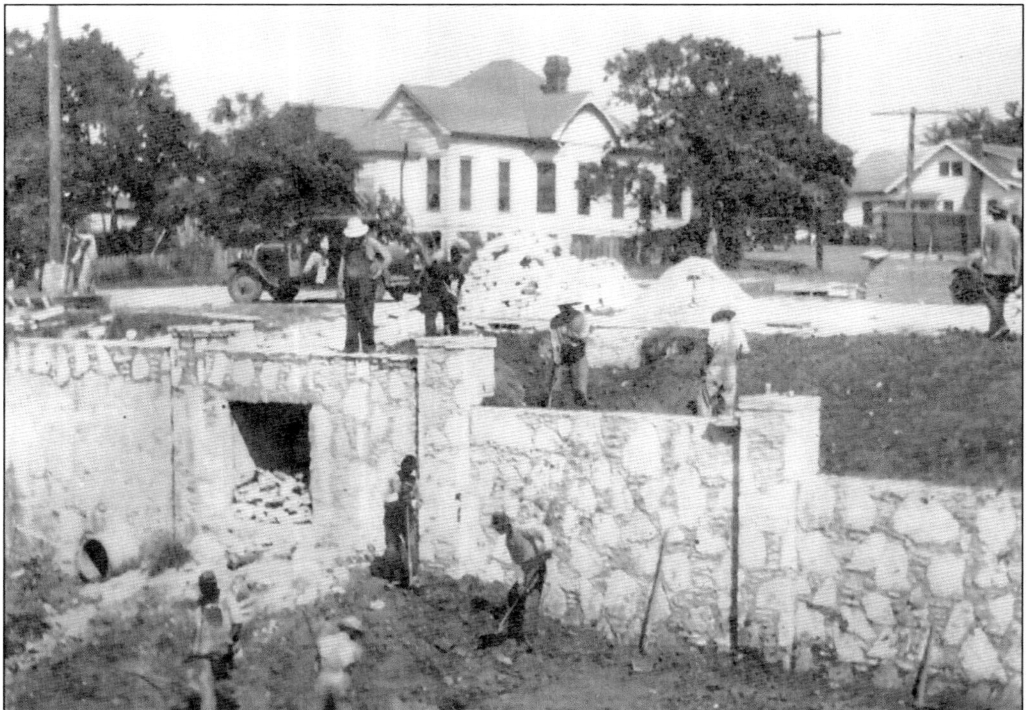

These photographs feature stages of development of the city swimming pool. The photograph at right shows the WPA mules laying the groundwork for the swimming pool. Below, children are anxious to immerse themselves in the water. Meanwhile, adults look on determining the security measures to be implemented for this new stage of the city's progress. The choice of Brule Park for the location of the pool was the result of innovation and imagination on the part of city leaders; the surroundings contribute to a feeling of security and relaxation. (Both, courtesy Russell Cushman Collection.)

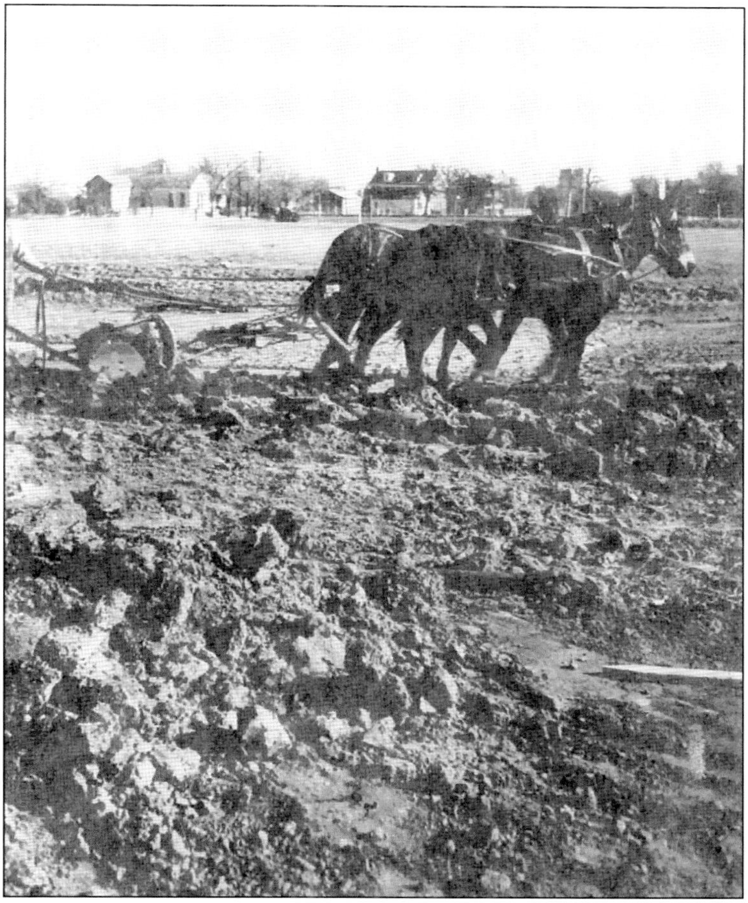

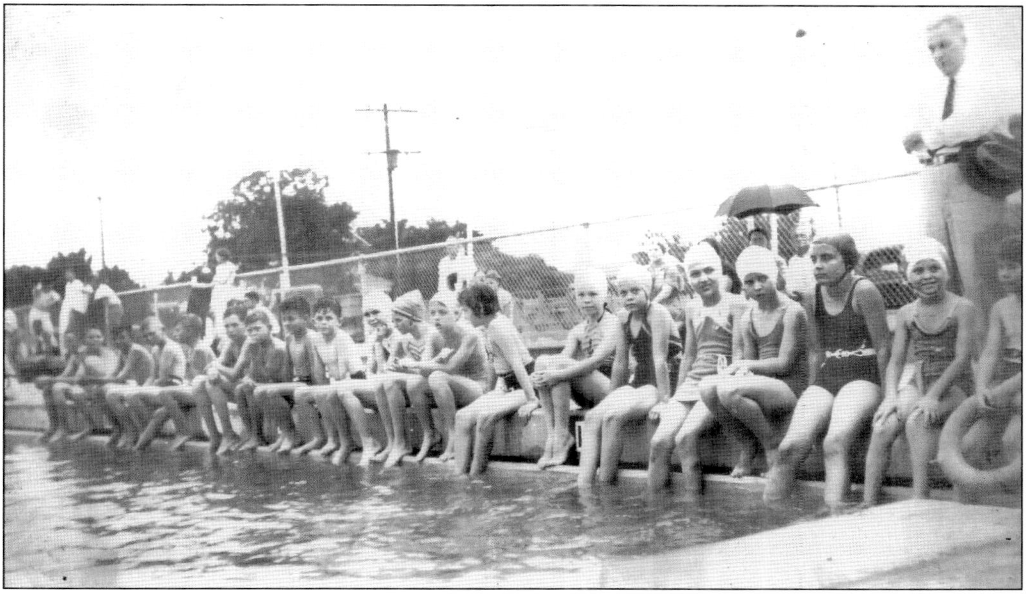

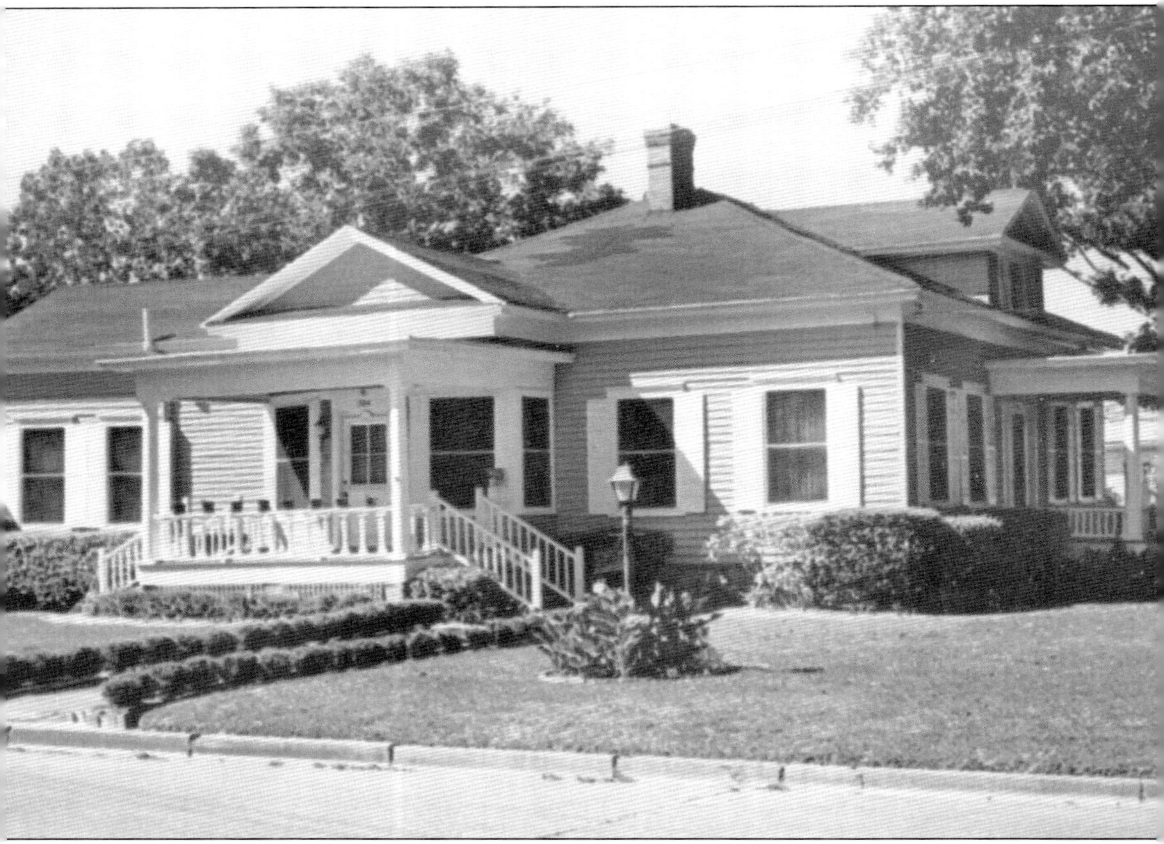

George D. Neal, a major figure in state-level politics, once lived with his family at 504 Church Street in Navasota. Between his birth in 1853 in Virginia and his death in 1916, he held multiple political offices in Texas, including deputy county clerk of Austin County, county judge of Grimes County (from 1884 to 1886), city attorney of Navasota (from 1888 to 1896), and member of the Texas Senate (from 1896 to 1902). In his last term in that body, he served as president pro tem. Finally, from 1903 until 1907, he held the high office of Lieutenant Governor of Texas. Along the way, in 1880, he married Fannie C. Brooks. Upon moving to Navasota one year after their marriage, the couple was blessed with three children. (Courtesy J.D. Dickenson.)

Five

Education and Religion

In Navasota's early days, there were no public schools. Private schools or at-home tutors were the mark of the times. The setting was laid for the modern school system when Dickson Greer built a log house in his field and hired a teacher to teach his three children. In time, other children were taken on for a fee. On February 19, 1853, Greer and Jackson Duke deeded four acres to the trustees of the Union School Society. The property was located on the south side of present Washington Avenue near the entrance to present Church Street. The next year, the first school was built. During the Civil War, the student body was greatly reduced. The postwar yellow fever epidemic ended its stint as the major focus of Navasota education.

By the end of the Civil War, efforts to found a new school came to fruition in 1872 with the Atchison Institute. The institute lasted with that name until 1949. It became relegated to an elementary school when the Victoria Felder Manual Training School emerged in 1910.

Education of African Americans advanced in 1870 when Ira Malcolm Camp, owner of Camp Inn, donated property for a one-room school for African American children, built in 1875. Fire destroyed this building in 1910. In 1928, a modern structure was built just south of the present fire station. In 1942, this became the elementary school when, nearby, several new buildings were christened the George Washington Carver High School.

In 1947, the Navasota Independent School System was established, and by 1969, it was fully integrated racially. Now, the system covers some 312 square miles and includes a high school, junior high, intermediate school, and two elementary schools.

Meanwhile, the first religious services were held in the Union School, built in 1854. This marked the beginning of the Methodist, Presbyterian, and Baptist churches.

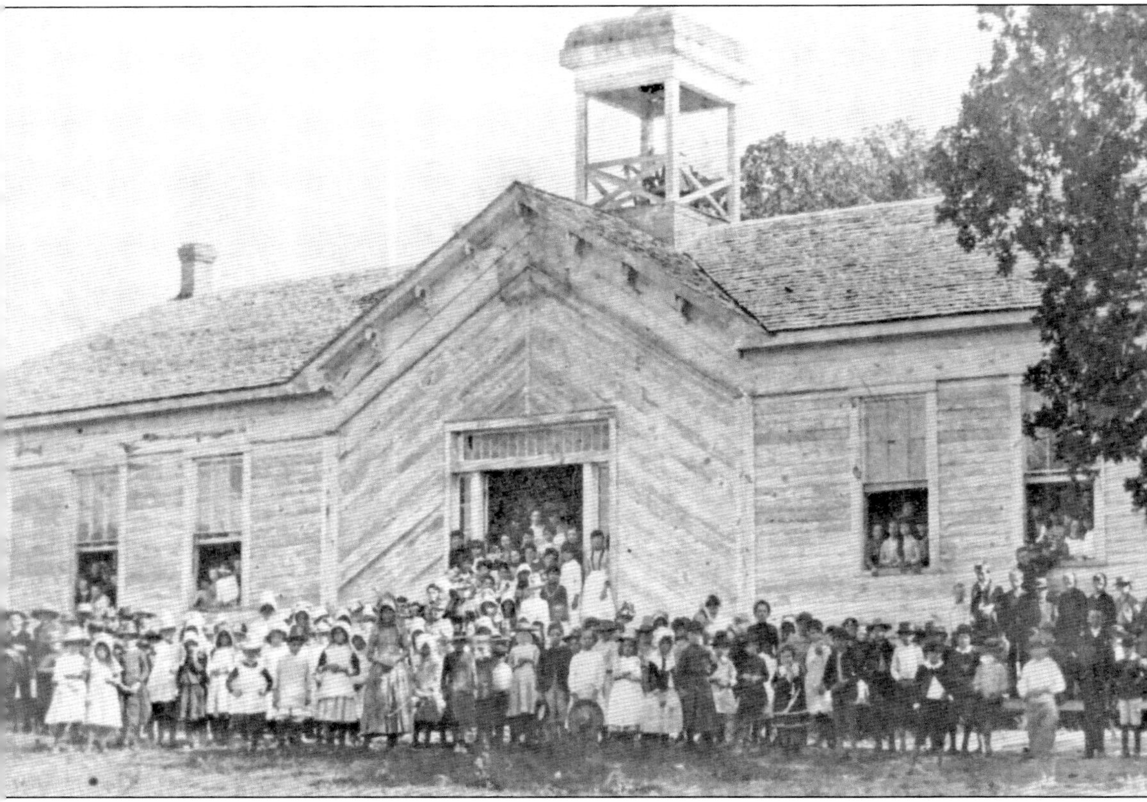

This was the first Atchison Institute. The necessity for this school lay in the decline of the original 1854 Union School. Seeing the need for a larger school, the Union Society Trustees obtained a court order granting them permission to sell off part of the four acres the society had received in 1853 from associates of D.D. Greer and Company for the purpose of public education. The funds from such a sale were slated for a better school. In addition, Capt. D.D. Atchison donated $1,000, enabling the society to put $2,600 toward a good frame building. Joseph Brooks was the architect of Atchison Institute, named for Captain Atchison's generous donation. The school opened in 1872. Sometime in the 1880s, the school burned down, ironically, during a rainstorm. For a while afterwards, school continued on an ad hoc basis until the advent of the second Atchison Institute. (Courtesy Marcus Mallard, Russell Cushman Collection.)

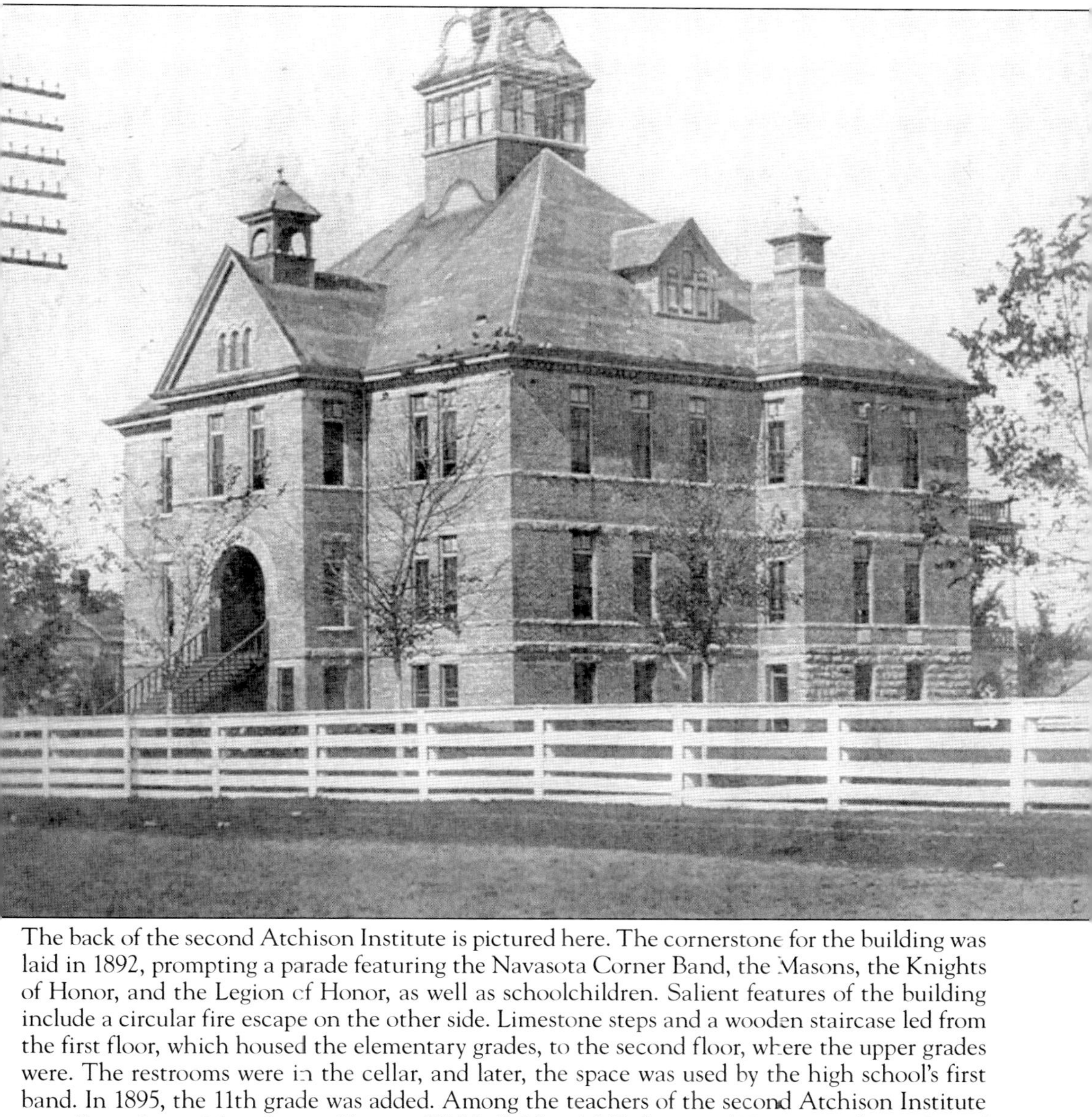

The back of the second Atchison Institute is pictured here. The cornerstone for the building was laid in 1892, prompting a parade featuring the Navasota Corner Band, the Masons, the Knights of Honor, and the Legion of Honor, as well as schoolchildren. Salient features of the building include a circular fire escape on the other side. Limestone steps and a wooden staircase led from the first floor, which housed the elementary grades, to the second floor, where the upper grades were. The restrooms were in the cellar, and later, the space was used by the high school's first band. In 1895, the 11th grade was added. Among the teachers of the second Atchison Institute were Gertie Lang, Mary Spann, Virginia Walthall, Nina McFarlane, and Hattie Matthews. One of the deficiencies of the school was the excessively high ceilings, which made heating the building difficult. The school bell eventually made its way, for awhile, to the belfry of St. Patrick's Catholic church. (Courtesy Russell Cushman Collection.)

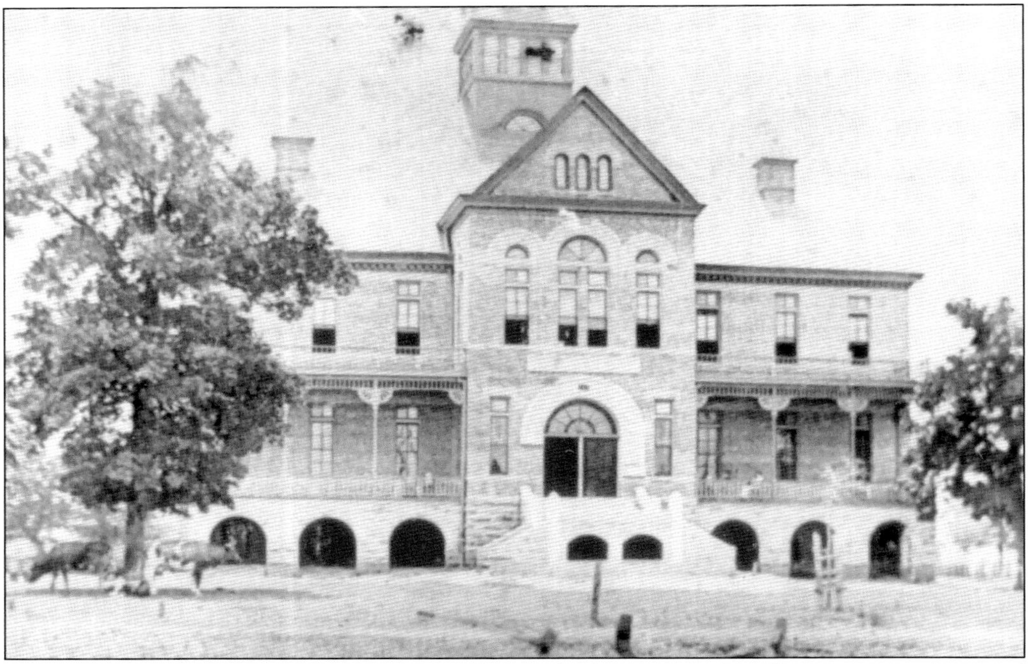

Here is the second Atchison Institute, viewed from the front. Note the split staircase and covered porches with pillars on either side. Also interesting are the cows resting under the shade of the large tree in the spacious front yard. (Courtesy Navasota Public Library.)

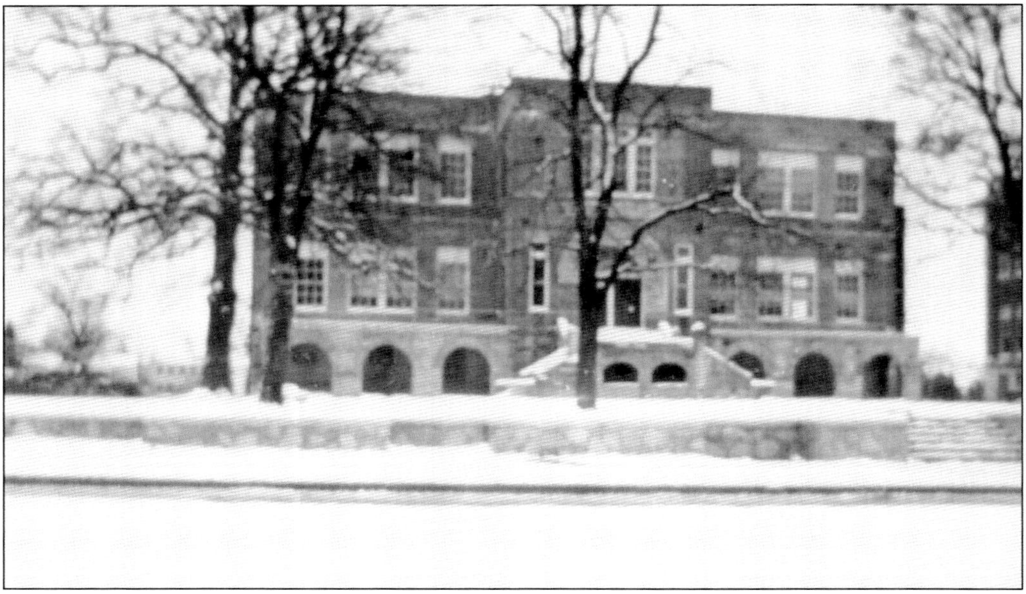

Here is the same Atchison Institute in 1940, by then serving just as the elementary school. Note the differences from the school that was launched in 1892. The porches and the extended roof are no longer there. Even so, a portion of the fire escape is visible far to the right. (Courtesy Navasota Public Library.)

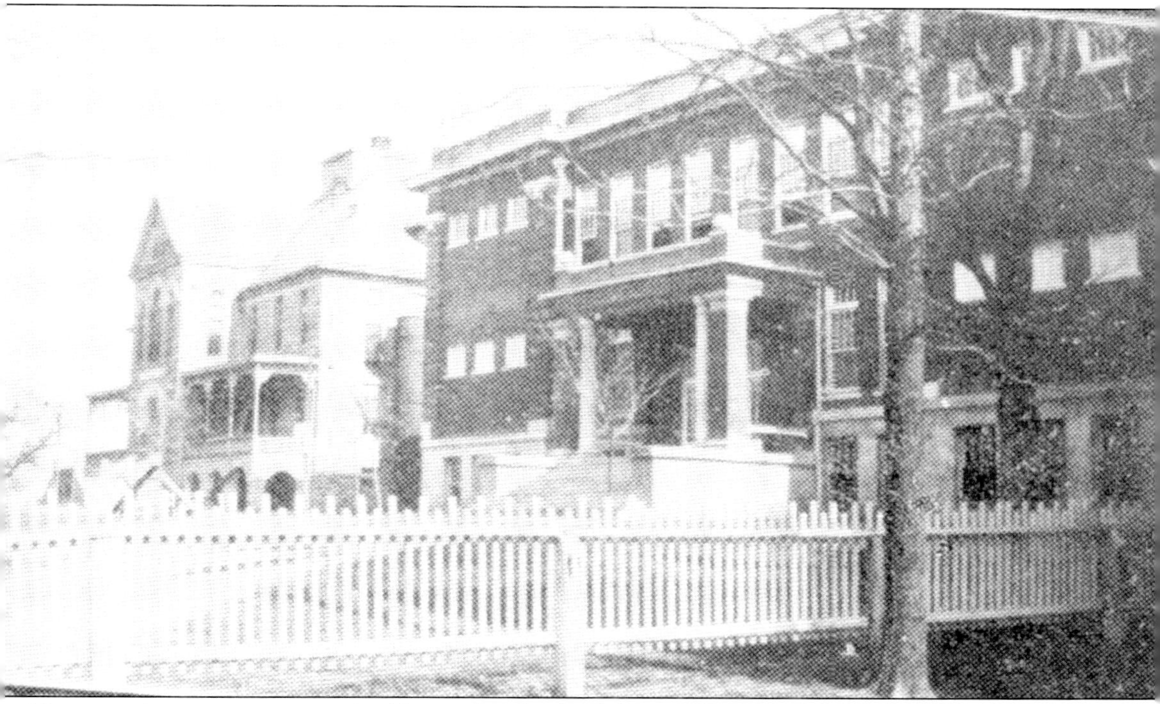

Here are the two impressive buildings that bridged the gap between old Navasota and the modern era. Both of these schools were placed on the lot bracing the south side of Washington Avenue, where it now intersects with Church Street. On the left is the second Atchison Institute, razed in 1949, while on the right is the Victoria Felder Manual Training School. The latter was dedicated with grand fanfare in 1911 and served as the high school until 1930. In 1912 or 1913, the upper division classes had been moved from Atchison Institute to the Victoria Felder School. The school received its name from the wife of J.H. Felder, who donated land to the schools. The land was sold to subsidize a new high school. On the main floor of the new high school were well-lit and spacious classrooms. The upper floor was used entirely as an auditorium, while the basement held a workshop, a science laboratory, and a home economics room. (Courtesy Navasota Public Library.)

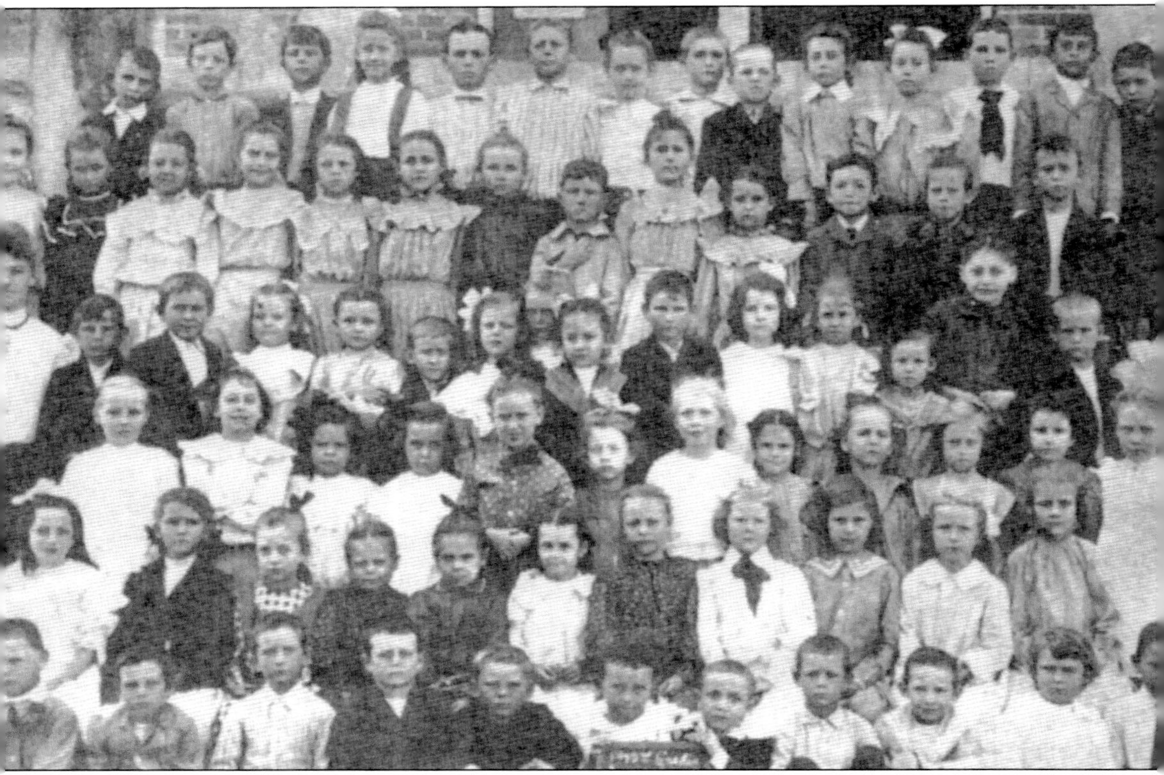

Pictured here in October 1905 are first and second grades of the Atchison School. The teachers are Emma Froelich and Hattie Matthews. From left to right are (first row) Kemper McHaney, Sandord "Pete" Elliott, Willie Haschke, Harold Hamilton, Leslie Bosse, Nelson Lake, Barnett Weatherly, W.J. Kelley, James Smith, David Bradley, and Jeff Jones; (second row) Dora Wehner, Melba Camp, unidentified, Albert Allen, Elise Dickie, Louise McKay, Sallie Kate Allen, Mary Roberts, Lois Fahey, and Maggie Bradley; (third row) Autumn Weatherly, Agenes Millroy, Algere Myrich, Reba Mickelborough, Johnnie Hutchins, Mary Ackerman, Kate Stratton, Susie McKay, Mildred Tribble, Bessis Johnson, Maggie Gooch, and Maggie Deason; (fourth row) Lee Roy Heard, Adele Peachock, May Rucker, Clay Floyd, Milton Calloway, Alick Noak, Aline Rowland, Carrie Jones, Cecil Heard, unidentified, Ruby Harrison, Venita Scott, Fannie Rick, unidentified, and Barnet Riesto; (fifth row) Kathleen Blackshear, Minnie Haschke, Myra Kelly, Bess McAlpine, Hallie Showalter, Georgia Miller, Martha Kriese, Muldrew Wilderson, Claudia Lake, Jessis Miller, Lem Shipley, Lila Morris, and John Henry King; (sixth row) Ernest West, Willie Heil, Arthur Noack, Jessie Baker, Eugene Coe, Wilks Herbert, Allie Coe, Harold Fore, Robert Watkins, Hallie Bolton, Claudia Steele, Henry Wesson, Leonard Keller, and James Alexander. (Courtesy Linda Evans.)

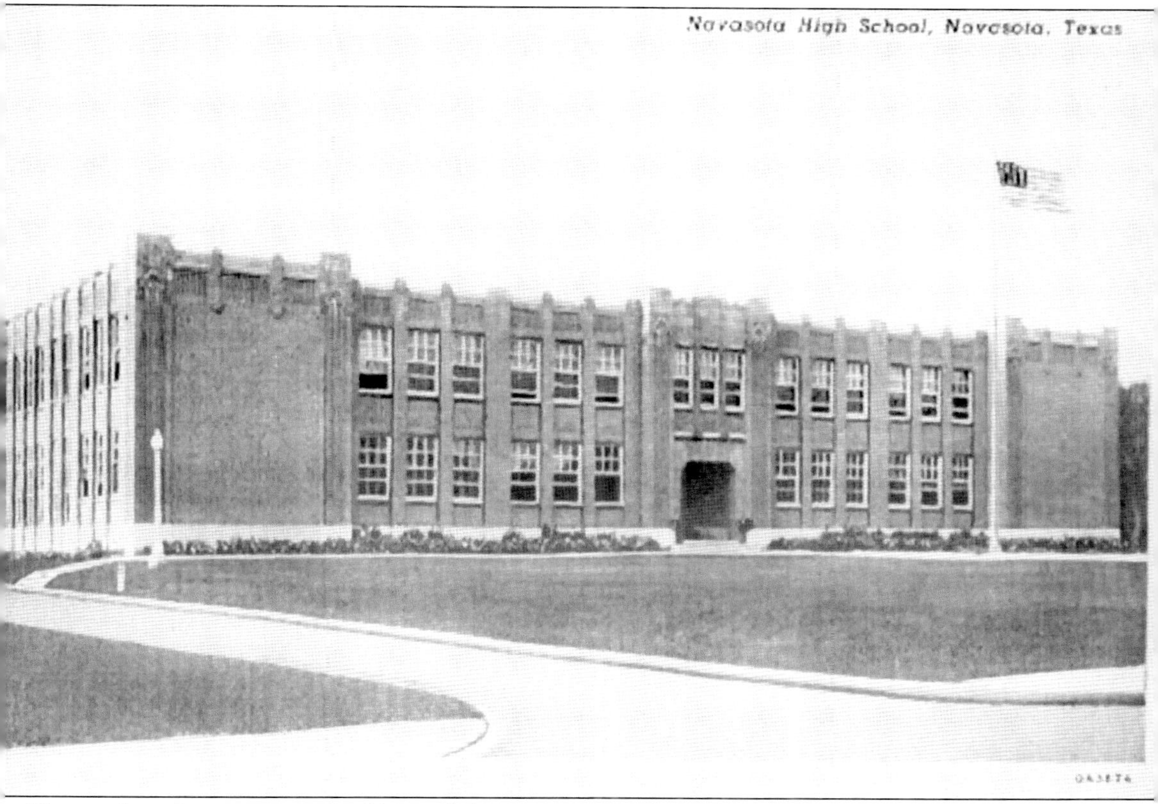

This is the administration building of the Navasota Independent School District (ISD) off Washington Avenue. Classes for African Americans had been held on a limited basis until 1865. In 1875, a small school was constructed on property donated by Ira Camp, next to the current fire station. This school burned in 1910. In stages, by the early 1940s, there was a modern elementary and high school for African Americans on the property; the high school was called George Washington Carver. In 1947, Navasota became an independent school district, and by 1969, all schools in the system were integrated. In 1976, the new high school was ready for business, leaving the old high school, pictured here, as the administration building. The Navasota ISD now features a high school, junior high, intermediate school, and two elementary schools. These operate in conjunction with a Navasota Educational Learning Center. (Courtesy Russell Cushman Collection.)

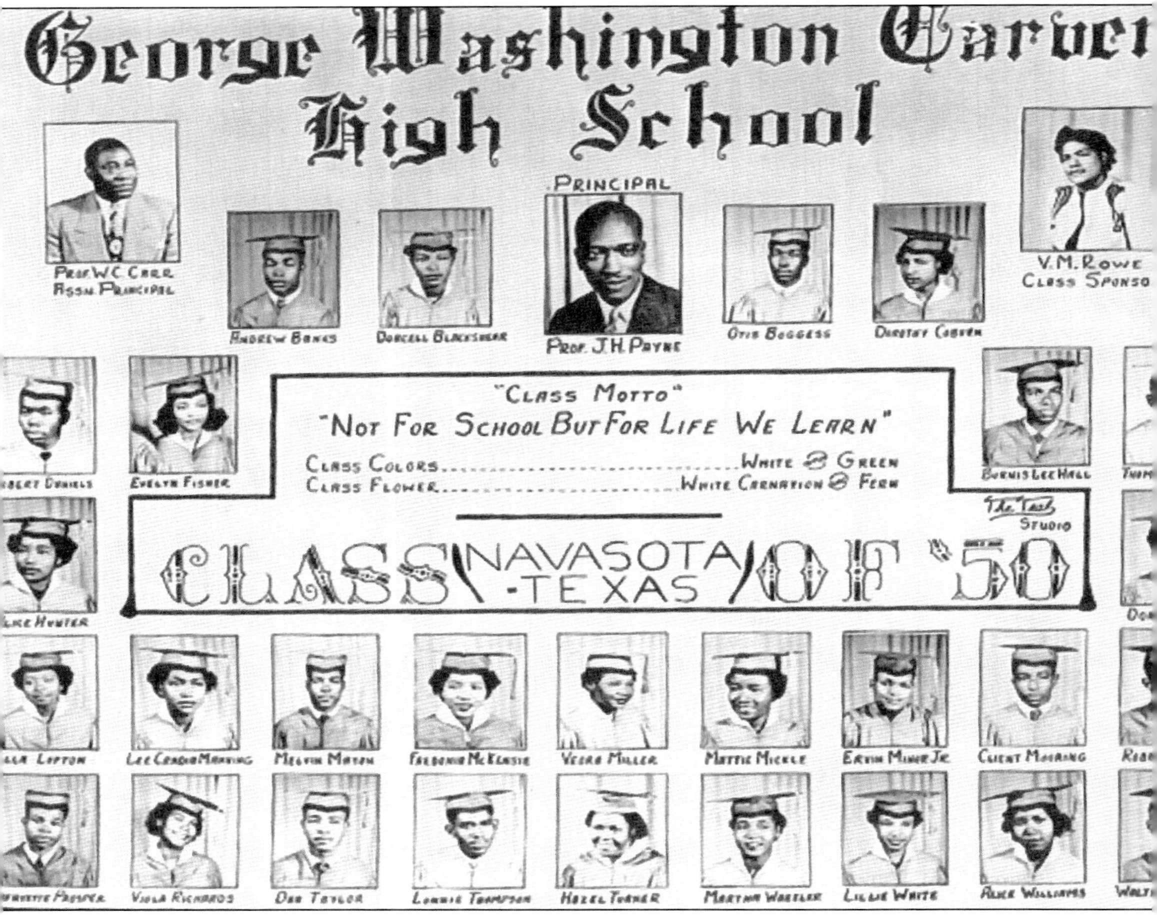

The 1950 graduating class of George Washington Carver High School is shown here. Note the impressive motto, "Not for school but for life we learn." (Courtesy Pamela Vance.)

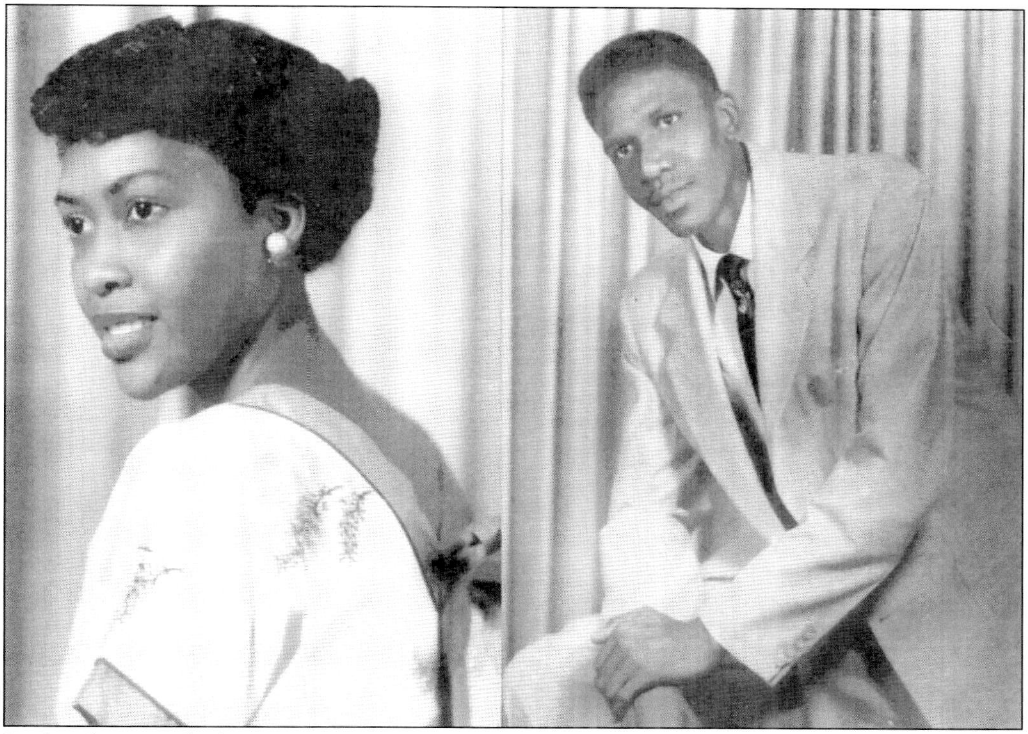

In the photograph above are two members of the George Washington Carver class of 1950. They were high school sweethearts and later married. She was Lee Cradia Manning, Miss Wildcat (similar to a homecoming queen) and the eldest of 12 children. She grew up in the Blackjack community. He was Burnis Lee Hall Jr., co-valedictorian of the class. Both went on to graduate from Prairie View in 1954. They are now retired, he as a lieutenant colonel. Helen Beatrice Washington appears in the photograph at right, the daughter of Rena and George Washington. Helen graduated in 1928. She is seen here in front of her home at 1102 Farquhar Street, across from George Ashford's home, now the Ashford and Oliver Funeral Home. (Both, courtesy Pamela Vance.)

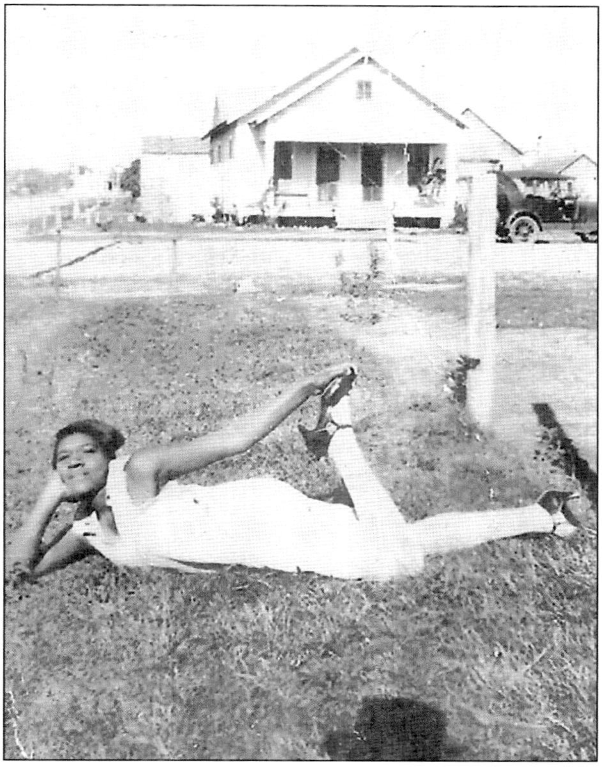

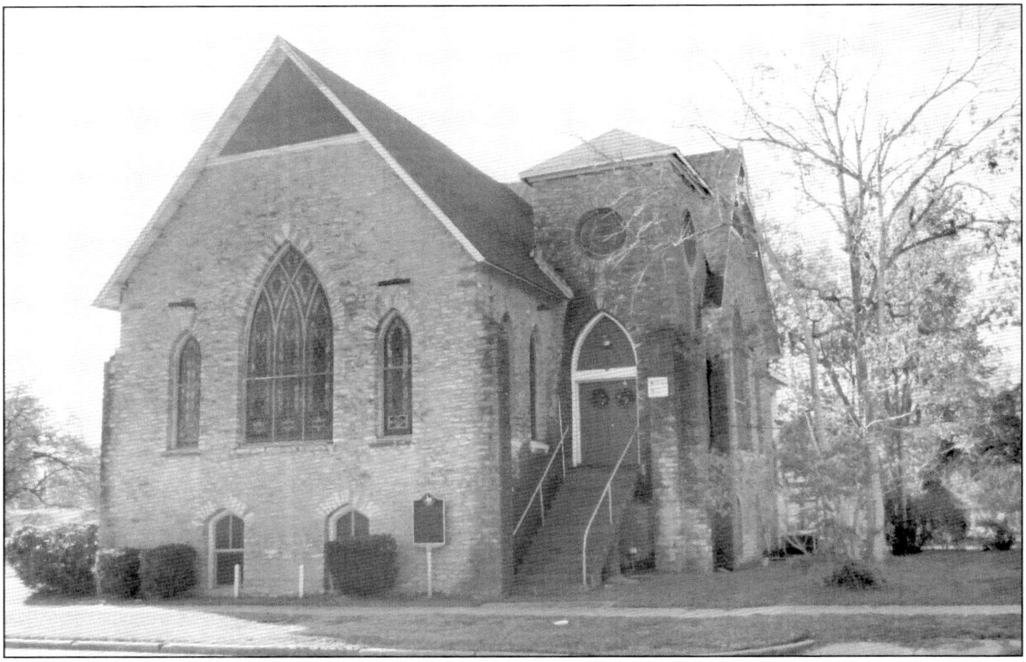

The photograph above shows Lee Tabernacle Methodist Church at 302 Teague Street. This congregation was founded in 1860, and it worshipped with Baptists in shared facilities. In 1866, the congregation erected a church building in what was called "Freeman's Town." The Methodists separated and formally organized in 1876, building a separate facility. The present building dates to 1896. When the structure was completed, the congregation assumed the name "Lee" in honor of then pastor Rev. Edward Lee. This is a fine example of a Gothic Revival church, with arched windows, a tower entry, stained-glass windows, double wood paneled doors, and a gabled roof. The photograph below shows the Lee Tabernacle United Methodist Church group on June 4, 1942. (Above, courtesy Joy Montgomery; below, courtesy Navasota Public Library.)

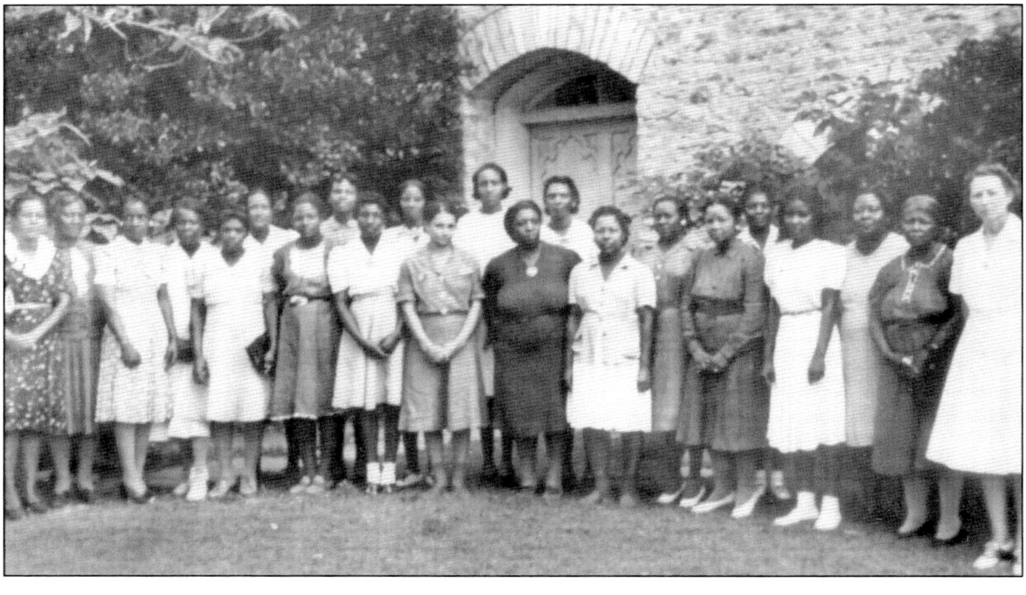

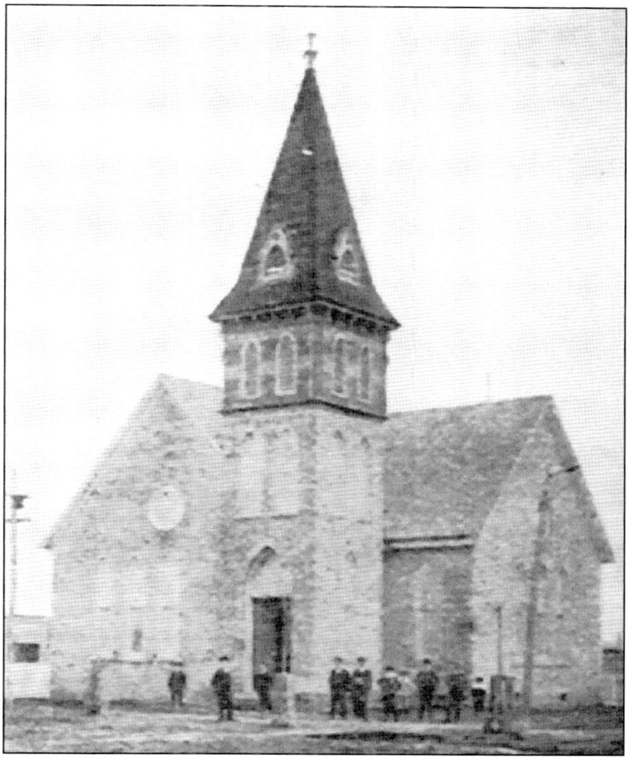

The First United Methodist Church was built in 1959 on 616 Holland Street. In 1866, the Houston and Texas Central Railroad deeded land for this site, where a frame building with shuttered windows was originally constructed. In 1891, a stone building, shown here, replaced the frame structure, and in 1912, a brick sanctuary was built, the forerunner of the present structure. (Courtesy Russell Cushman Collection.)

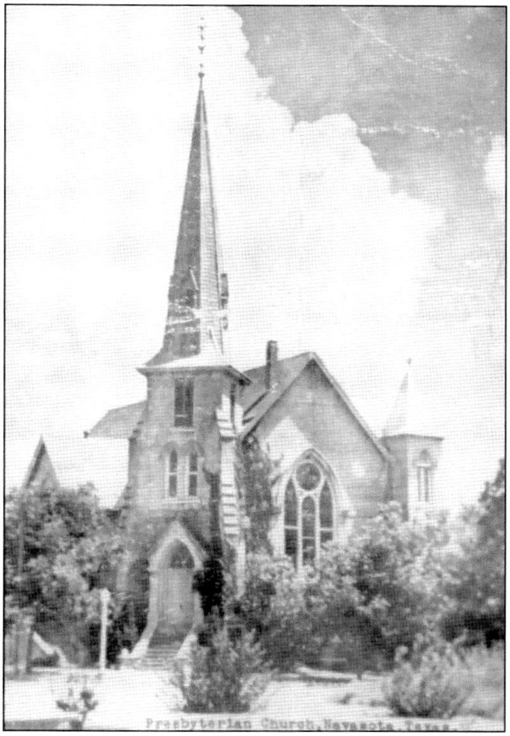

The First Presbyterian Church was organized in 1866 or 1867. Fire having destroyed the original records, the exact date is uncertain. By 1876, the church of Washington-on-the Brazos had been dismantled and rebuilt in Navasota, as the city's first stone church. In 1893, the church was torn down. The present structure was erected the following year on 302 Nolan Street. (Courtesy Russell Cushman Collection.)

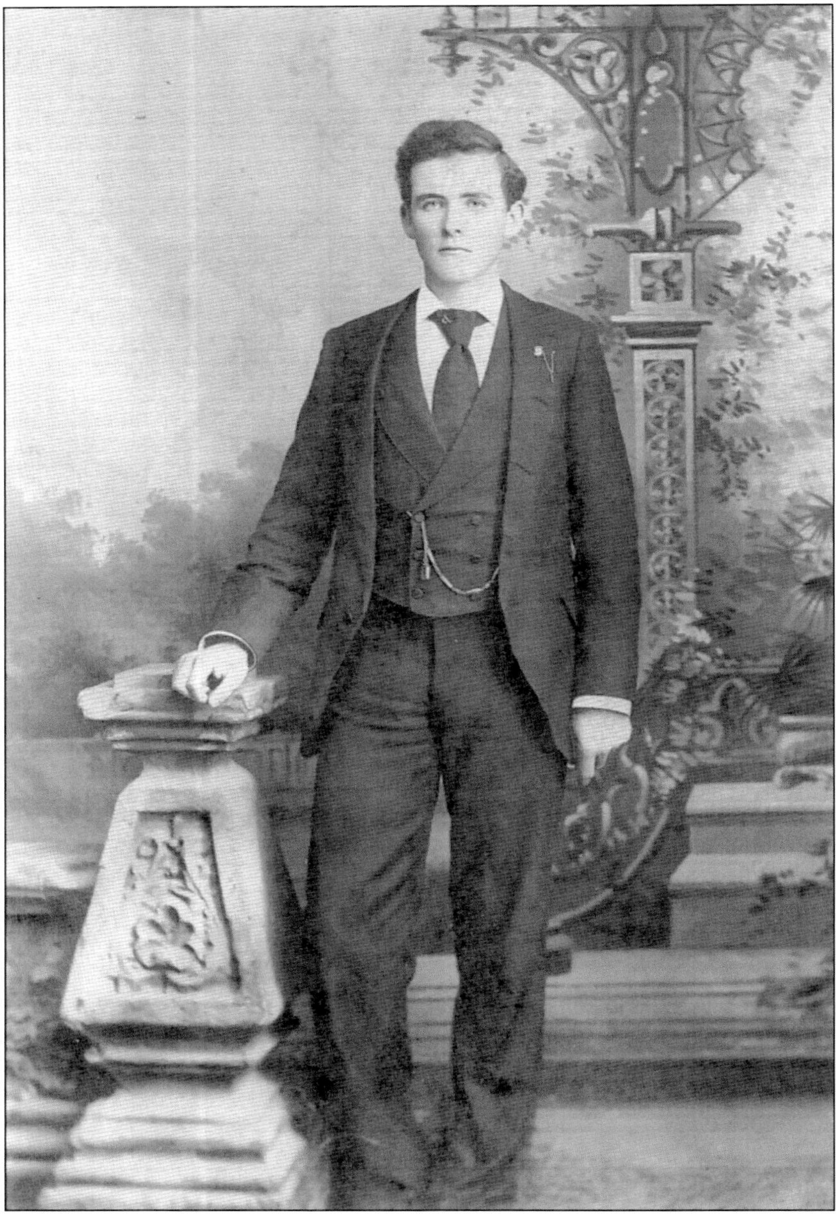

George White McDaniel, a citizen of Navasota, rose to become the president of the Southern Baptist Convention in 1926. Born in 1875 in Grimes County to Francis Asbury and Letitia Anne White McDaniel, he attended school in Navasota but became an orphan at age 16. He was baptized at First Baptist Church in 1892. He was later educated at Baylor University and the Southern Baptist Theological Seminary. He held pastorates in Kentucky and Texas but made his mark on the larger stage while pastor of First Baptist Church of Richmond, Virginia (1905–1927). In his presidential address, he set Baptists on a defining course. He asserted that "This Convention accepts Genesis as teaching that man was a special creation of God, and rejects every theory, evolution or other, which teaches that man originated in, or came by way of, a below animal ancestry." (Courtesy Russell Cushman Collection.)

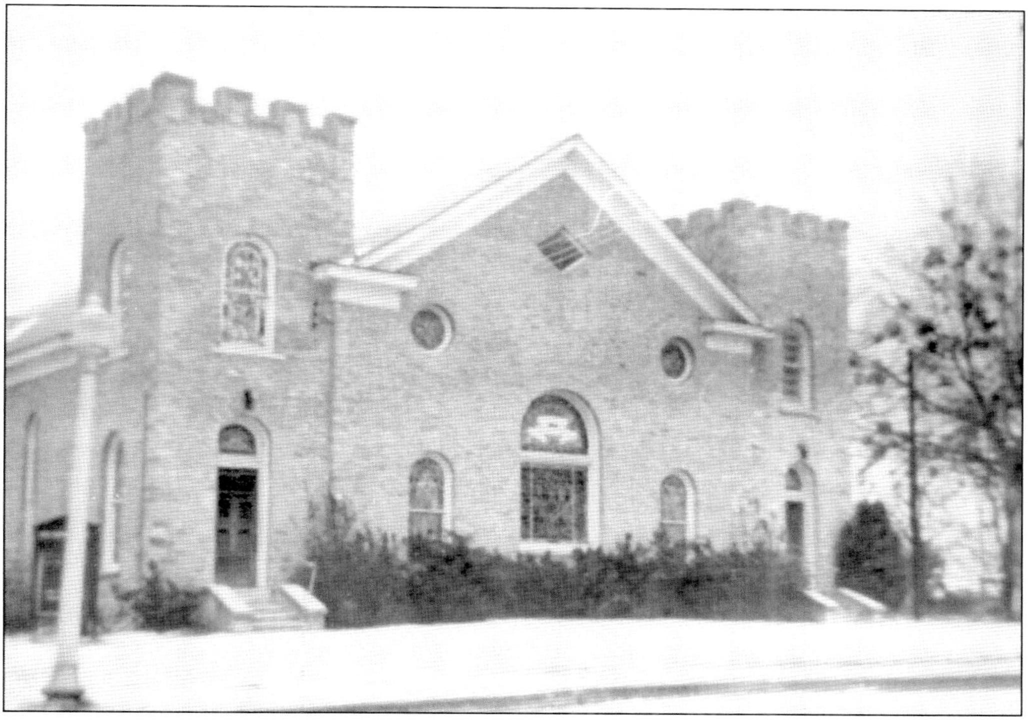

Organized in 1860 with six men, the congregation of First Baptist Church grew quickly, necessitating a new frame structure in 1872. By 1890, after a fire, a stone building with a steeple was erected, and by 1925, a two-story annex was added. Although a larger structure was built in 1955, the 1890 building is still in use. (Courtesy Russell Cushman Collection.)

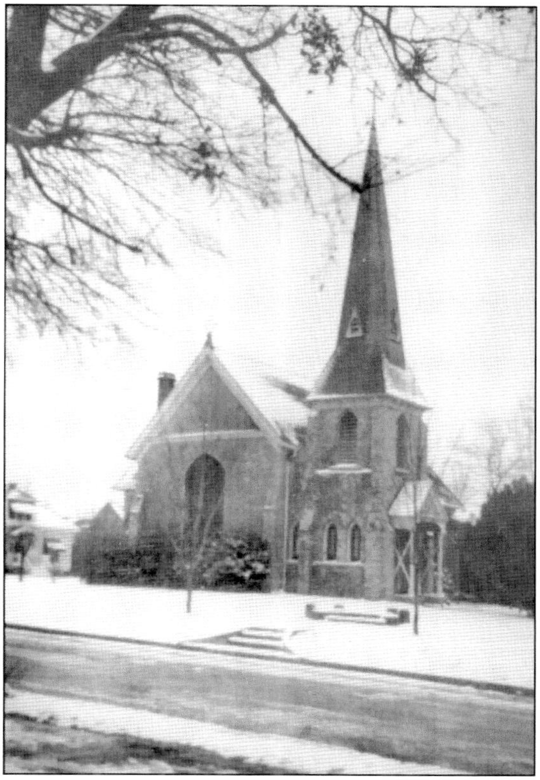

St. Paul's Episcopal Church is located on 414 East McAlpine Street. An Episcopal Parish had been formed in 1866 under the name of the Holy Comforter. When St. Paul's in Washington-on-the Brazos relocated to Navasota in 1870, it assumed the same name at its new site. The congregation completed its new church in 1891. (Courtesy Russell Cushman Collection.)

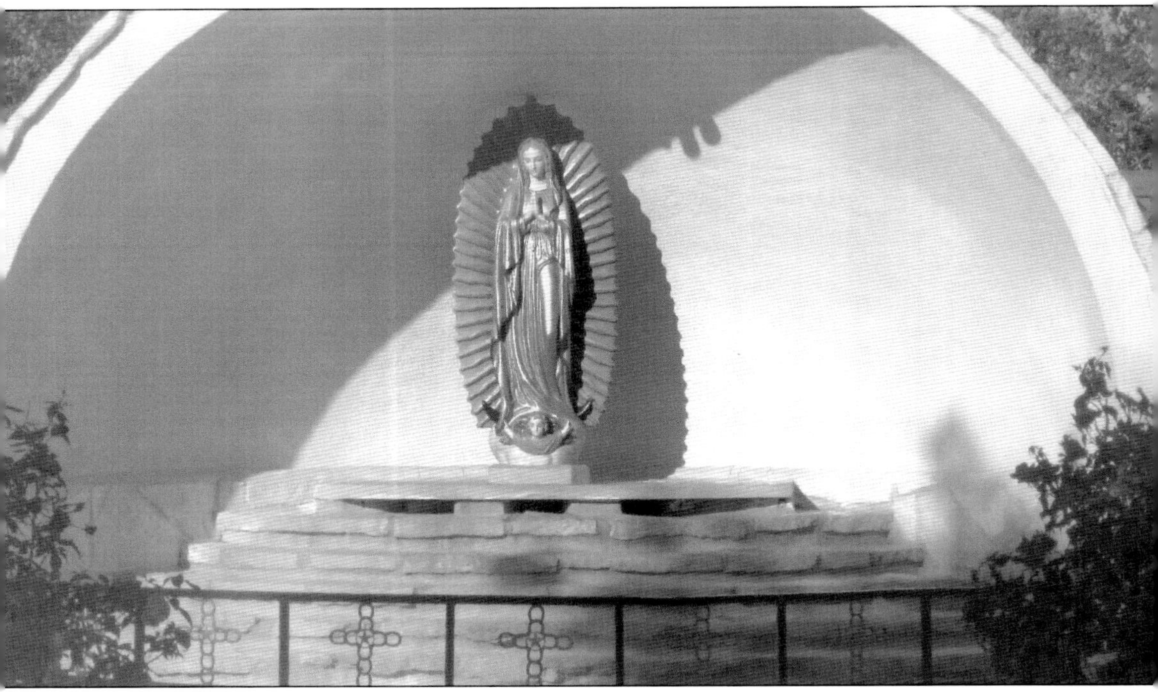

Our Lady of Guadalupe of Christ Our Light Catholic Church was donated by the Torres family. Catholicism in Navasota dates to the Civil War years when the Catholic Diocese of Galveston would occasionally minister to Navasotans. In the early 1870s, the Houston and Texas Central Railroad donated property near the present city hall where the first St. Patrick's church was built. By 1896, that church had burned, and services were held in private quarters. In 1896, property was purchased in the IM Camp Survey, where the second St. Patrick's church was constructed. In 1946, two lots were purchased from Herbert Youens on Church Street. During the next year, an Army chapel in Laredo was dismantled and brought to Navasota. In 1949, consequently, the cornerstone for the third St. Patrick's church was poured. Soon afterwards, the second St. Patrick's church was renewed, largely to serve the emerging Hispanic community. By 1958, that church had been razed and the new Our Lady of Guadalupe was dedicated. In 1982, this church was expanded and renovated, now called Christ Our Light Church. (Courtesy Joy Montgomery.)

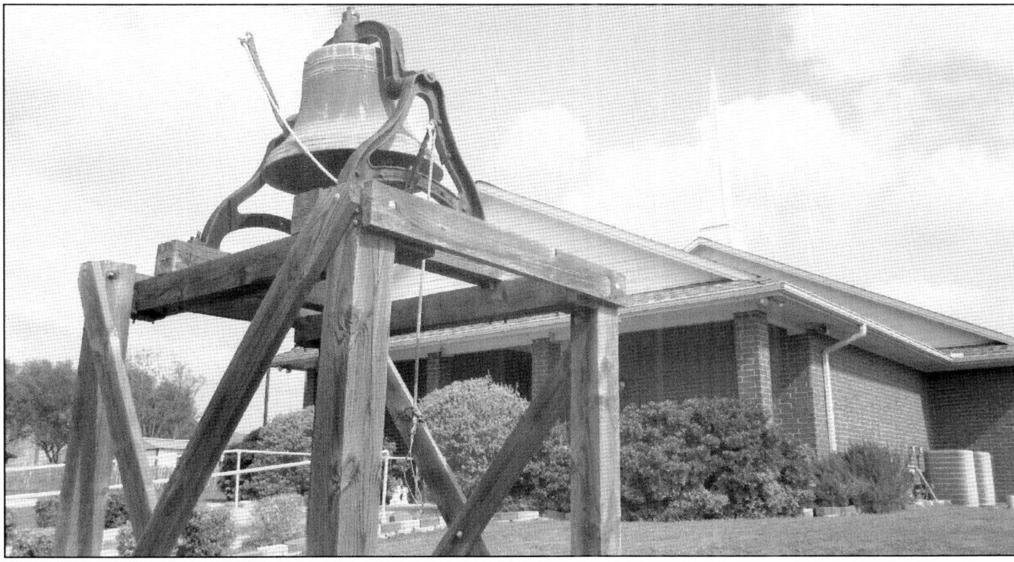

Pictured above is a closeup of the historic bell. The present-day Missionary Camp Baptist Church is pictured below. Organized in 1880, the first services were in a brush arbor on the Blackshear Place southwest of Sand Prairie. Later, Manson Reese donated land for the church at Sand Prairie, about two miles south of the present location. A log cabin was built on the land, named Missionary Camp Baptist Church. The church received the nickname "Sand Prairie" because it was located on a sand bar in the middle of a prairie. Later, a wood-frame building was erected on the site. In January 1991, the church began regular Sunday services with a full-time pastor. In September 2003, under the leadership of Rev. James Mable Sr., the congregation filed into their new and most impressive sanctuary off 105 West. (Both, courtesy Mildred Edwards.)

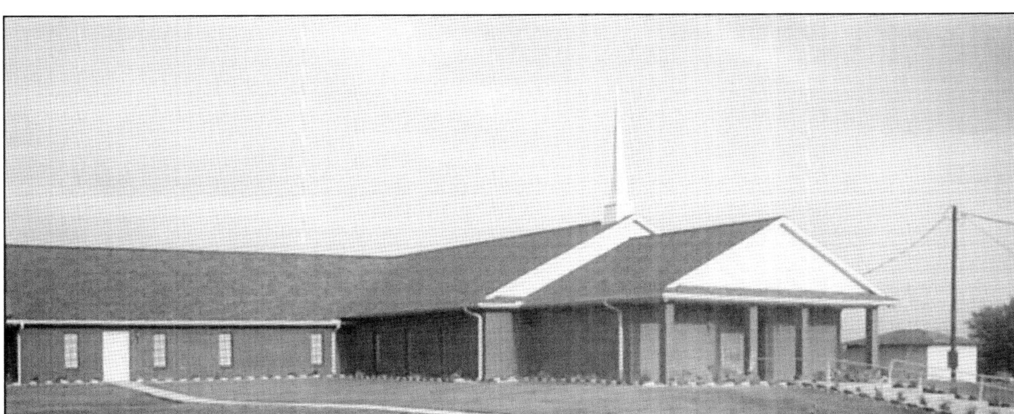

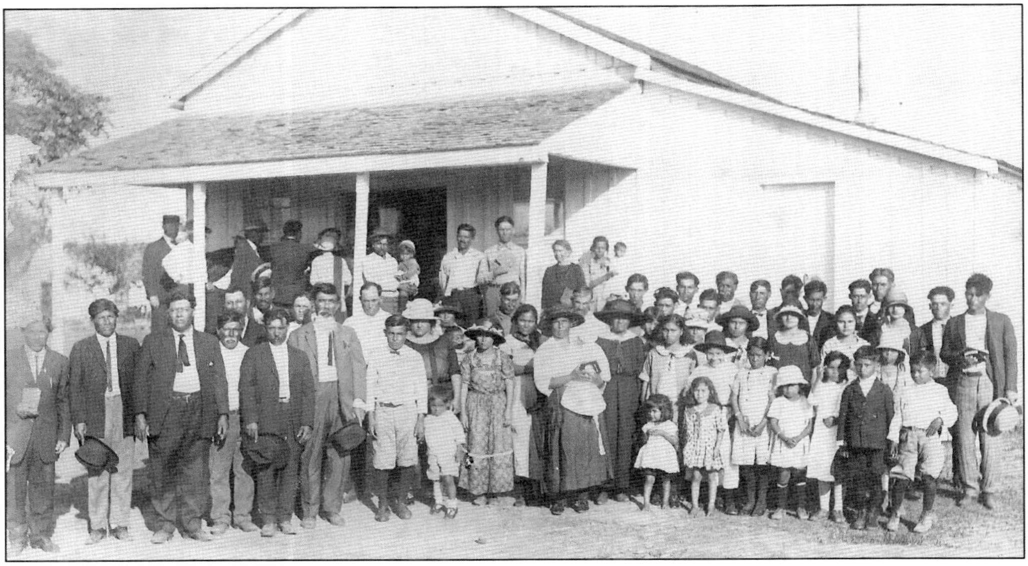

Shown here in 1927 are the Iglesia Mexicana Bautista and congregation, established in 1919. The church was independent yet Southern Baptist in doctrine. From 1934 to 1995, it was a "Mexican Mission" to First Baptist Church. Incorporated in 2008, it is now known as Iglesia Bautista de Navasota. Plans call for the establishment of a new structure off the Highway 6 Bypass 797 sometime in 2012. (Courtesy Pastor Jose Maldonado.)

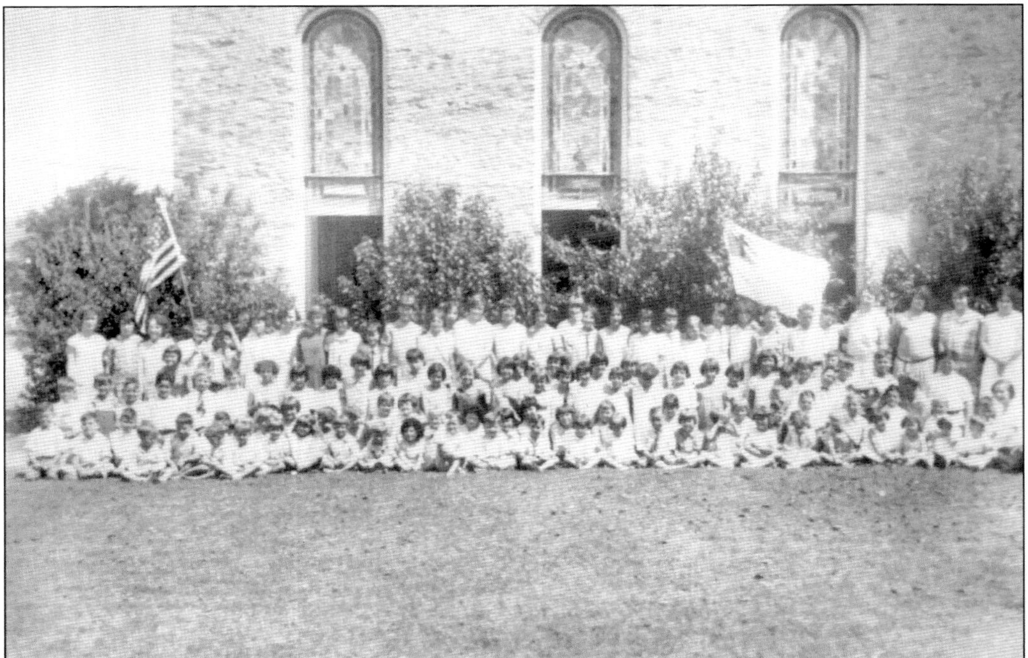

Formed during the early days of Navasota, the Methodist, Baptist, Presbyterian, and Episcopal churches had much in common. Respect for their common heritage is evident in this photograph. Pictured here is First Baptist Church. The occasion is a daily Vacation Bible School, sponsored by all four of these churches in the 1920s. (Courtesy Navasota Public Library.)

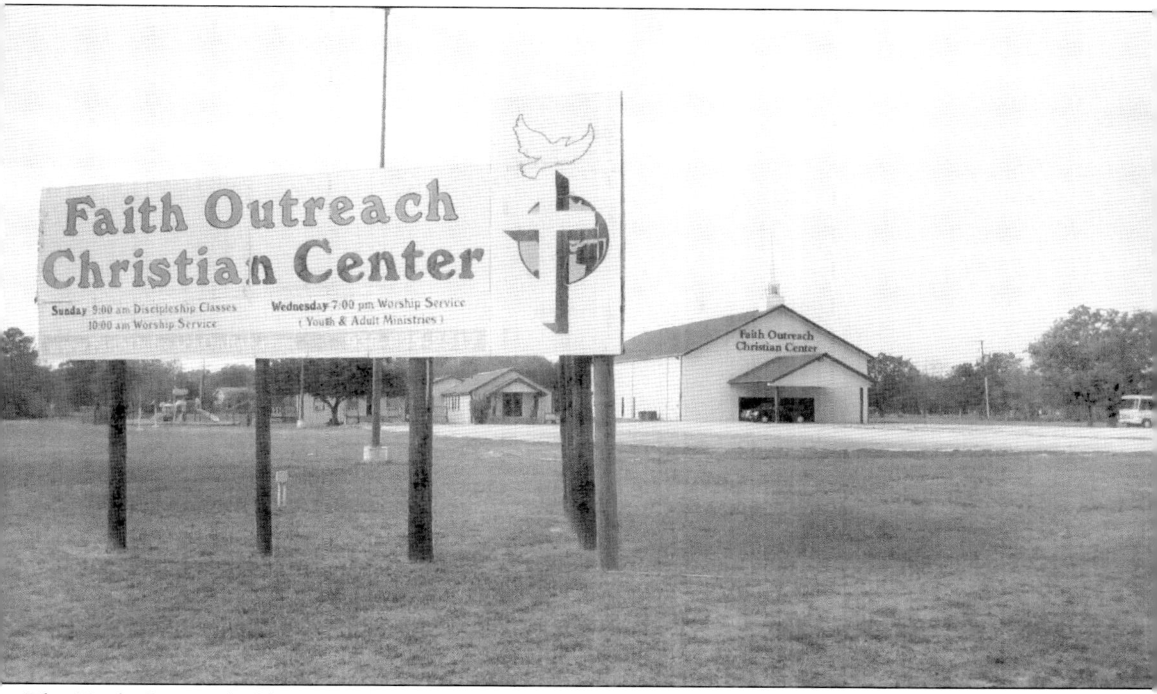

The Faith Outreach Christian Center is an interdenominational spirit-filled fellowship of New Testament believers. The church is located about a mile south of Navasota off the west side of Highway 6. Feeling a calling, pastors Henry and Naomi Sanders founded the church in 1976. The vision of the church is summarized on their website in three phrases: "A Servant-Hearted Family Church," "A Spirit-Filled Teaching and Training Center," and "A World Outreach Center." The purpose of the outreach is stated thusly, "We believe a Great Commitment to the Great Commission and Great Commandment will build a great church for our heavenly father." The church supports many local and foreign ministries. Faith Outreach Christian Center is not a denomination. Rather, it acknowledges all born-again believers around the world as being a part of the body of Christ. (Courtesy Faith Outreach Christian Center.)

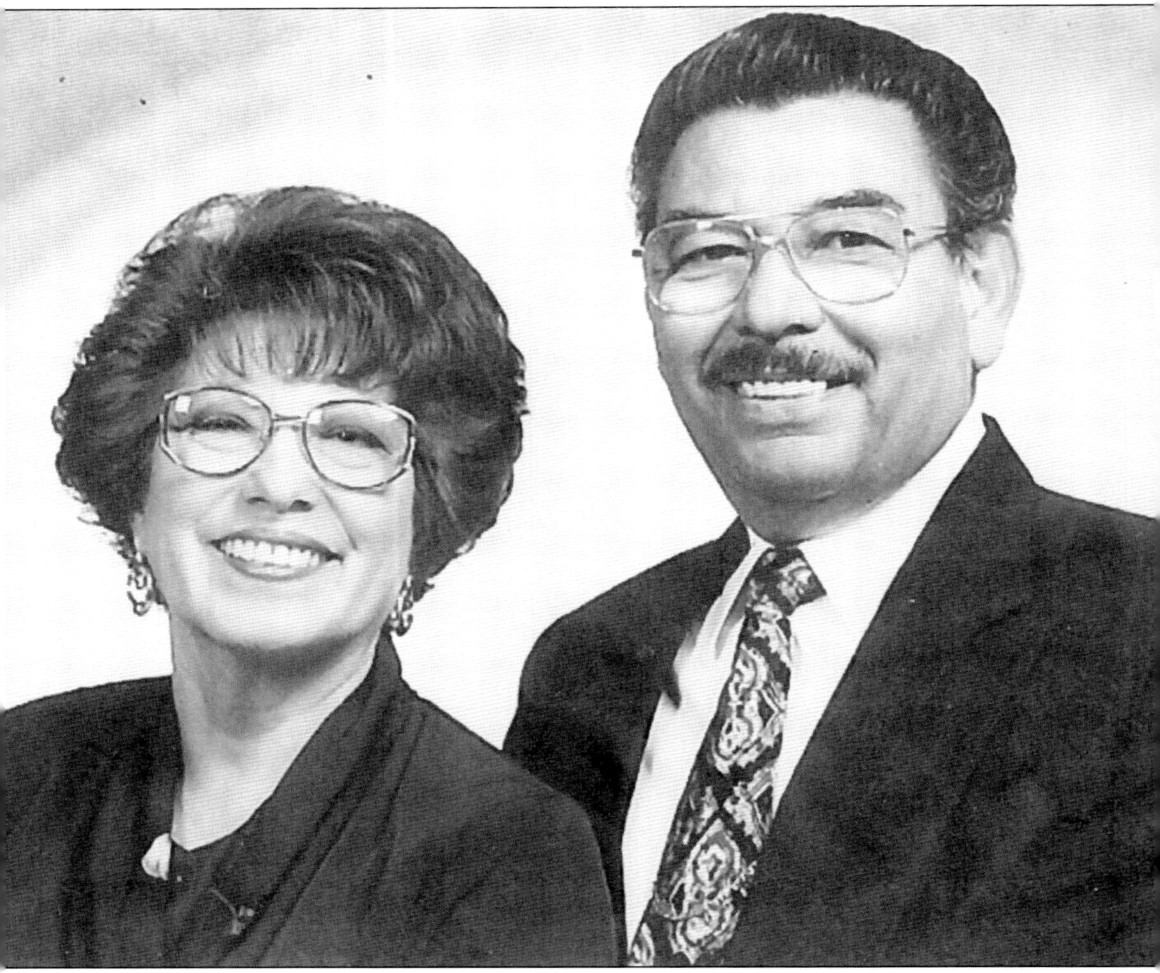

Faith Outreach Christian Center has missions in many places, both nationally and internationally. One of these places is Mexico. Pictured here are pastors Henry and Josie Zaragoza, missionaries in Mexico. When available in the United States, they conduct services in Spanish. (Courtesy Faith Outreach Christian Center.)

Six

Street Scenes

Old Navasota was far to the east of the later railroads. In 1876, in a "Brief Sketch of Navasota," Dr. Andrew Robert Kilpatrick writes, "Where the city of Navasota is, was a forest and open prairie till about 1855, when James Nolan built a double log house at the eastern end of town . . . Mr. Nolan cultivated a field of 15 acres in cotton in 1858–59. Extending from his (then) residence down around [the Union School]. Embracing the land where the Methodist, Baptist, and Presbyterian churches and adjacent buildings now are." Kilpatrick also tells how Col. J.K. Holland tried and failed to establish a town called Hollandale. Verplanck Ackerman received an appointment as postmaster of Hollandale but only for a while.

There was also an attempt to place the town on the Daniel Tyler land just south of the present center of town. Kilpatrick noted that this was "a much more desirable place for a town, but the parties concerned could not agree on the terms." Kilpatrick states that, "it has been estimated that the owners . . . of city property in Hempstead, feared the prospective rivalry with Hempstead, and would make no effort to foster a town that would compete with Hempstead."

Ira Camp invested a fortune financially in an effort to start a railroad to the east, but alas, when the railroad came, it came to the west, along present Railroad Street, so the center of Navasota merged to the west to accommodate it.

This chapter focuses on businesses and houses primarily along Washington Avenue but also on other avenues, moving from the old town of the east, to the business center of the west.

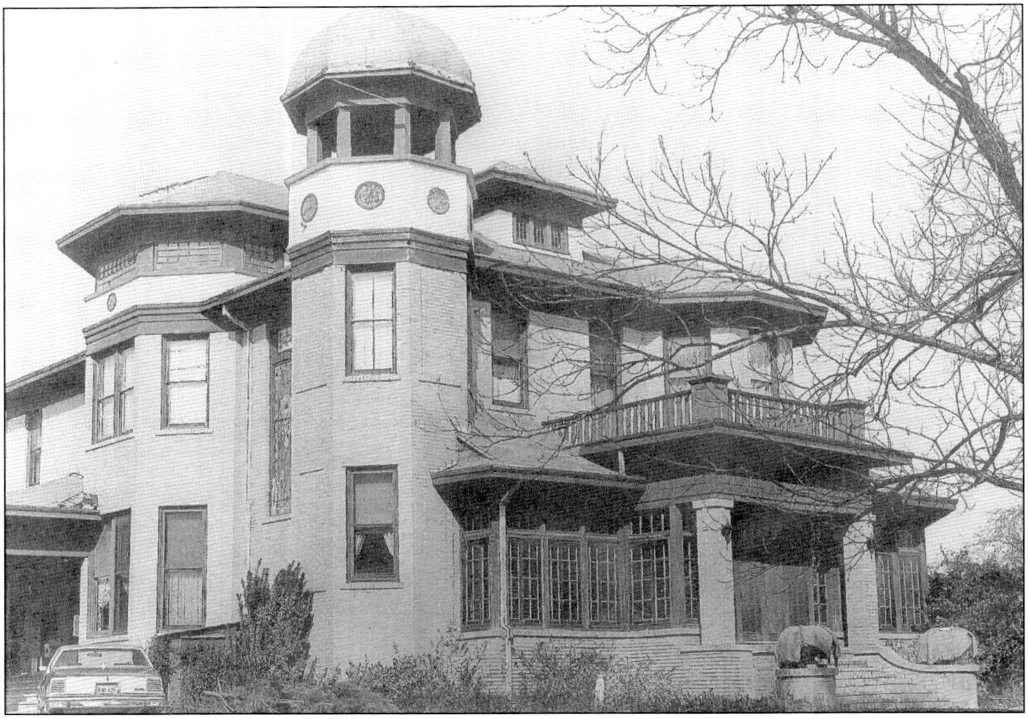

The Templeman House is located on 1403 East Washington Avenue. Known locally as "the Castle," the house was built in the mid-1890s for newlyweds Ward B. and Annie Foster Templeman. Originally of Queen Anne design, it was modified to suit the Prairie School style of architecture in the early 20th century. (Courtesy J.D. Dickenson.)

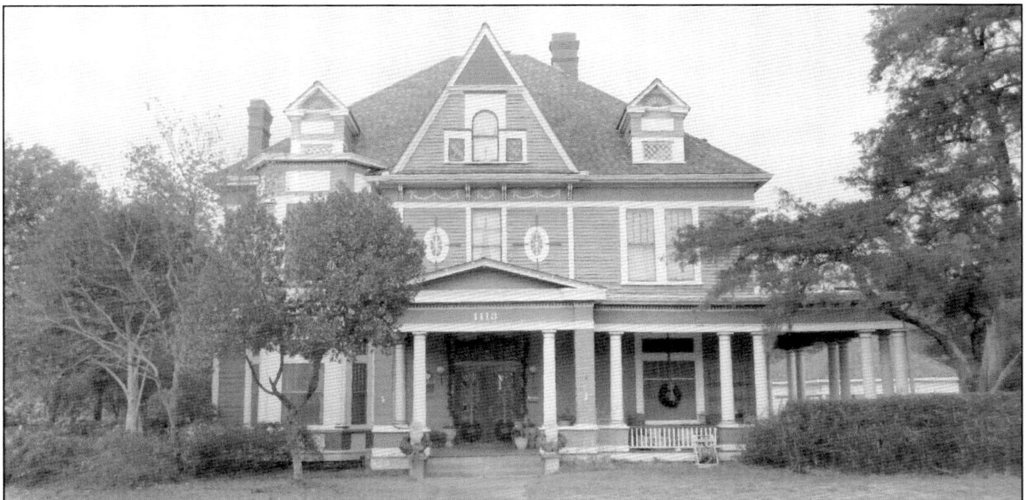

Robert Andrew Sangster, using a portion of the proceeds from a winning lottery ticket, built the pale blue Sangster House at 1113 East Washington Avenue in 1902. The Queen Anne Revival style is featured with Classical Revival elements on the exterior. The 12-room interior is decorated with curly and red-pine woodwork. (Courtesy Texas Center for Regional Studies.)

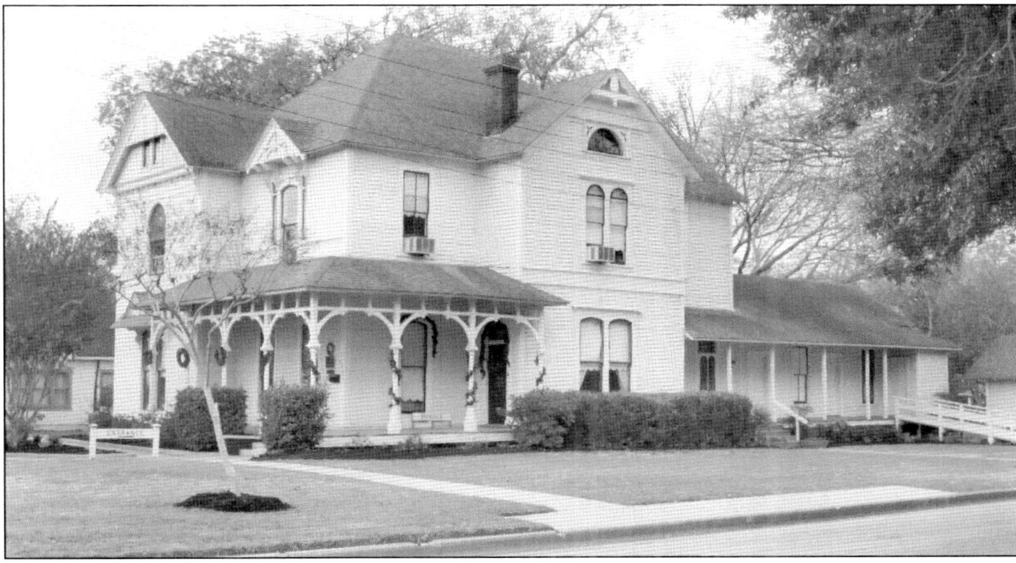

The Robert Augustus Horlock House stands at 1215 East Washington Avenue. A prominent businessman and civic leader, he and his wife, Agnes White Horlock, had this house built in 1892. It stayed in the family for nearly 100 years, when it was eventually turned over to the city of Navasota. (Courtesy Texas Center for Regional Studies.)

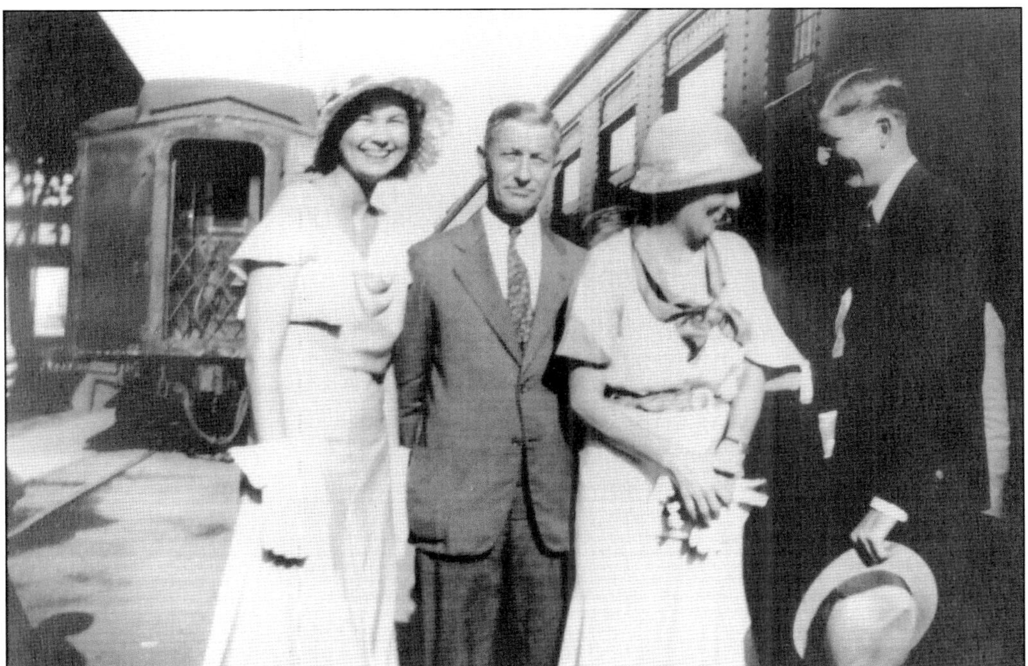

Second-generation Horlocks enjoy a sunny day on the platform of the train station. From left to right are Lillian, her husband Arthur, Lillie, and Fisher Horlock. (Courtesy Horlock History Center.)

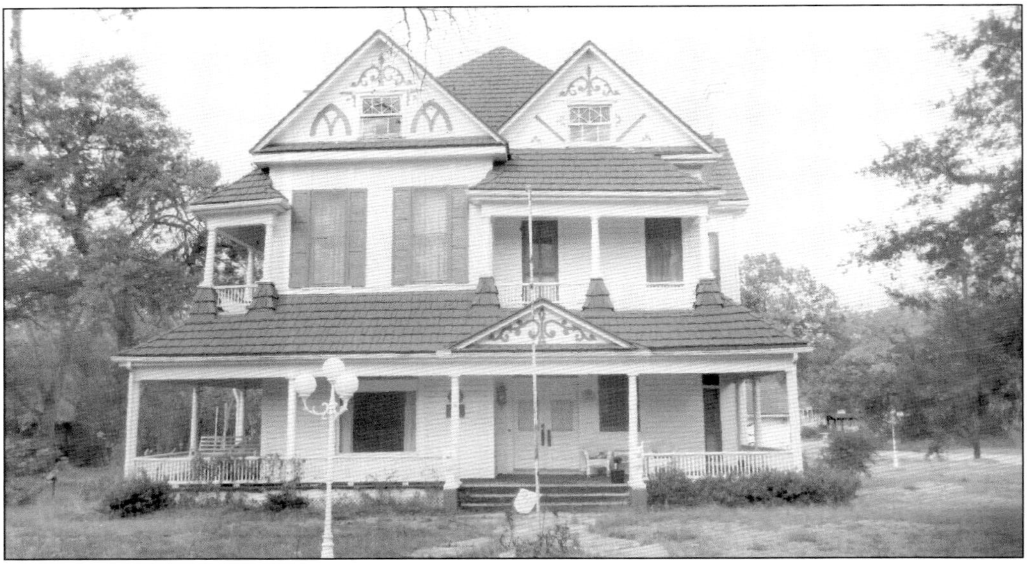

This turn-of-the-20th century home at 1015 East Washington Avenue was built in 1900 under the auspices of Mattie Brigance Foster, daughter of early Grimes County settler Franklin Brigance. Incorporating Colonial Revival and Shingle style in a cypress-frame construction with a gabled roof, the house was built soon after the death of her husband. (Courtesy Texas Center for Regional Studies.)

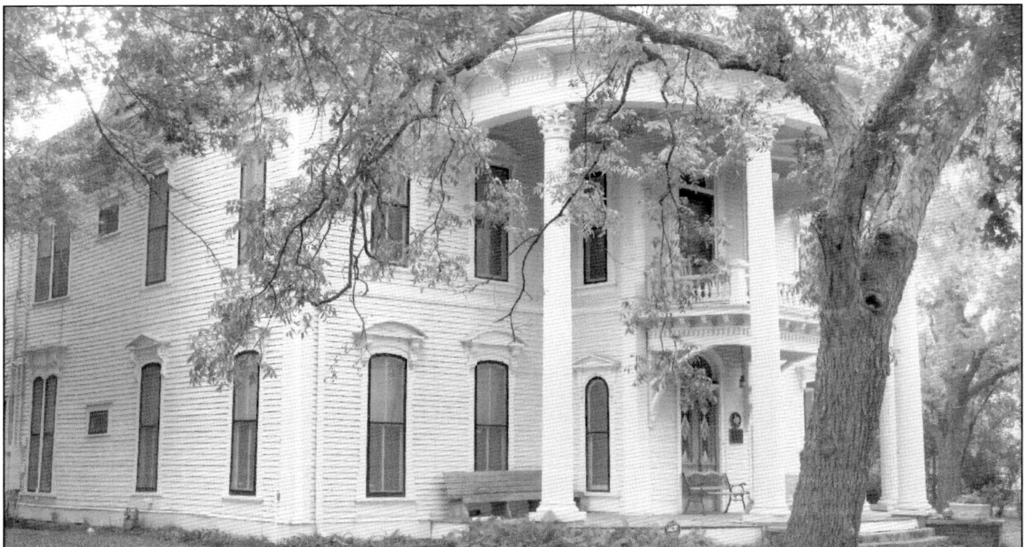

This home at 612 East Washington Avenue is known as the Joseph Brooks Home. A Confederate veteran of the Civil War, Joseph Brooks also survived the yellow fever epidemic of 1867 and went on to become a successful and leading area lumberman. Originally in the Victorian design, Brooks built this home in the 1870s. In the first decade of the 20th century, the style was streamlined to Classical Revival. (Courtesy Texas Center for Regional Studies.)

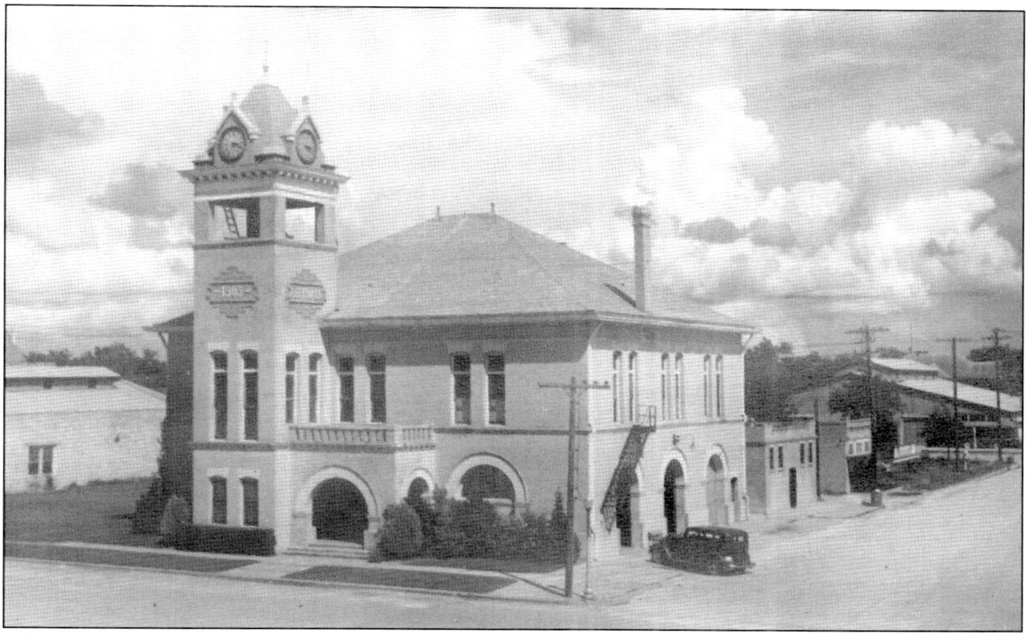

The city hall was built in 1903 and demolished in 1957. It went down in a blaze of international glory thanks to photographer Bob Whitten, who caught the tower in the act of falling. His photograph was featured in newspapers as far away as the *London Illustrated News*, and he received the *Headliners Club Award* for outstanding news photography. (Courtesy Bert Miller.)

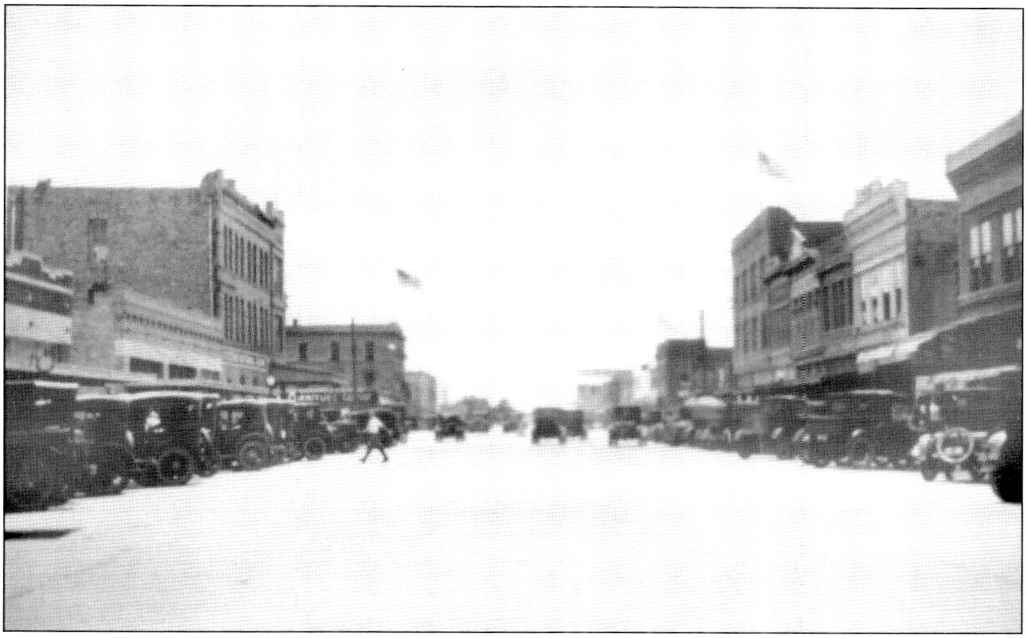

Pictured here in the early 1900s, Washington Avenue runs east to west in downtown Navasota, east of the railroads. Note the dated automobiles and lack of markers on the street floor. Also, there are several American flags flying high and free, reflecting the patriotism of the time. (Courtesy Navasota Public Library.)

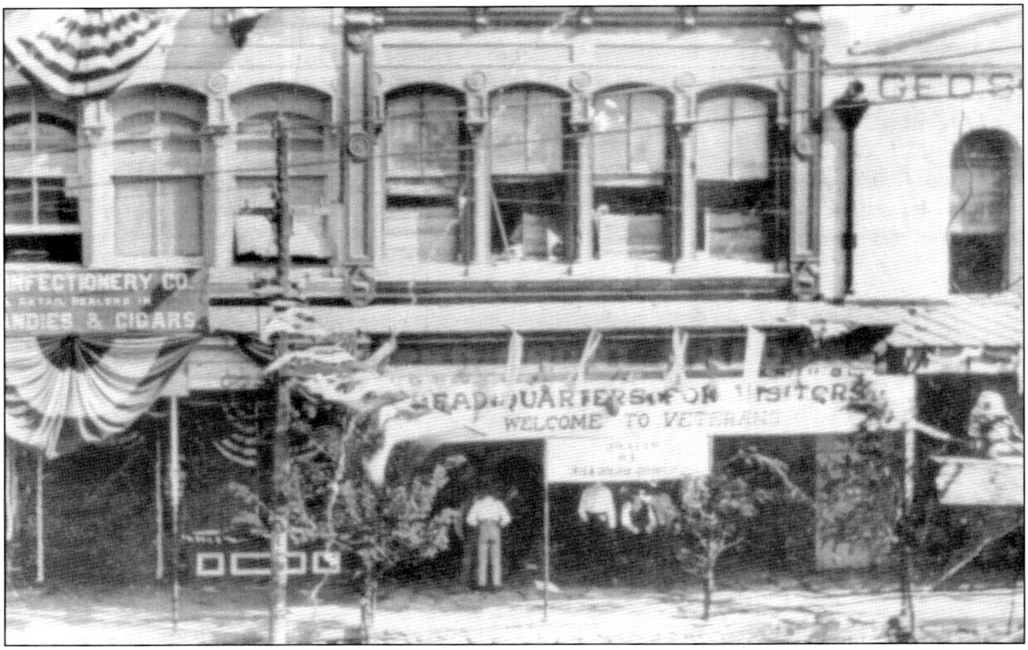

From left to right in the 1907 photograph above are Manos Confectionery Company, Jim Lee's Saloon, and the George Wood Store, respectively, at 107, 109, and 111 East Washington Avenue. Note that a banner in front of the saloon welcomes veterans of Hood's Brigade to one of Navasota's many parades and ceremonies in the day. In the early 20th century, saloons were popular and plentiful in Navasota. This was shortly before mighty Marshal Frank Hamer came to town to bring law, order, and stability to the region. The c. 1920 photograph below shows the inside of Manos Confectionery. The business dealt in both wholesale and retail, featuring "Fruits, Candies and Cigars." (Both, courtesy Navasota Public Library.)

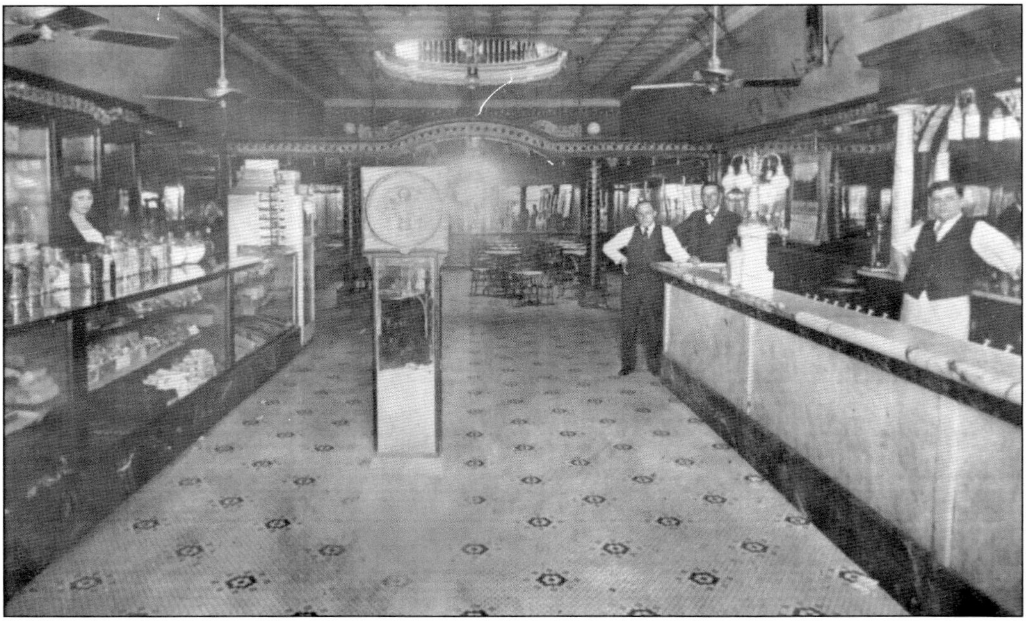

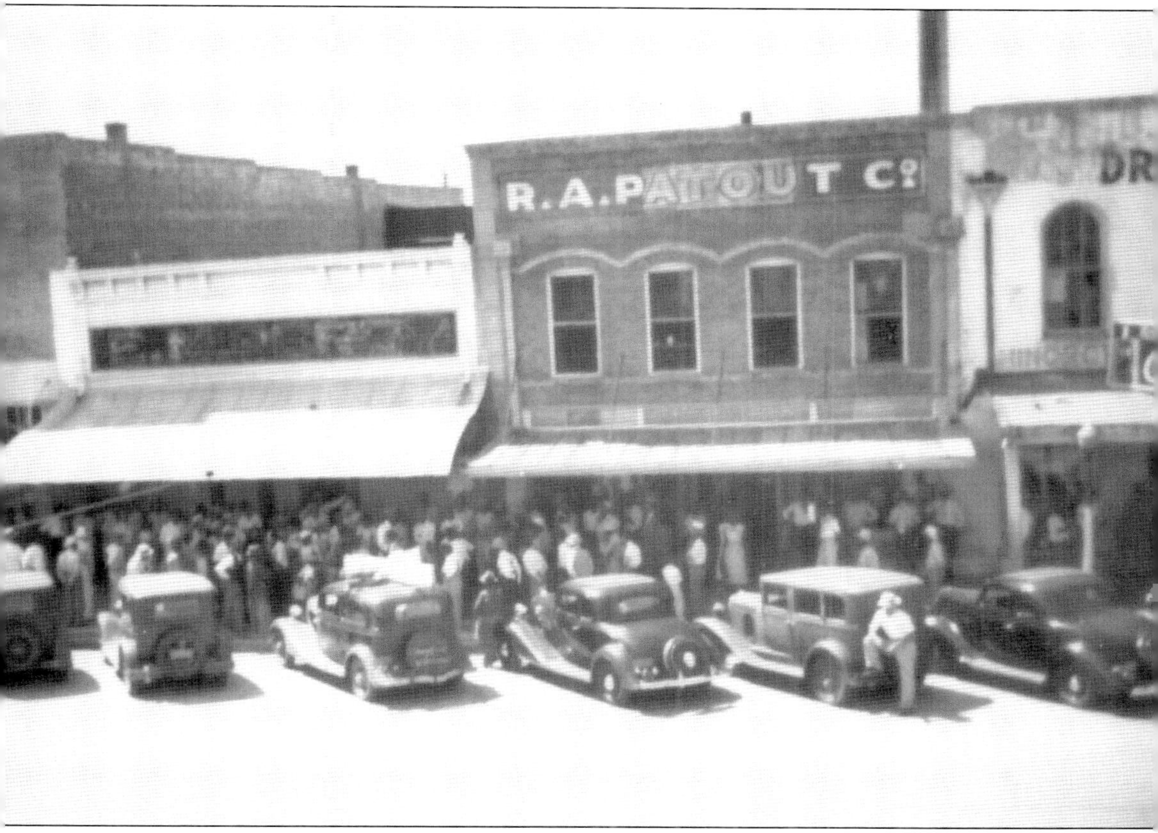

A Saturday afternoon in the summer of 1936 on Washington Avenue is depicted here. From left to right are the establishments of E.M. Perry, R.A. Patout Company, and Camp Drug Company. The property of the Patout store dates to very early Navasota, as evidenced by a cistern found during construction work in 1976. The supposition is that the cistern once belonged to C.S. Taliaferro, who bought the lot from the famous Judge James Nolan. Nolan, in turn, had bought the land as part of a larger tract from D.D. Greer and Company in 1856. Greer had purchased 1,054 acres from the grant of Daniel Arnold. Arnold was one of the original pioneers to establish a presence on the site later called Navasota. D.D. Greer, who purchased Arnold's land, was the source for the land on which the original Union School was built in 1854. (Courtesy Navasota Public Library.)

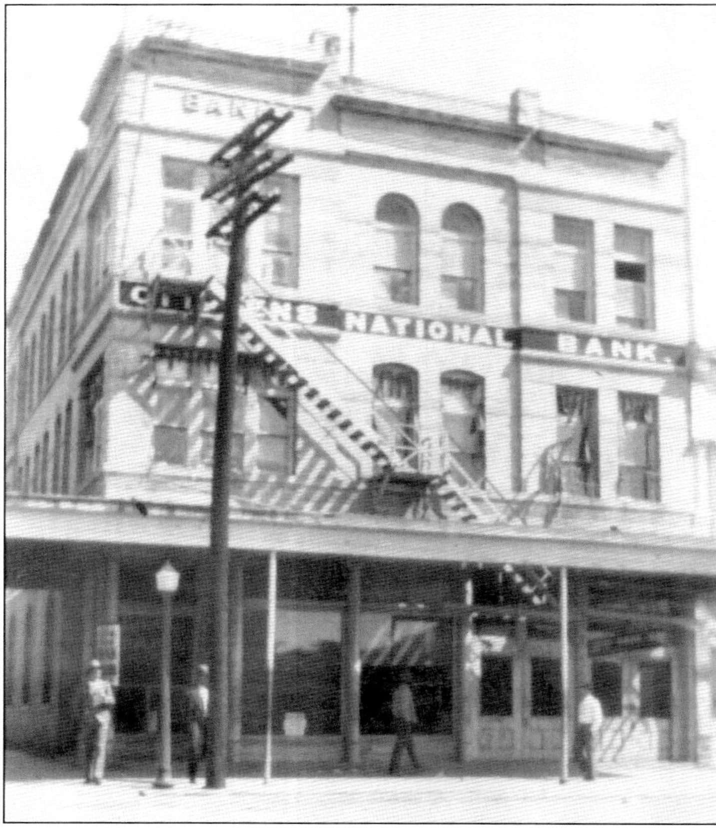

Pictured at left in the 1920s, the side of Citizen's National Bank is visible at the intersection of Railroad and Washington Streets. In the photograph below, the front of the same building is visible, when it was the site of the Hotel Bluebonnet. Other businesses shown here are Buckalew's Grocery and Market, a café to the left, and a glimpse of the building that was once the Smith Hotel to the right. Note the large advertisement for ice cream. Also interesting are the cars parked along the busy thoroughfare. This intersection has ever been a pivotal area of Navasota. (Left, courtesy Navasota Public Library; below, courtesy Terrell Collection.)

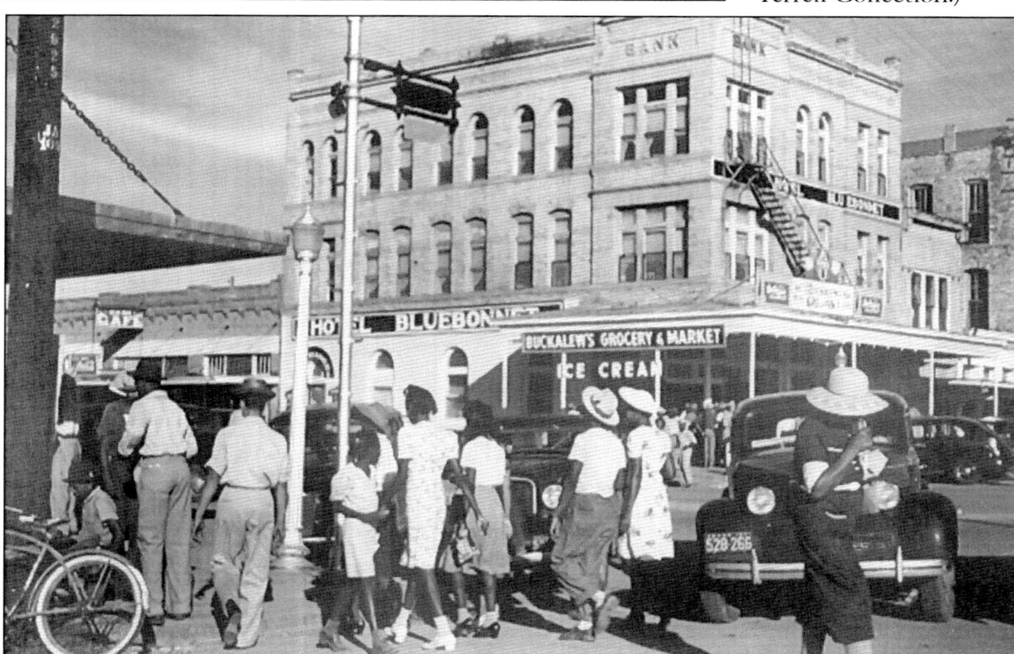

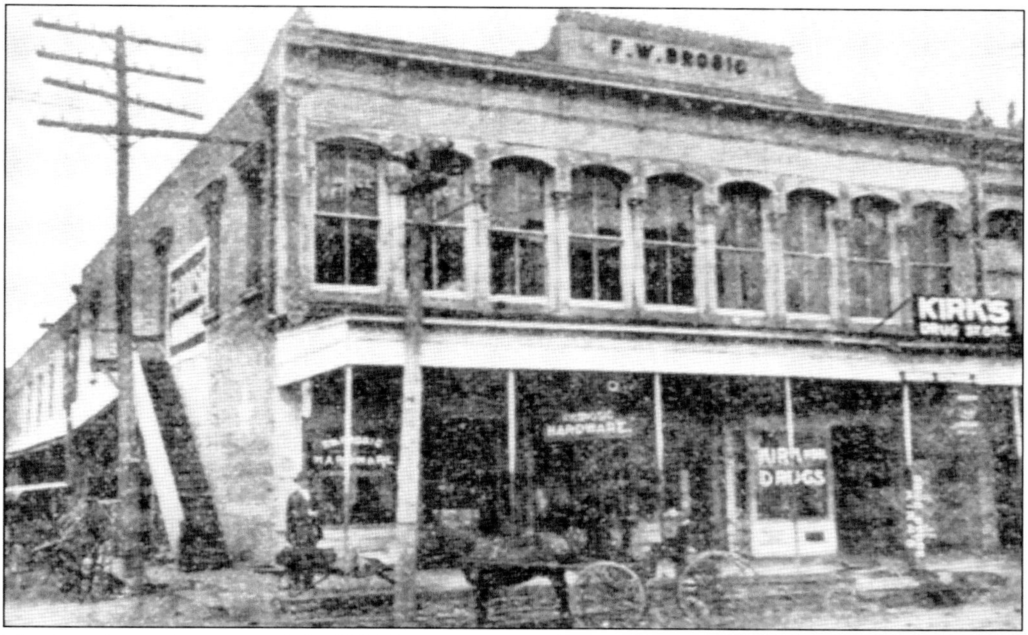

The interior and exterior of the F.W. Brosig store are featured in these photographs. The store was located off East Washington Avenue on the site of the earlier Judge Nolan Hotel and across the street from the Citizen's Bank. A German by birth in 1842, Brosig spent most of his childhood in Houston. Later he served in the Confederate army, ultimately being stationed in Anderson. In 1867, he married Josephine Shafer and moved to Navasota. Soon thereafter, she died of yellow fever. Meanwhile, Brosig had taken over his father-in-law's store. Though suffering three serious business losses by fire, Brosig, a giant of his community, persevered until 1893. (Above, courtesy Marcus Mallard; below, courtesy Navasota Public Library.)

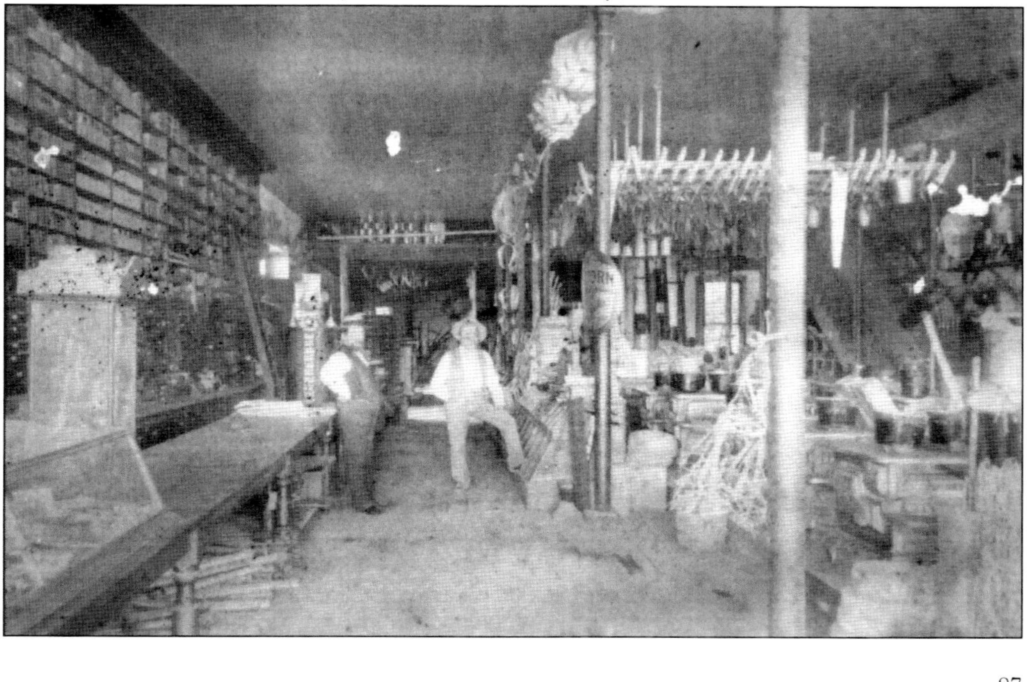

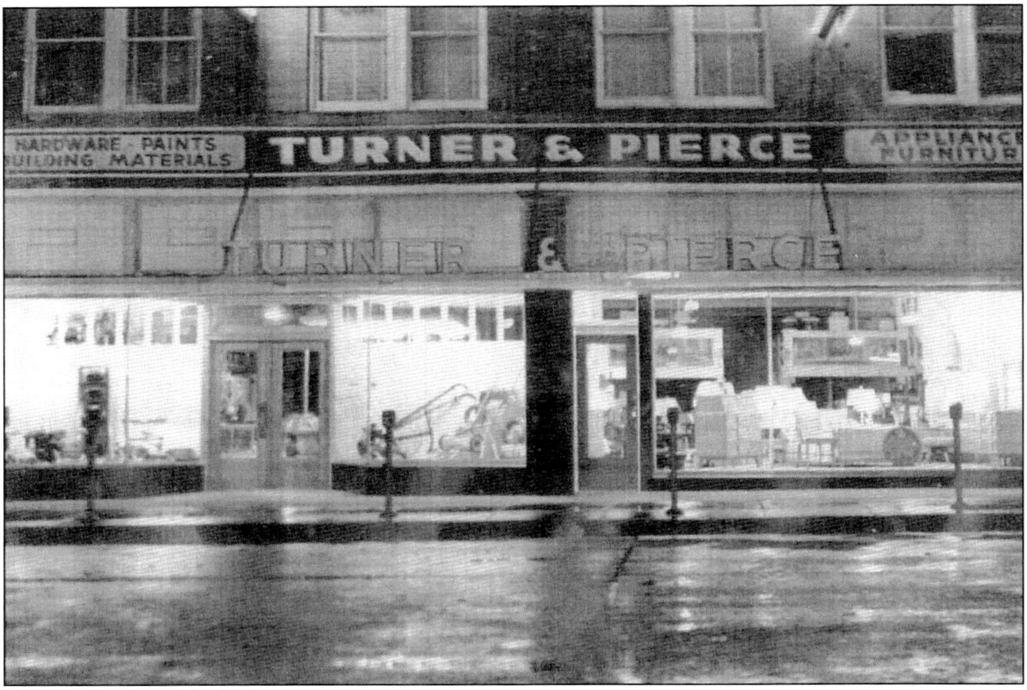

In the photograph above, Turner Pierce and Fultz Hardware occupied the site of the Brosig Building from 1934 until 1974, when the business moved to its present location west of the tracks down Washington Avenue. The original store also had branches on the west side of the tracks. In the photograph below, from left to right, are Harvey R. Turner, G. Schaeffer Pierce, and Joe K. Fultz Sr. This threesome owned the store at the time of the move of the main store to the west side of the tracks. (Above, Courtesy Marcus Mallard; below, courtesy Joe King Fultz.)

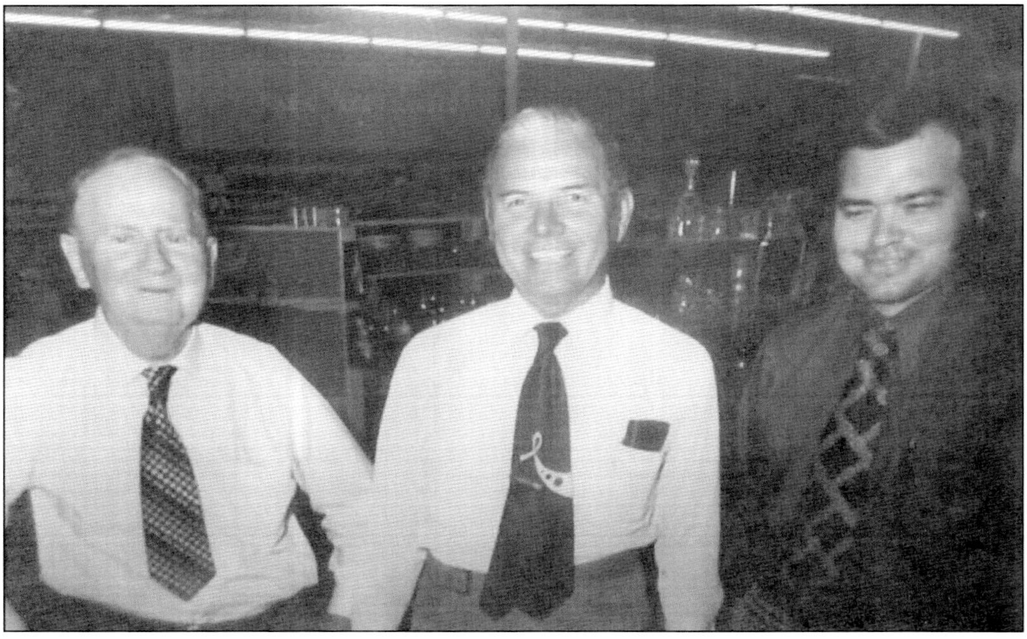

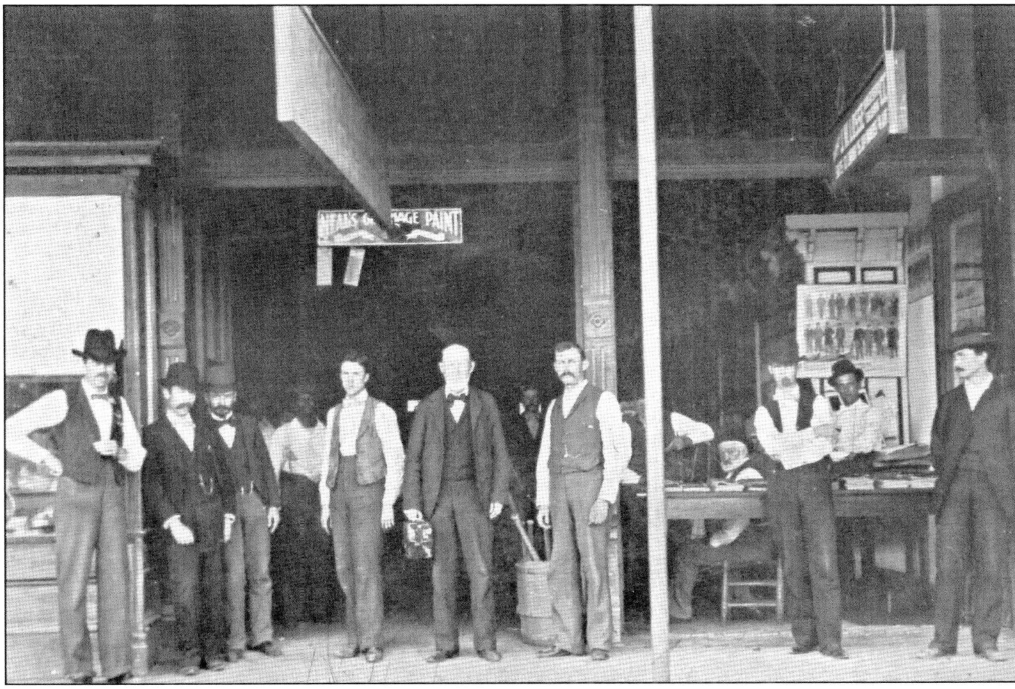

The pharmacy of Dr. A.R. Kilpatrick was next to the Brosig store. Ketchum's Drug now occupies the site of the Kilpatrick store. (Courtesy Russell Cushman Collection.)

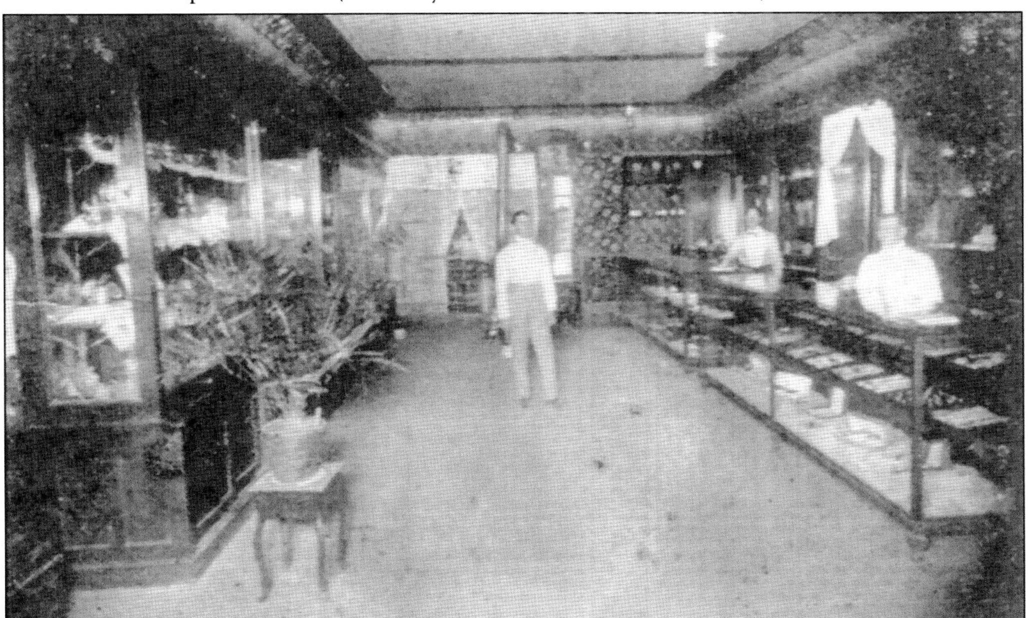

W.E. Wilson started this jewelry store in about 1898. A distinctive feature of the store, popular with the public, was that all goods were marked with one price prevailing for all alike. A large array of diamonds, watches, clocks, silverware, rings, bracelets, and spectacles, among other items, were carried here. (Courtesy Russell Cushman Collection.)

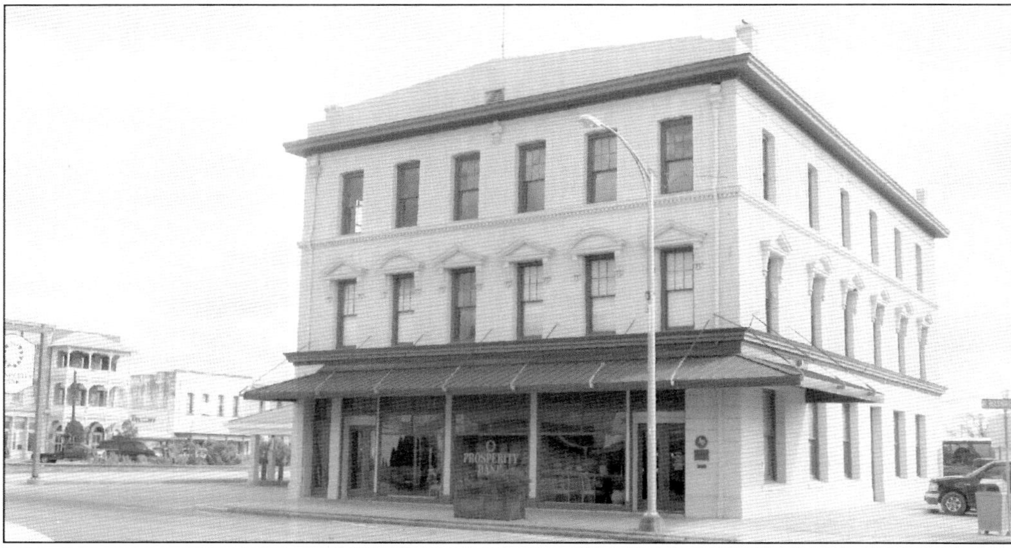

The First National Bank Building was once located across the tracks from the old Citizen's Bank Building on West Washington Avenue, just across the street from the present Theater Building, itself on the site of the former gigantic Templeman Store. (Courtesy Russell Cushman Collection.)

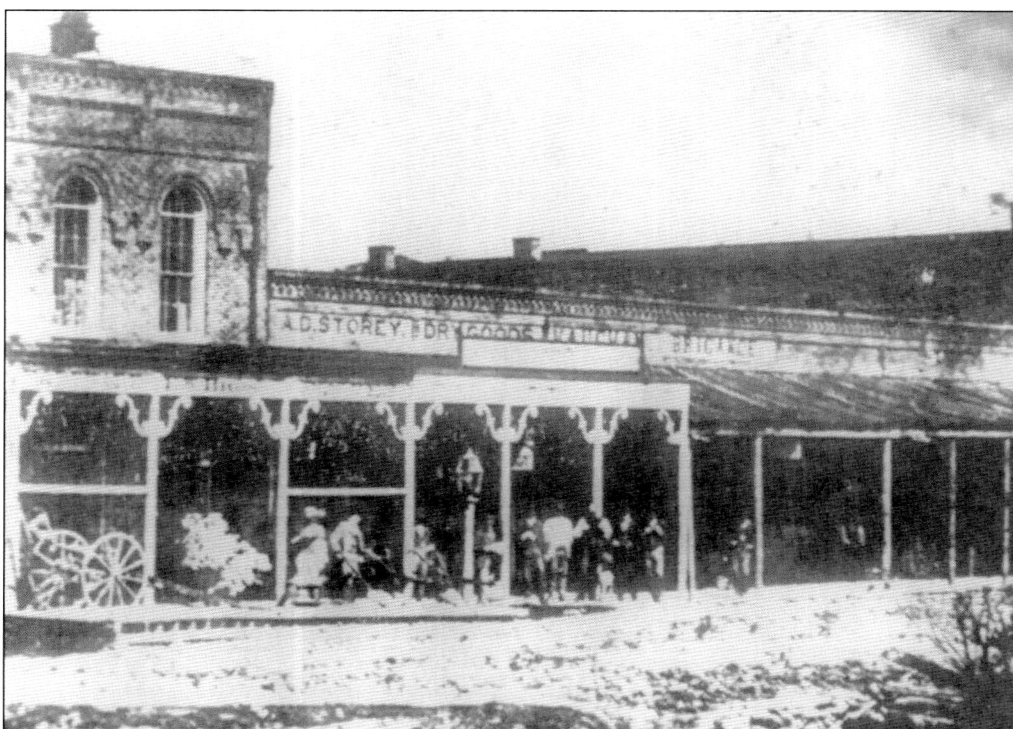

A.D. Storey Dry Goods appears here in the 1880s; Brigance is nearby. Note the huge buggy wheels on the porch, the large number of patrons crowding the walkway, and the apparently muddy streets. (Courtesy Russell Cushman Collection.)

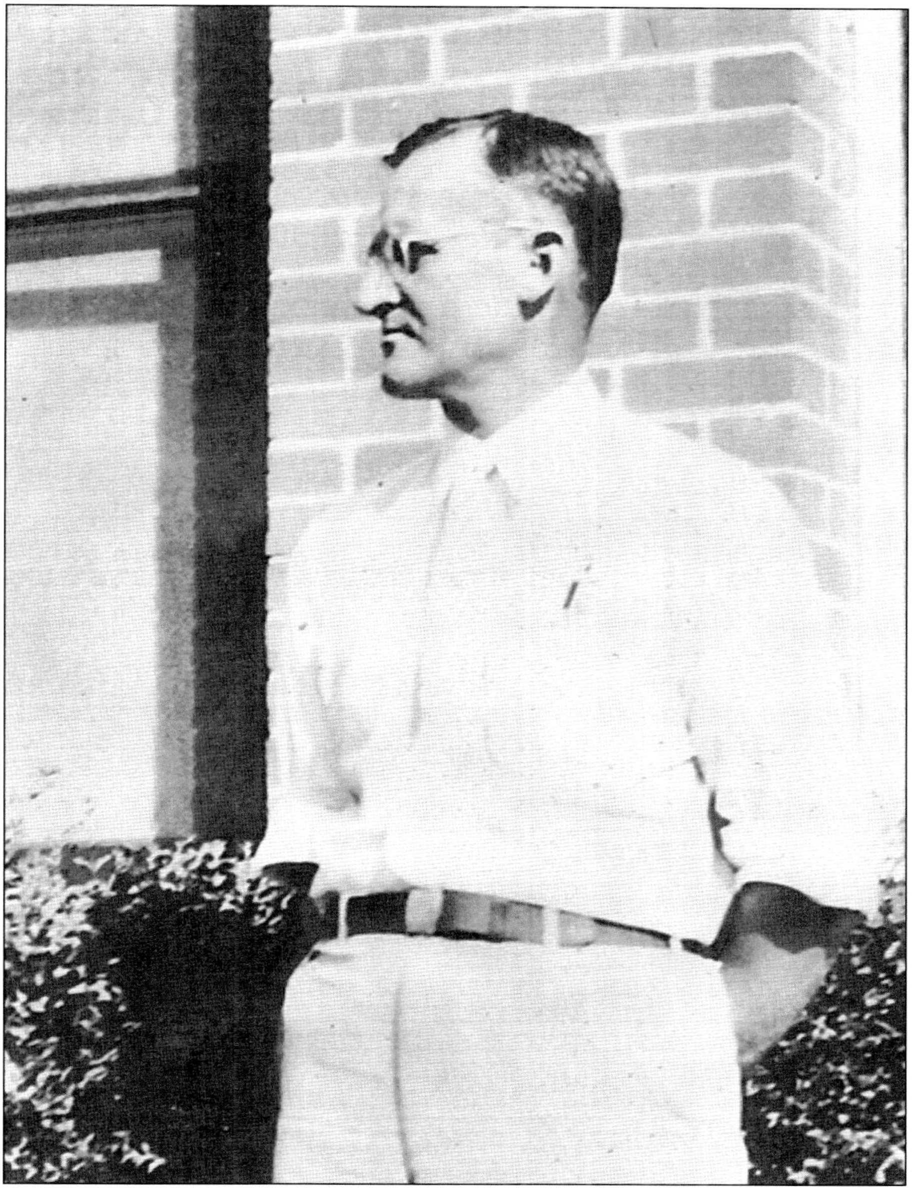

Arthur Youens was manager of the Youens Lumber Company located between Railroad and Tenth Streets. Among his services to Navasota, he was Sunday school superintendent at the Presbyterian church for many years. He was on the city council and then served as mayor from 1930 to 1937. In 1942, he served as interim city manager. Arthur Youens, husband of Blake Gibbs, had an illustrious ancestry. His father, Jesse Youens, was an immigrant from England, who served nobly in the Confederate army during the Civil War then came to Navasota during the terrible time of the yellow fever. He partnered for many years with Joseph Brooks before becoming head of the lumber company. Then called J. Youens and Company, sold was lumber, sashes, bricks, doors, blinds, water closets, caskets, fencing, and bicycles, among other items. (Courtesy the Russell Cushman Collection.)

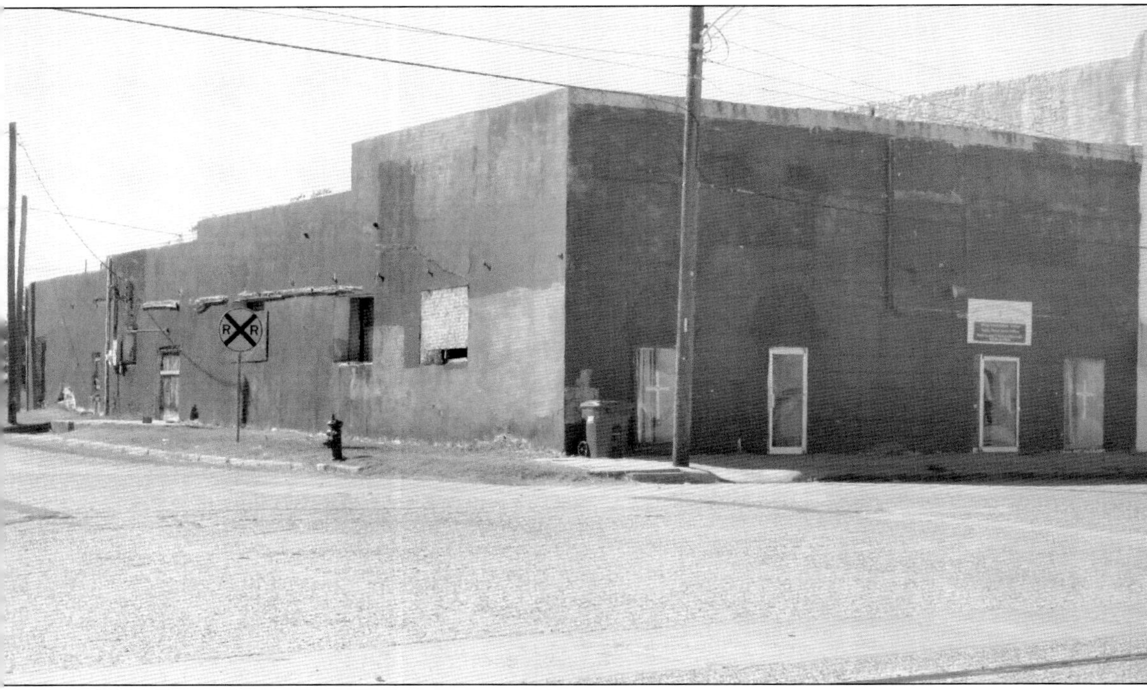

Not far to the north of Youens was the opera house on Tenth Street, pictured here in its present form. Operas were also held in the former city hall, now razed, off East Washington Avenue. One of the more famous acts to perform in Navasota was "Blind Tom" in 1876 and in 1895. According to Maurine Chinski's book, *Navasota Bluebonnet*, Blind Tom "played for Queen Victoria and in all the capital cities of Europe, as well as those in the United States." Blind Tom composed several of his own musical pieces—a remarkable feat for a blind man who was also perceived to be severely mentally challenged. An African American, he was born a slave on a plantation near Columbus, Georgia. One day, he simply went to the piano and began to play—essentially, whatever he desired. (Courtesy Texas Center for Regional Studies.)

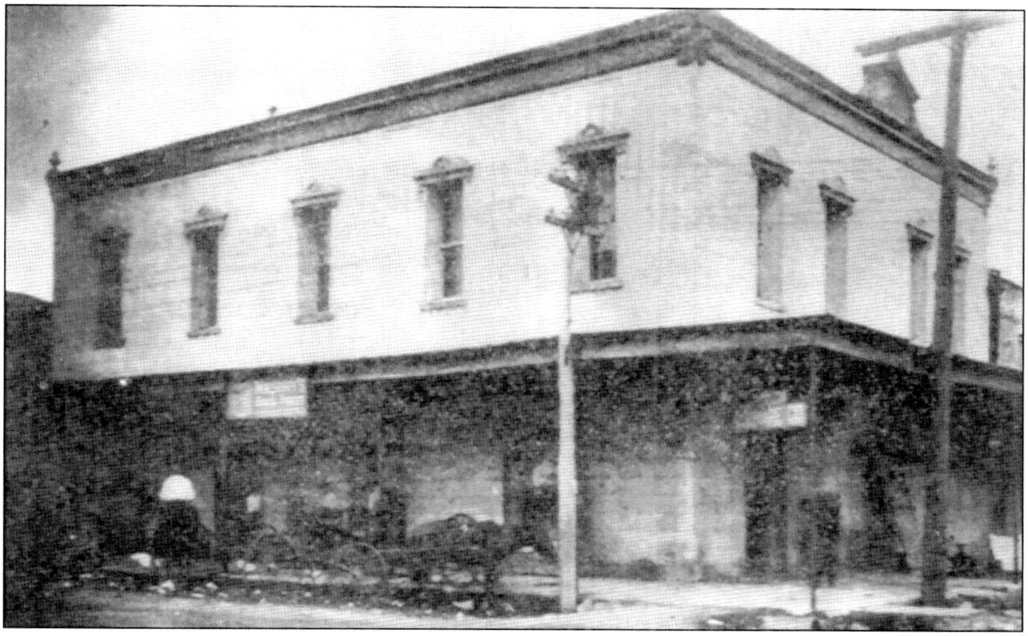

Pictured is the Ahrenbeck Hardware Company at Washington Avenue and Tenth Street. *The Examiner-Review* ran an article on this store on December 16, 1909. It stated, "this business was established over forty years ago." It also stated that manager E.L. Ahrenbeck had great faith in the future of Navasota and had "invested his money freely." (Courtesy Russell Cushman Collection.)

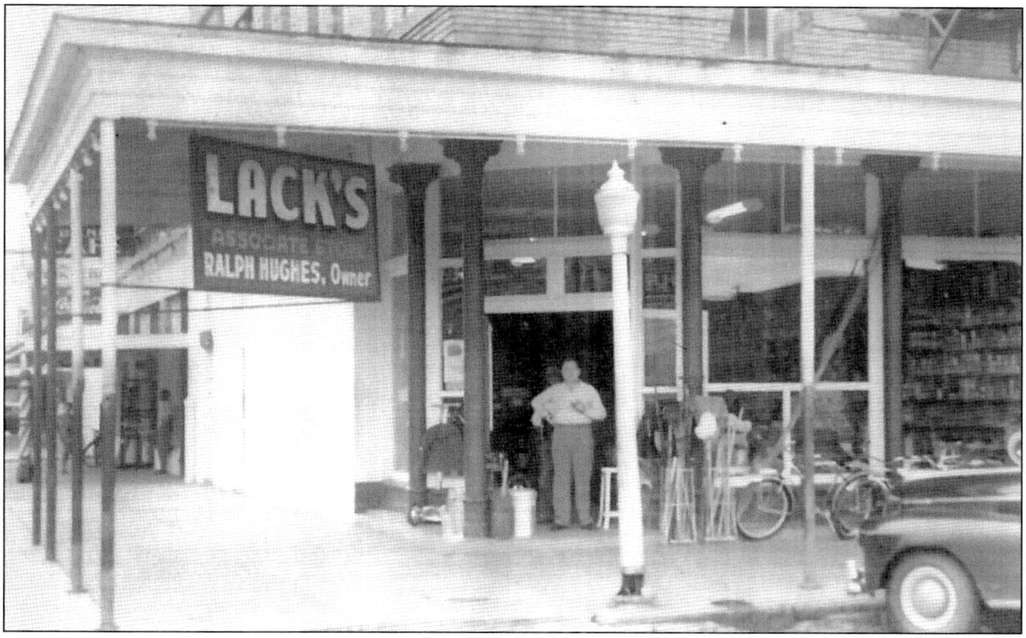

Lack's Associate Store occupied the lower floor of the Citizen's Bank Building at the corner of East Washington Avenue and Railroad Street in the mid-1940s. The owner pictured here is Ralph Hughes. Walking east at the time, one would have passed White's Barber Shop, Bank Café, and Minsky's Bakery. (Courtesy Navasota Public Library.)

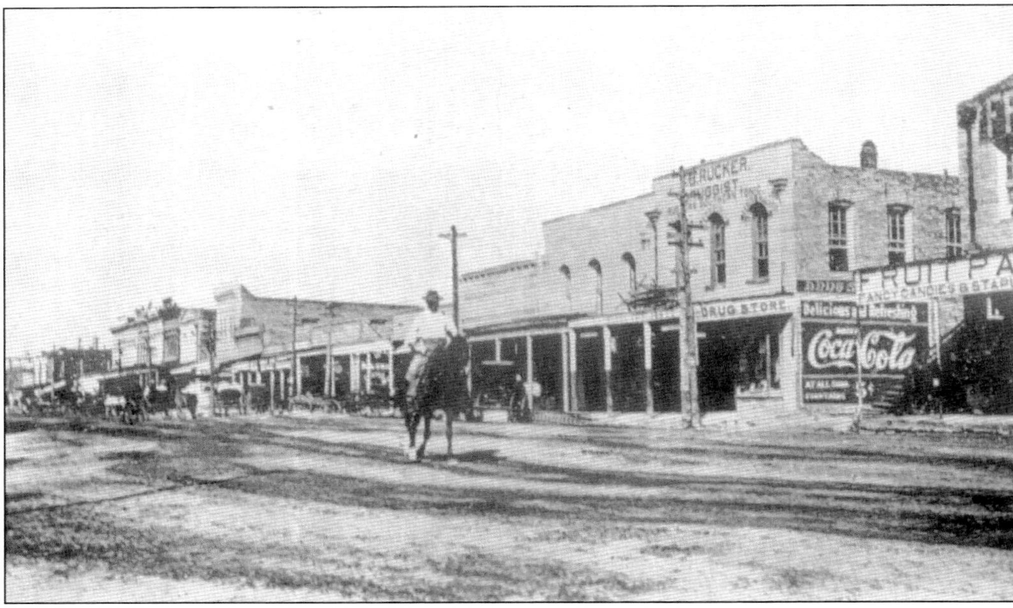

S.B. Rucker's drugstore was located on Washington Avenue on the site of the present Tejas Antiques. The photograph above places the store in the larger context of a broader Washington Avenue in the days of dirt roads, horses, and wagons. Even then, as seen here, the ever-present Coca-Cola was a popular drink, deserving a huge sign on the side of the building. In the photograph below is a closeup of the store. Note the lettering on the front of the building promising cures for chills, fever, and malaria. (Both, courtesy Russell Cushman Collection.)

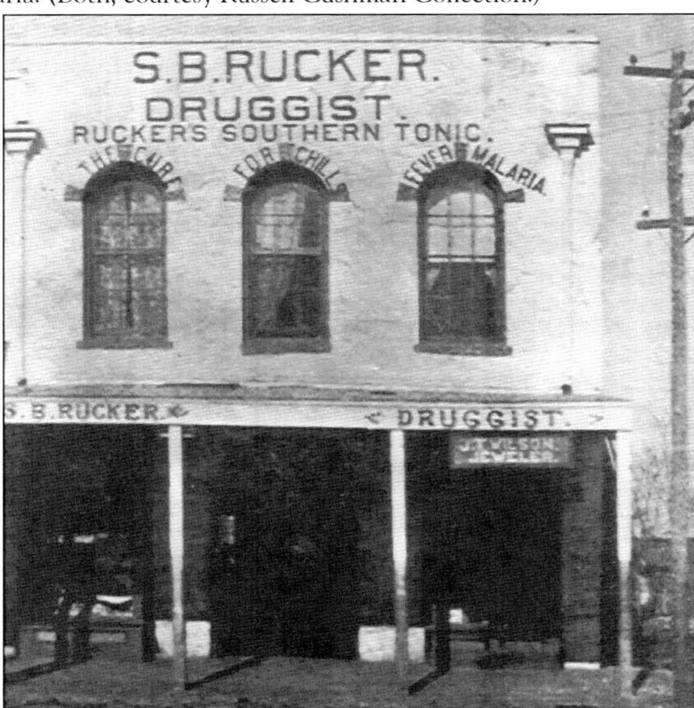

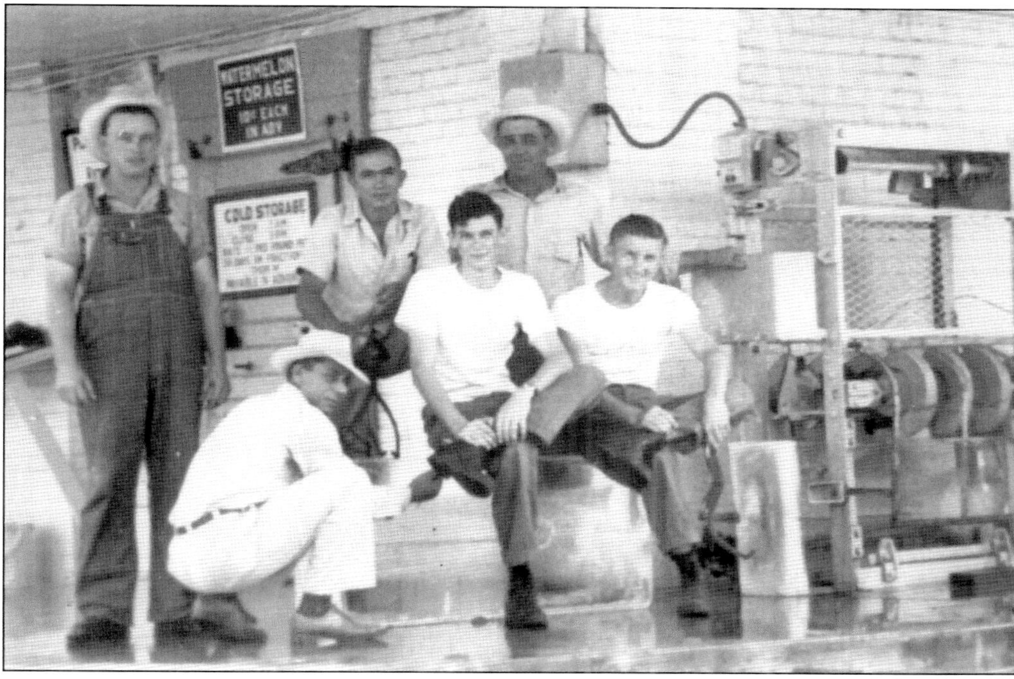

Here is the dock of Gulf States Ice House off Malcolm Street in the early 1940s. On the left is Emory Shed. Grover Mitchell wields an ice pick, while "Dub" Haney and Tommy Trant are "cooling" on the block of ice. Standing in back are Harvey and Fritz Wehmeyer. (Courtesy Navasota Public Library.)

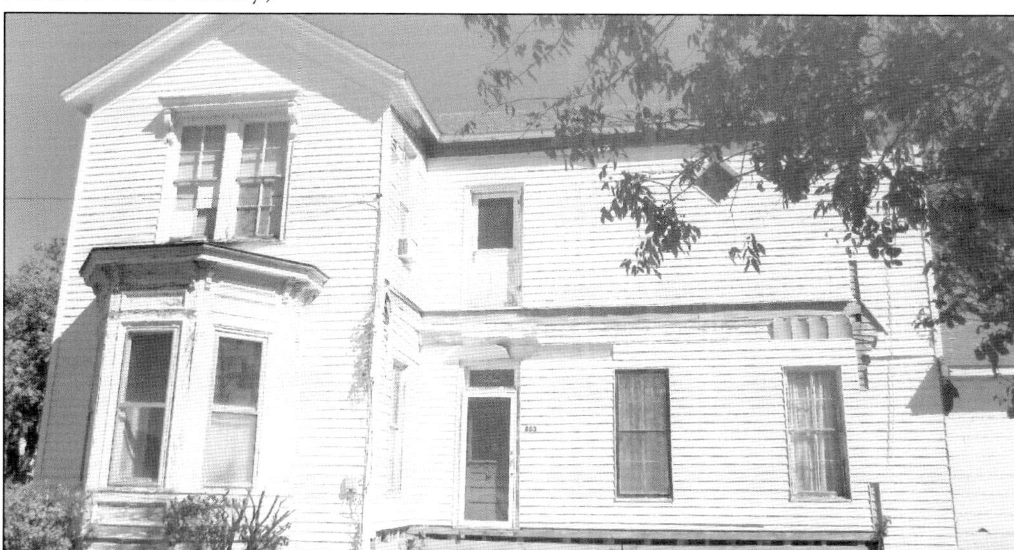

Charles Waters Stewart, a man with an illustrious lineage in Texas history, moved into this home at 808 La Salle Street in 1890. He was alternately tax collector and treasurer of Montgomery County before coming to Navasota, where he served for a while as mayor. He also served honorably in the Confederate army. His father, Charles Bellinger Stewart, was the first secretary of state in Texas. (Courtesy Betty Dunn.)

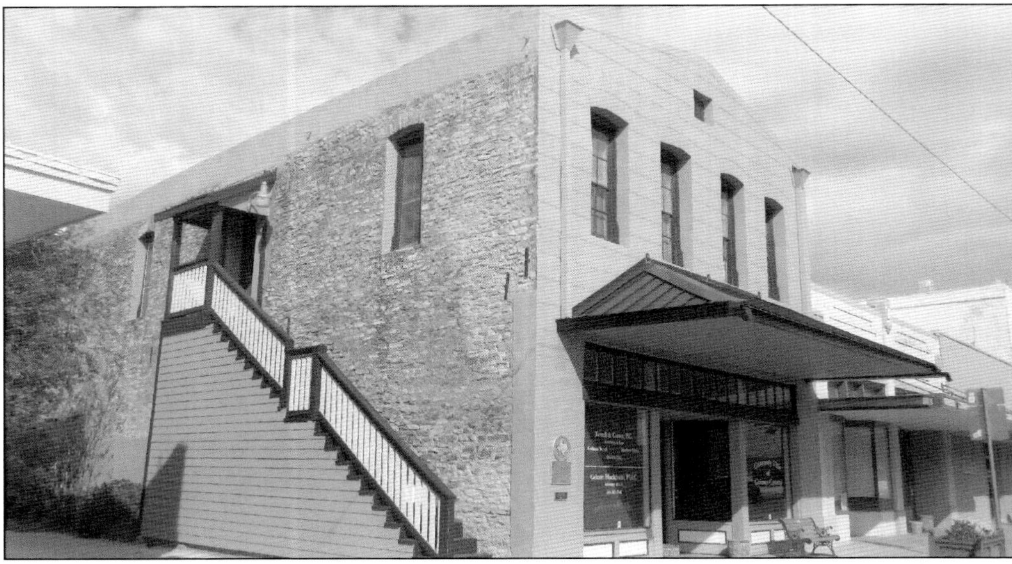

Walter J. and Julia C. Peterson built this one-story, frame Leaker Store building in 1873. In 1886, John Wesley Leaker purchased the store, enlarged it with native sandstone walls, and added a second story. Abraham S. Blumenthal occupied the store at the beginning of the 20th century. Around 1905, Blumenthal left Navasota only to drown on the ill-fated *Titanic*. (Courtesy Joy Montgomery.)

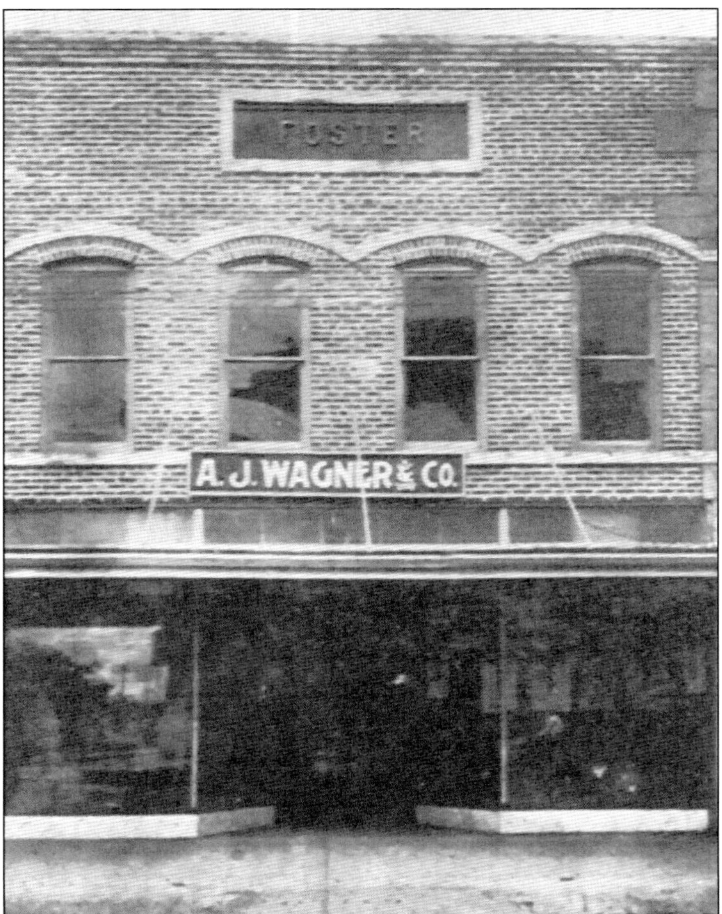

A.J. Wagner and Company, a dry goods and dress shop, opened around 1907. Men's, women's, and boy's clothing were sold here. (Courtesy Russell Cushman Collection.)

A horse-drawn buggy winds its way down Farquhar Street off Washington Avenue to the right. Note the 1920s automobile is advancing from behind, seeking an opportunity to pass in the narrow street. In the right foreground is R.M. Love's Food Market. (Courtesy Navasota Public Library.)

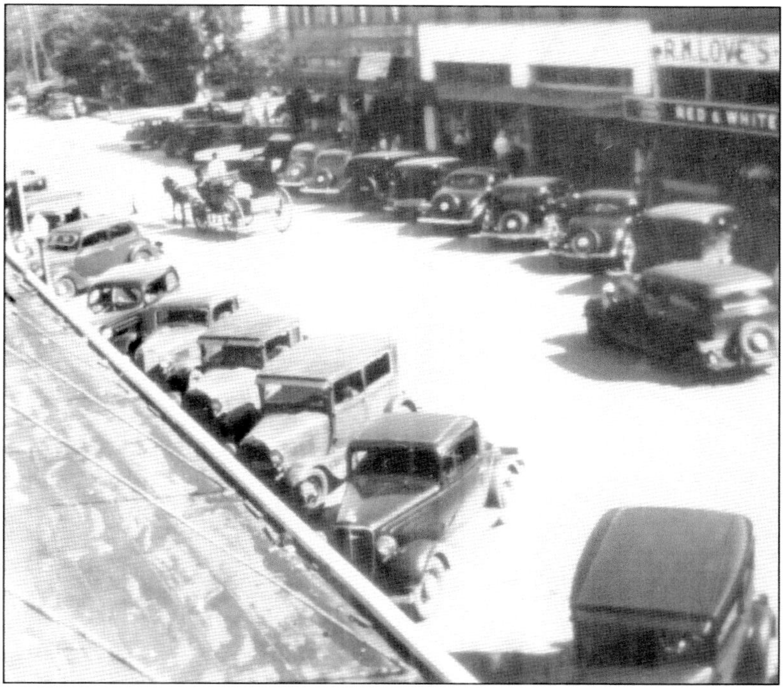

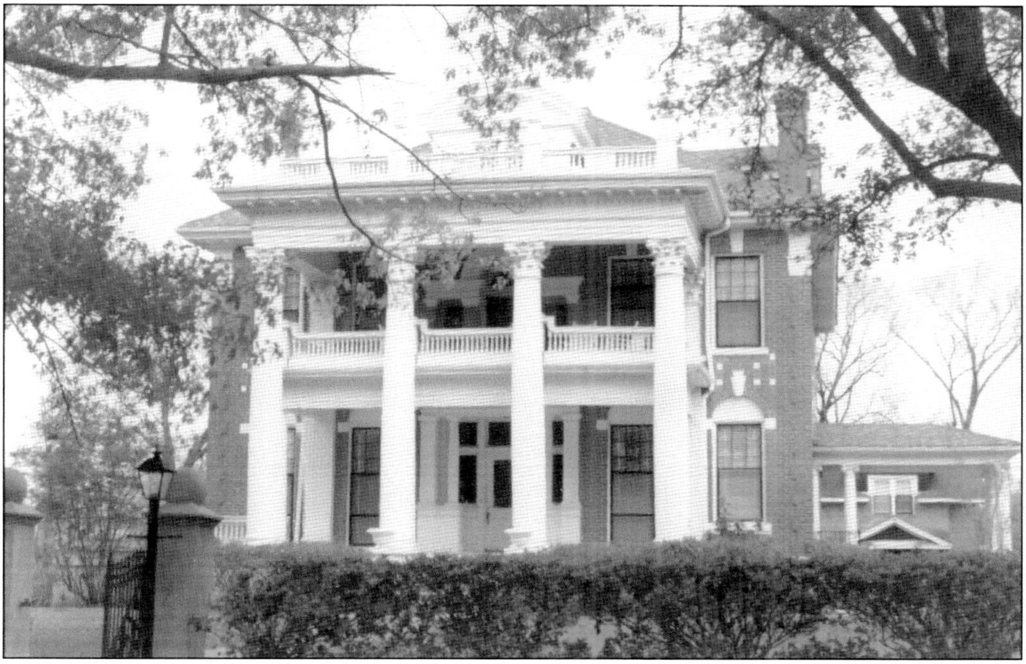

The house on 415 Johnson Street is referred to as the "W.J. Terrell place." The Terrell family purchased the house in 1962. It was built between 1904 and 1907 by R.B. Templeman for his daughter. This was the same Templeman who lived in the house off Washington Avenue known as "the Castle." The architecture here combines Greek Revival with Paladin and Victorian details. (Courtesy J.D. Dickenson.)

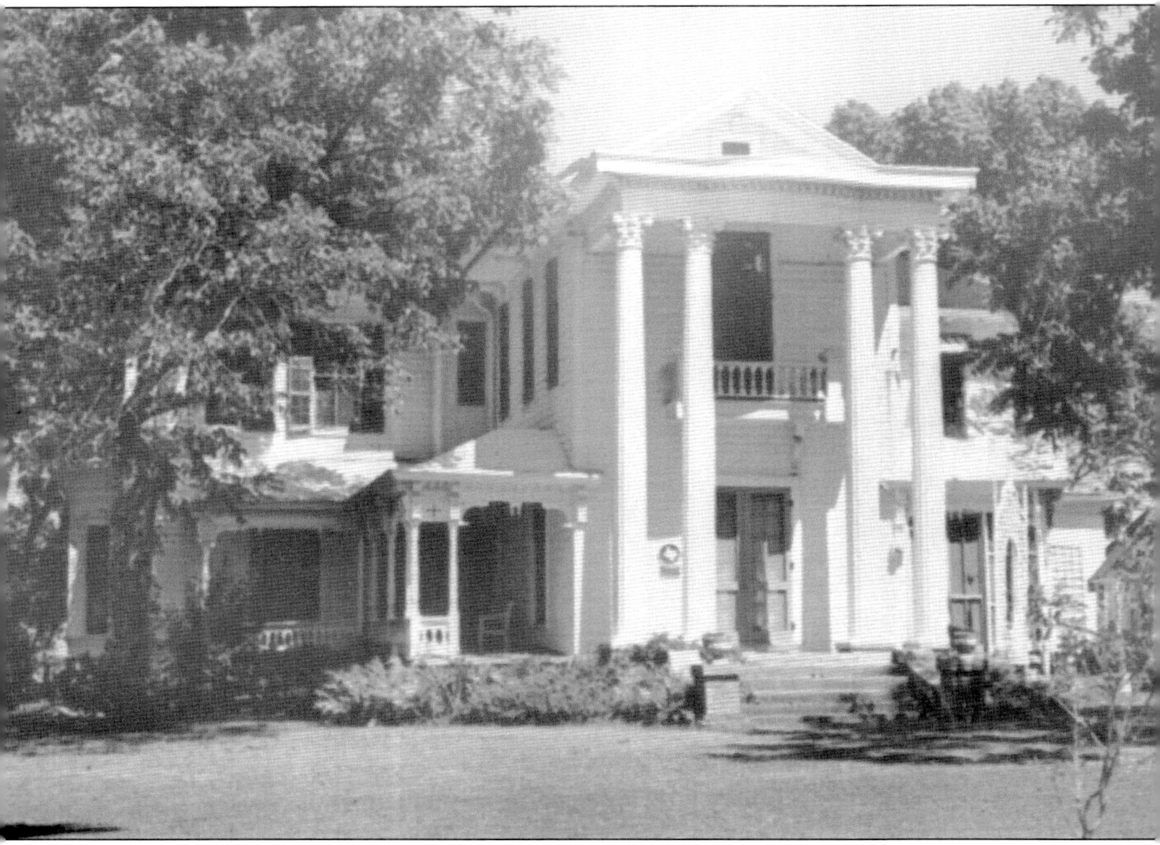

Jesse Youens built this house on 708 Holland Street in 1871, using his ancestral home in Dartford, England, as a model. The house underwent a remodeling process in 1893 and again in 1907. In later years, it was known as the Puryear house, named for Pam Puryear, a local historian of note. (Courtesy J.D. Dickenson.)

Seven

Cultures

The Reconstruction years hit Navasota hard, impacting the cultural milieu. Trouble erupted in May 1865, when some Confederate veterans returning home congregated in Navasota. Disconcerted over the war and over the withholding of their pay, they looted a warehouse filled with cotton and munitions. A fire and a great explosion demolished several buildings nearby, leaving much of the town's commercial district devastated.

The consequent placement of federal troops at nearby Anderson, as well as Millican, led to further violence. As a result, the Freedmen's Bureau stepped in to support African Americans with franchise, court, labor, and education. This, in turn, led to further reaction from some disgruntled whites, and some local African Americans formed their own militias.

But not all culture rested on racial fragmentation. Out of the matrix of distrust, a Populist alliance emerged, with key figures working together on a multiracial level. It was this mixed legacy that generated a culture characterized by a degree of togetherness and mutual respect. Out of this emerged the legendary songster Mance Lipscomb, who would draw international attention to the culture of the Brazos Valley and make Navasota the "Blues Capital of Texas." And then there was the internationally known artist Kathleen Blackshear, who made her basic focus the regional black culture of the early 20th century. Currently going strong as stars in the arts, Leon Collins, his daughter Molly Bee, and Russell Cushman focus on the Brazos Valley culture.

This chapter will cover artists of sound and canvas and show some of the artwork that depicts local farm life. Additionally, an example of Navasota sports culture will be featured, along with a woman of multiple talents, scientist and historian Pam Puryear.

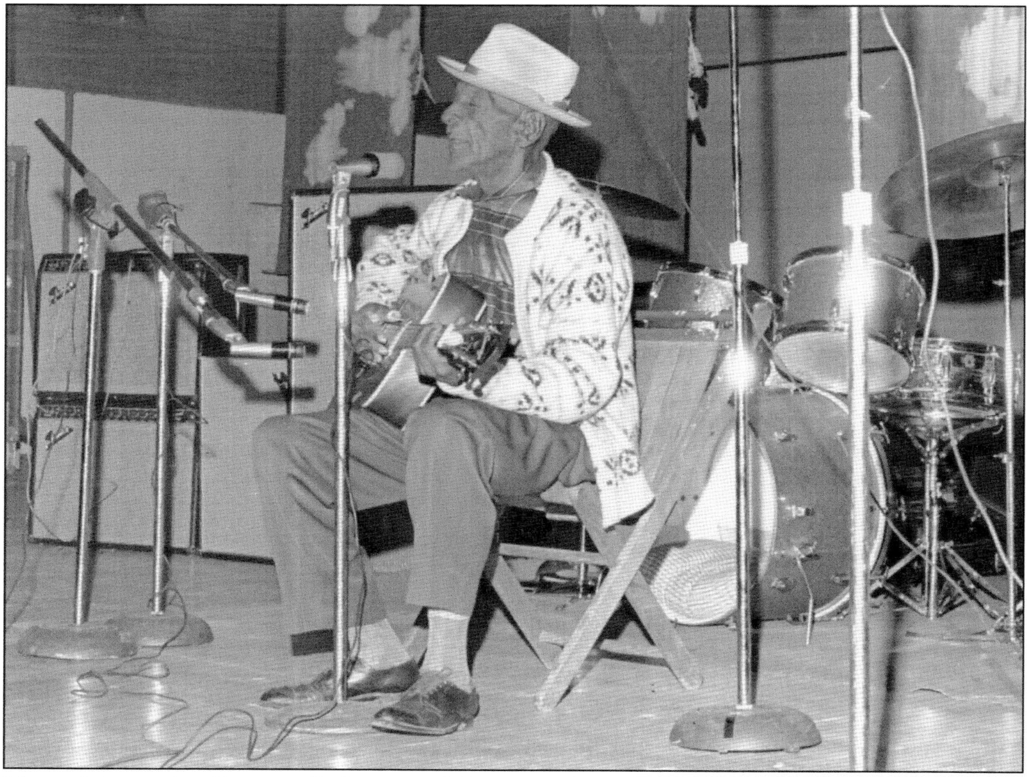

Mance Lipscomb, a "songster" who earned Navasota the title of "Blues Capital of Texas," appears in the photograph above. Lipscomb lived from April 9, 1895, to January 30, 1976. At birth, he received the name Beau De Glen Lipscomb, but as a youth, he assumed the name Mance as a play on the word "emancipation." It was late in life that he made several fine albums. On August 12, 2011, citizens of Navasota erected a statue of Lipscomb, sculpted by Sid Henderson of California, and placed it in the new Mance Lipscomb Park. Dr. Michael Birnbaum, psychology professor at California State University, appears with Mance in the photograph below. Doctor Birnbaum had studied under Lipscomb. He now gives demonstrations at the Navasota Blues Fest and was instrumental in the placement and dedication of the Lipscomb Statue. (Above, courtesy Marcus Mallard, below, courtesy Russell Cushman Collection.)

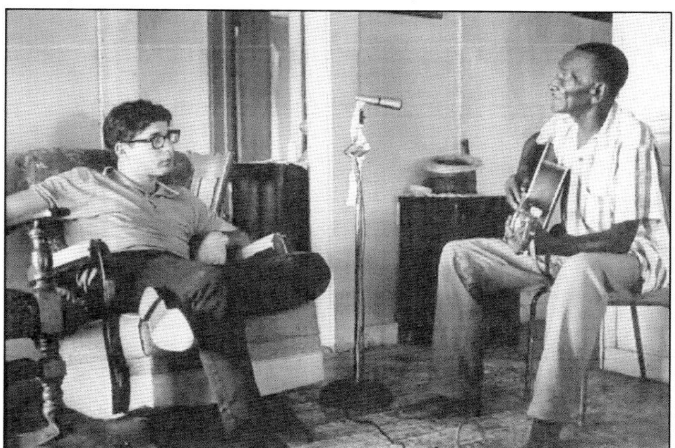

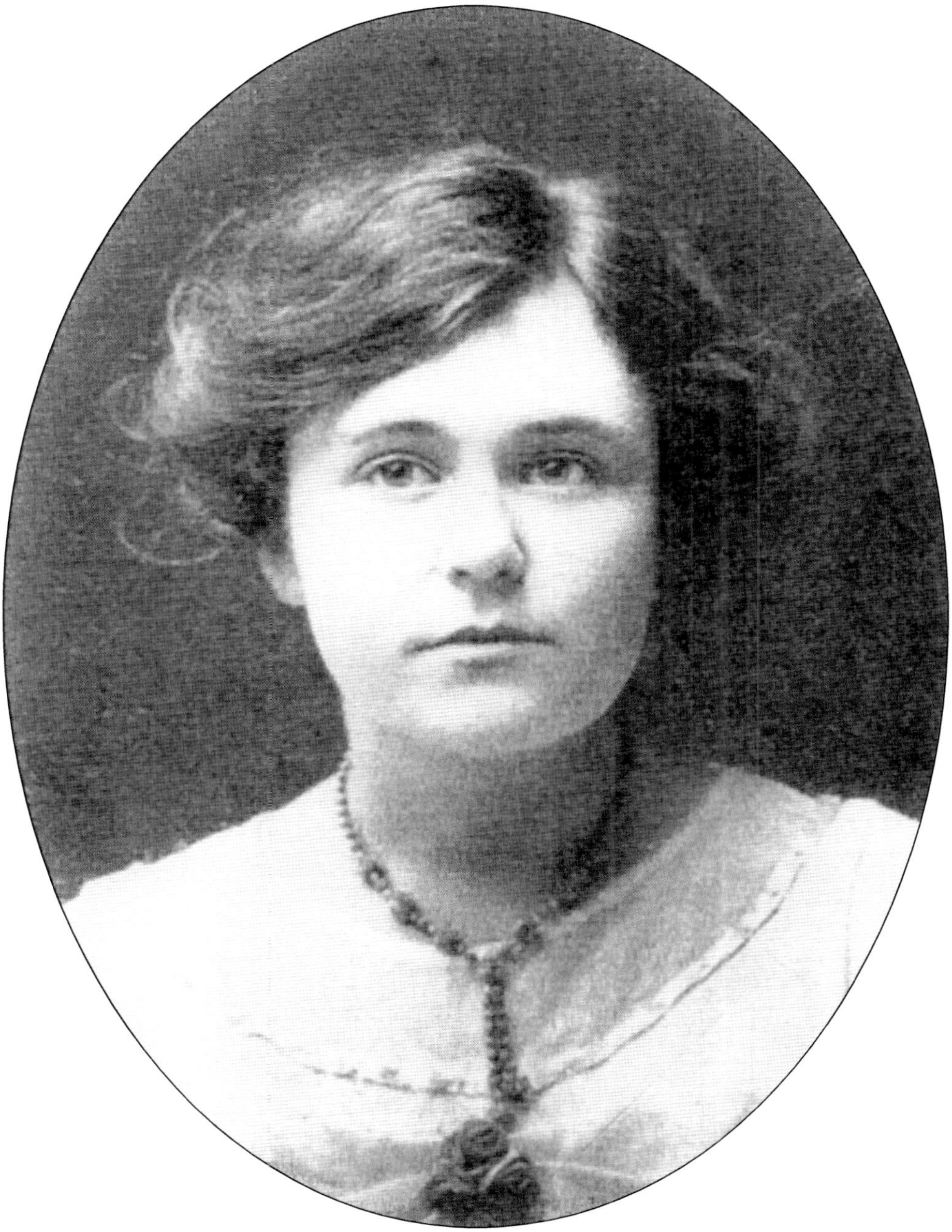

Kathleen Blackshear, an artist and teacher of international fame, rose to academic heights at the prestigious Art Institute of Chicago. Born to Edward Duncan and May Terrell Blackshear in 1897, she was raised in Navasota and educated at the Atchison Institute. She retired to Navasota and was buried in Navasota's Oakland Cemetery in 1988. Her primary focus was on Art Regionalism. Here, she returned to her roots, seeking to capture the essence of the African American tenant farmer's existence in the Trans-Brazos Region. Always an individualist, it is said that she was the first woman in Navasota to publicly wear men's pants. (Courtesy Russell Cushman Collection.)

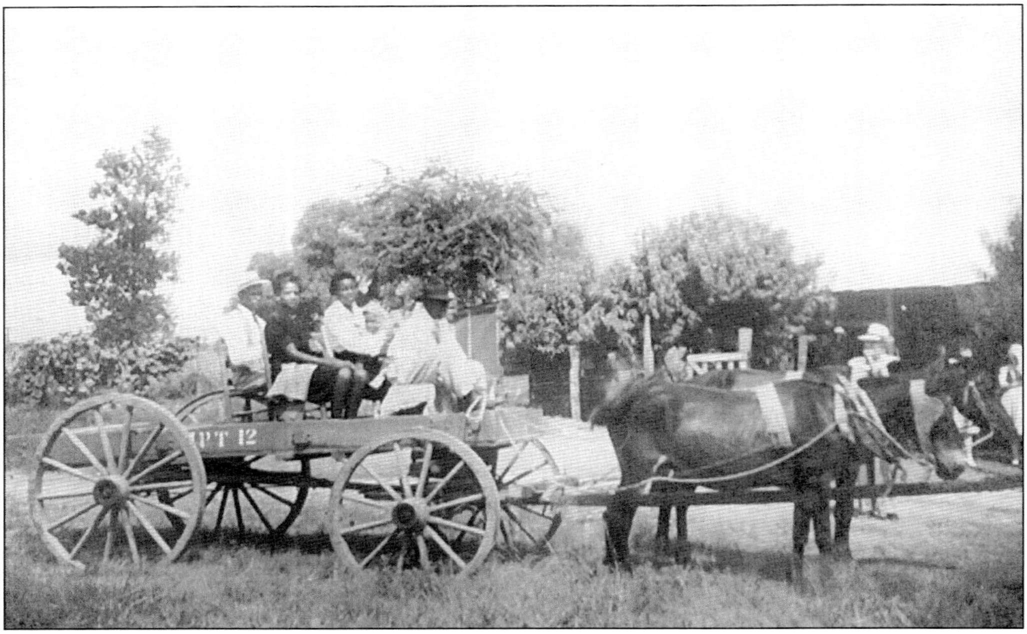

The photograph above comes from the collection of brother and sister, Bill and Kathleen Terrell, relatives of Kathleen Blackshear. Both are avid fans of local history, and Bill Terell is much in demand in the area as a dynamic speaker. This photograph reflects the local farm life that Kathleen Blackshear sought to depict in her Art Regionalism. The photograph below is a Blackshear watercolor of the Terrell cotton gin to the east of Navasota. (Above, courtesy the Terrell Collection; below, courtesy Navasota Public Library.)

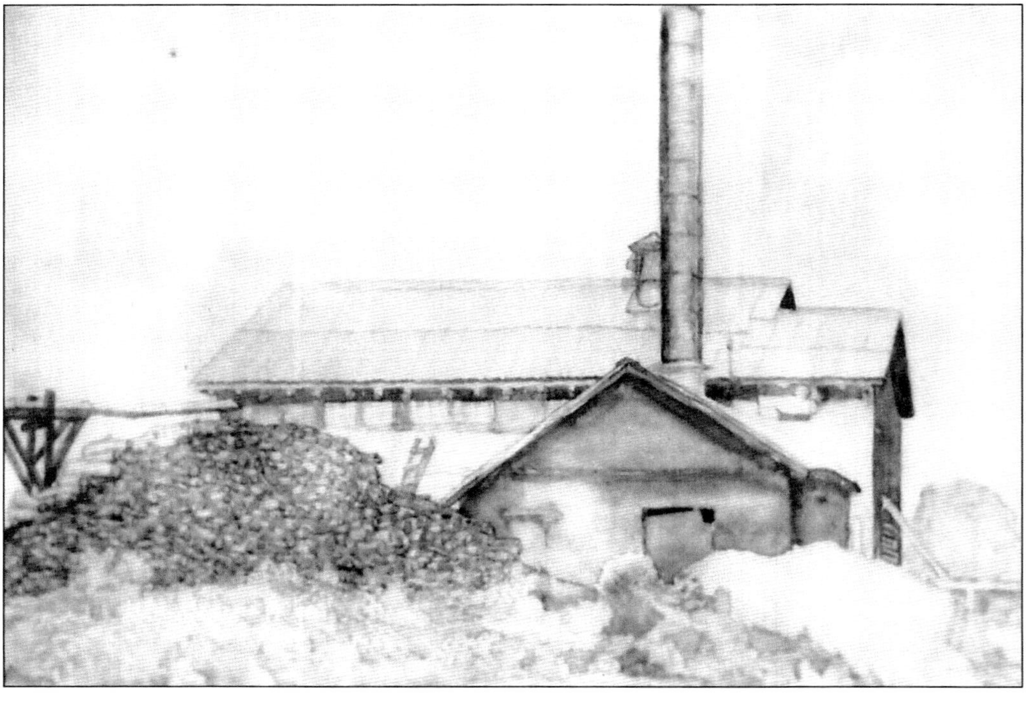

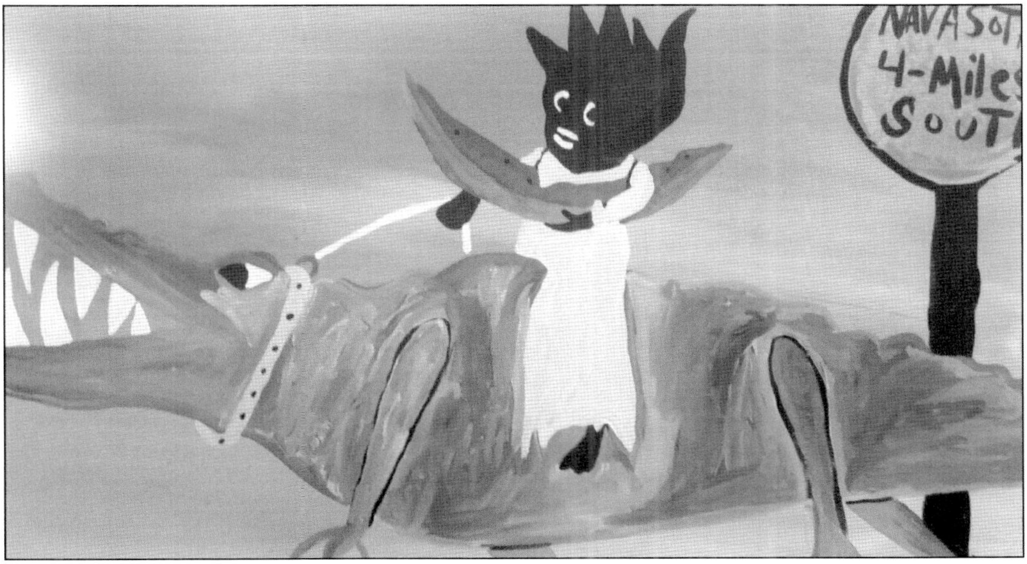

Leon Collins and his daughter Molly Bee are contemporaries of the authors. Their folk art is currently on display at Tejas Antics in downtown Navasota. Although centered on the Brazos Valley, their reach extends through such cities as Houston, Fort Worth, and New York. Leon Collins's primary inspiration is his great-great-grandmother, whom he lovingly called "Big Mama." A former slave, she lived to be 119 years old. Her stories still dominate his psyche. The characters these artists portray center on cotton fields and the folkways of the region. They are yet another grand example of Navasota's cultural gift to the world at large. (Both, courtesy Leon Collins.)

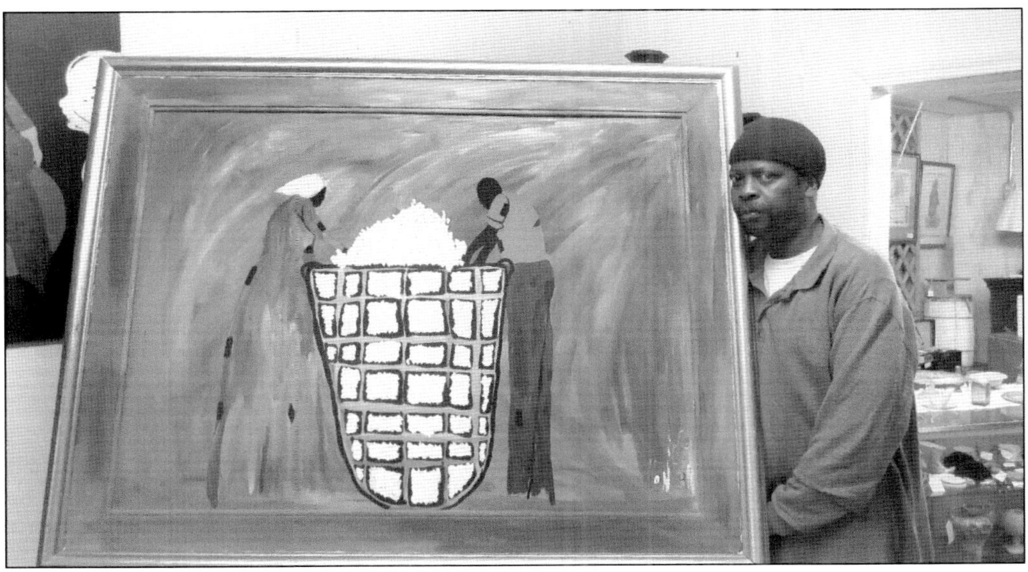

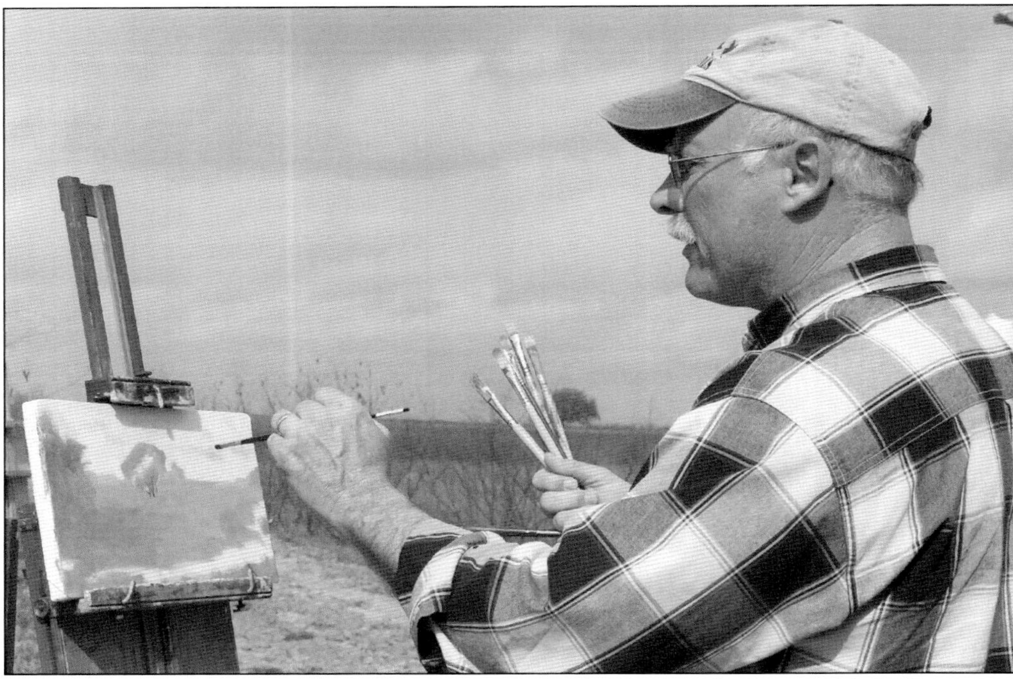

Russell Cushman is an artist, historian, and community leader who has established a massive legacy in American Art. Russell and his wife, Linda, love the beauty and heritage of the Brazos Valley. He has been instrumental in local historic preservation organizations, and twice has received election to the Navasota City Council. Cushman's sculptures and historical murals are landmarks in the Brazos Valley. A 140-foot mural depicting virgin Texas in 1845, found on the second-story interior of the Star of the Republic Museum at Washington-on-the-Brazos, is arguably the most famous of his pieces. Both photographs show Cushman and a sample of his work. (Both, courtesy Russell Cushman and the website of the *Navasota Current*.)

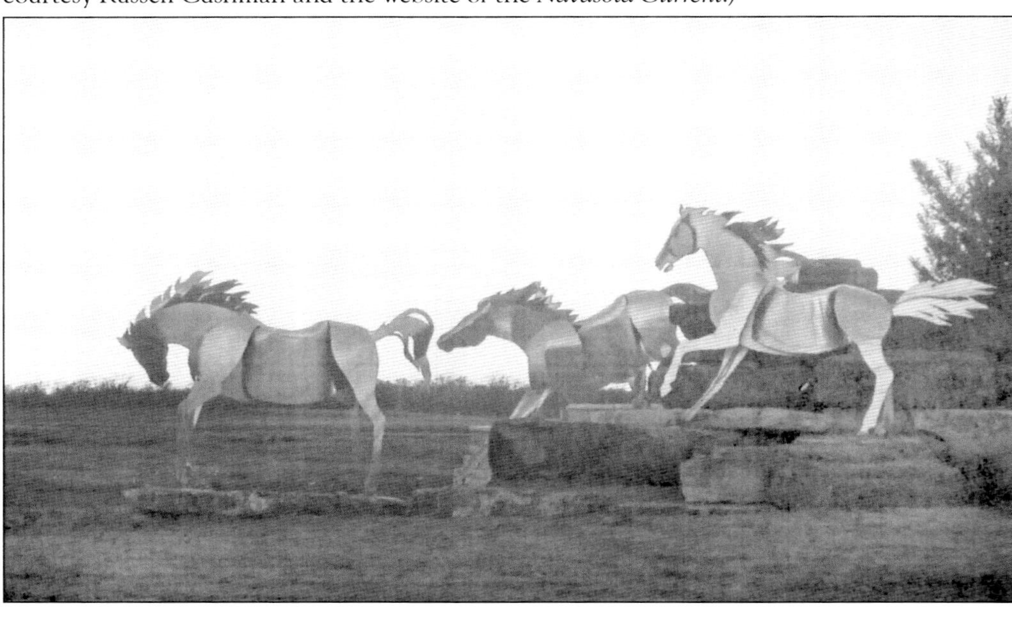

Some Navasotans were slow to adjust to the Civil War defeat as attested to in a song found in an old Navasota home, "I'm a Good Old Rebel." Supposedly, it was sung around the parlor. One line of the song is especially descriptive: "I don't want no pardon for what I was and am, I won't be reconstructed and I don't care a damn." (Courtesy Texas Center for Regional Studies.)

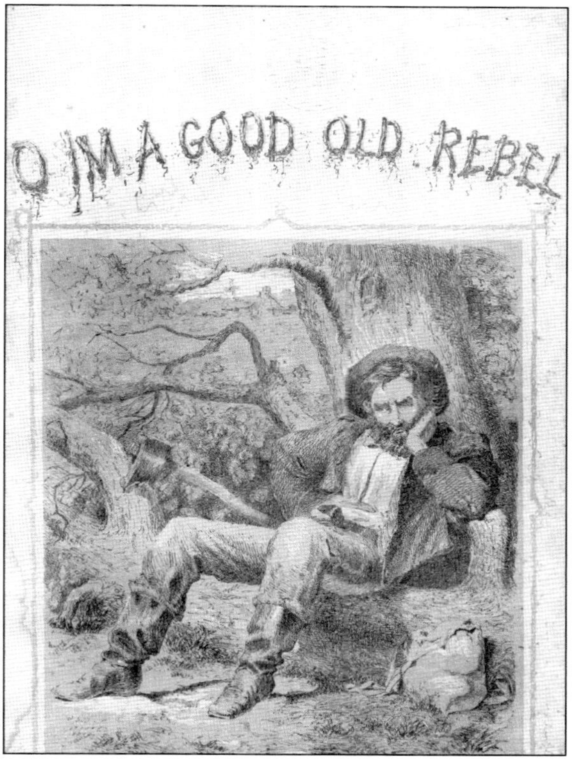

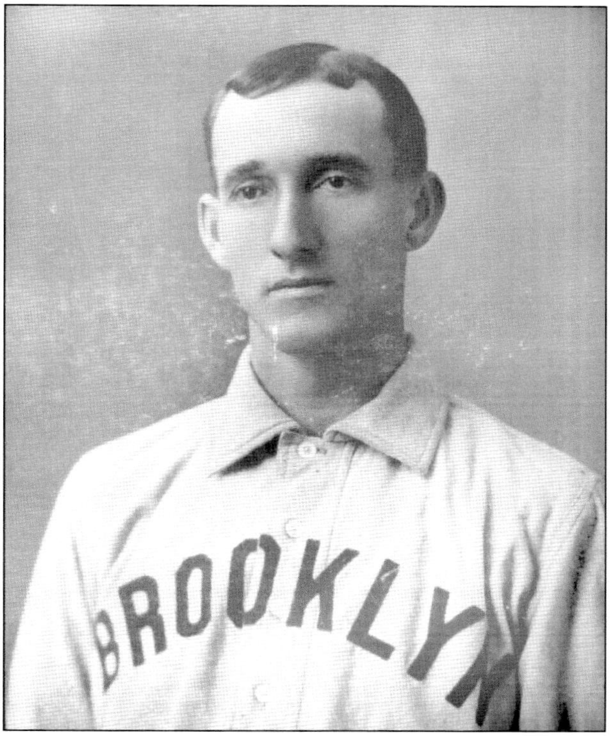

Virgil Lee Garvin was born in Navasota on January 1, 1874, and died June 16, 1908, in Fresno, California. From 1896 until 1904, he pitched 181 games with six Major League Baseball teams. His record was 57 wins against 97 losses. He had an earned run average of 2.72 with 612 strikeouts. (Courtesy Marcus Mallard.)

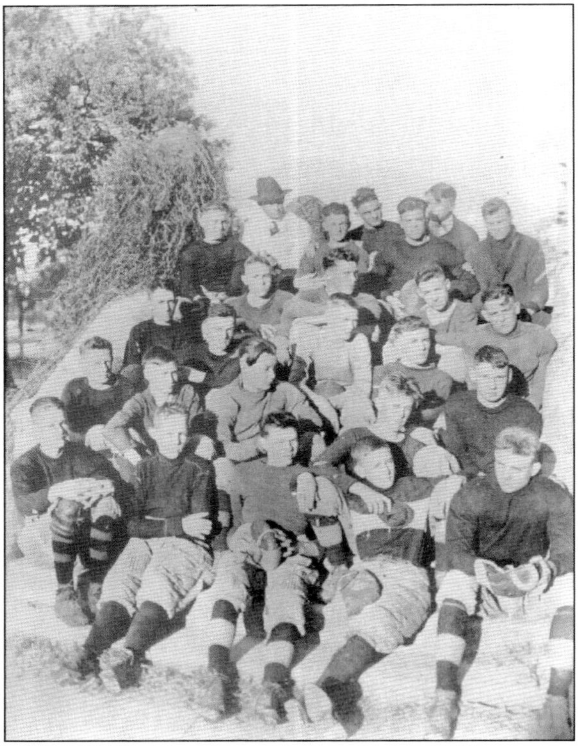

The Navasota High School Football Team players relax in 1919. They won six games, lost one, and tied one. Only one touchdown was scored against them all season. Their only loss was to Bryan, 2-0, though they beat a team that had beaten Bryan. Their tie was with Calvert, 0-0. (Courtesy Marcus Mallard.)

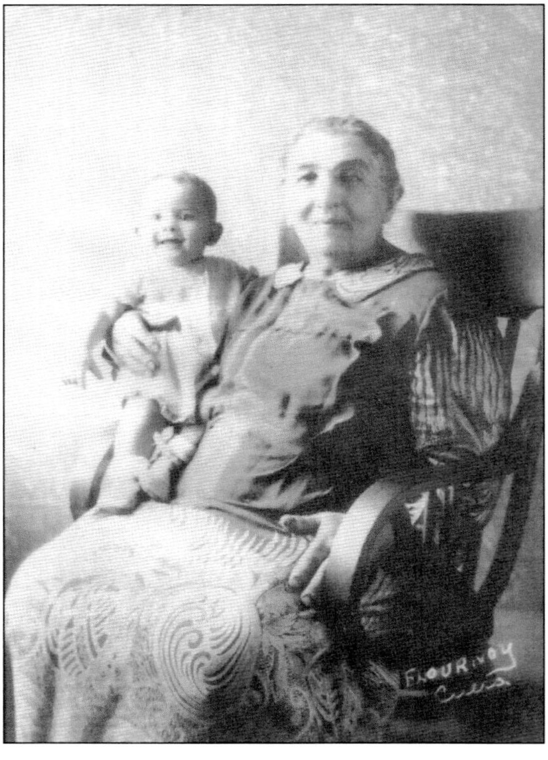

Sophie, wife of Ben Isenberg, holds her grandchild, Sarah Ann Silverstein, in 1926. The Isenberg's came to Navasota in 1912, having emigrated from Russia via Ellis Island in 1906. They established a produce business in a building on Tenth Street that had been the opera house before it was a laundry. (Courtesy Navasota Public Library.)

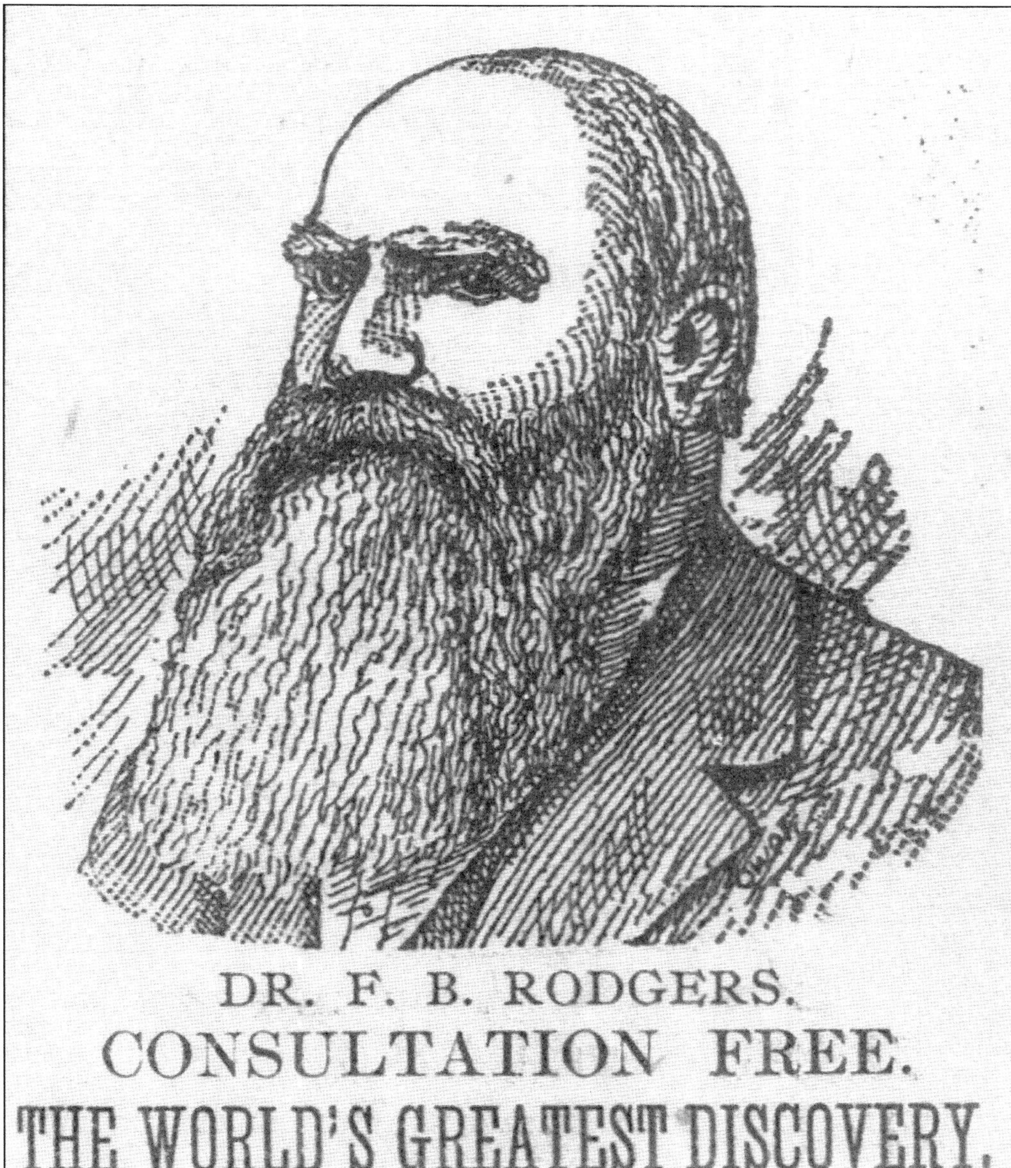

This cure-all was advertised as the "World's Greatest Discovery" in the *Daily Examiner* on January 14, 1896: "All are invited to call and investigate the New Process for the cure of all kinds of disease. A New principle, new process, new life, without disease and suffering. Causes removed, effects cease. Patients get well and remain so. Ninety percent of consumption cured, Catarrh, asthma, paralysis, blood and skin diseases, tumors, sores, ulcers, and all private diseases quickly cured; strict-est confidence." The doctor also claims to be a complexion expert, clearing "wrinkles, pimples and facial blemishes." Note the free consultations and the availability of testimonials. (Courtesy Horlock History Center.)

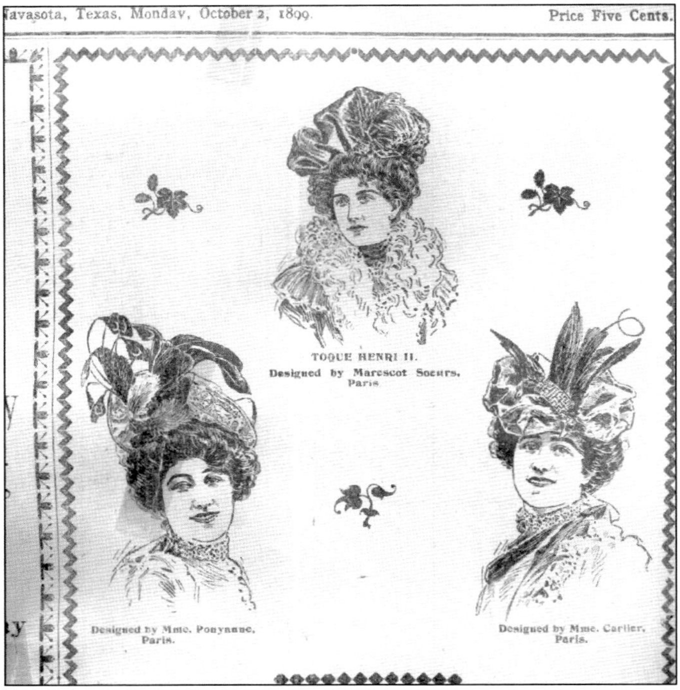

These advertisements were featured in the *Daily Examiner* on October 2, 1899. Pictured at left, Mistrot Brothers and Company advertises three hats from Paris. Note the names of the French designers. Pictured below, R.B. Templeman and Son advertises a similar assortment from New York and St. Louis. (Both, courtesy Texas Center for Regional Studies.)

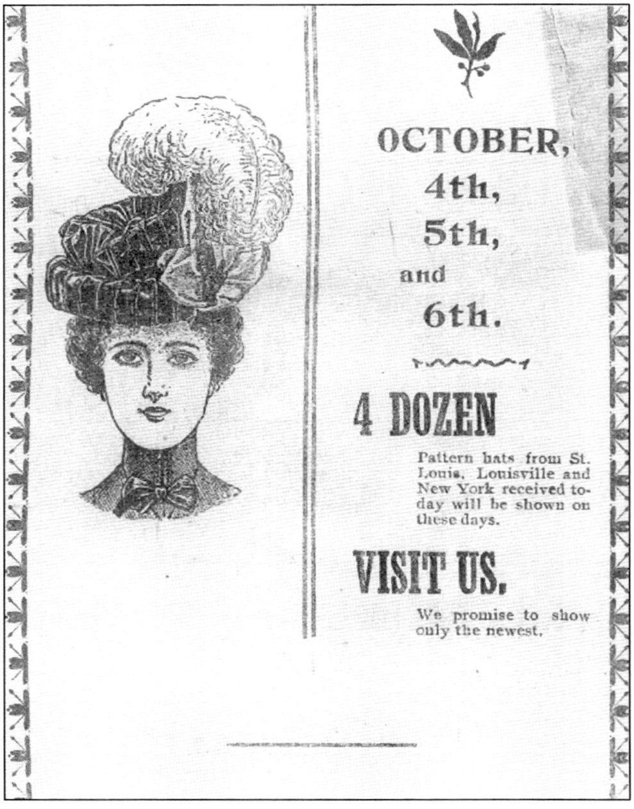

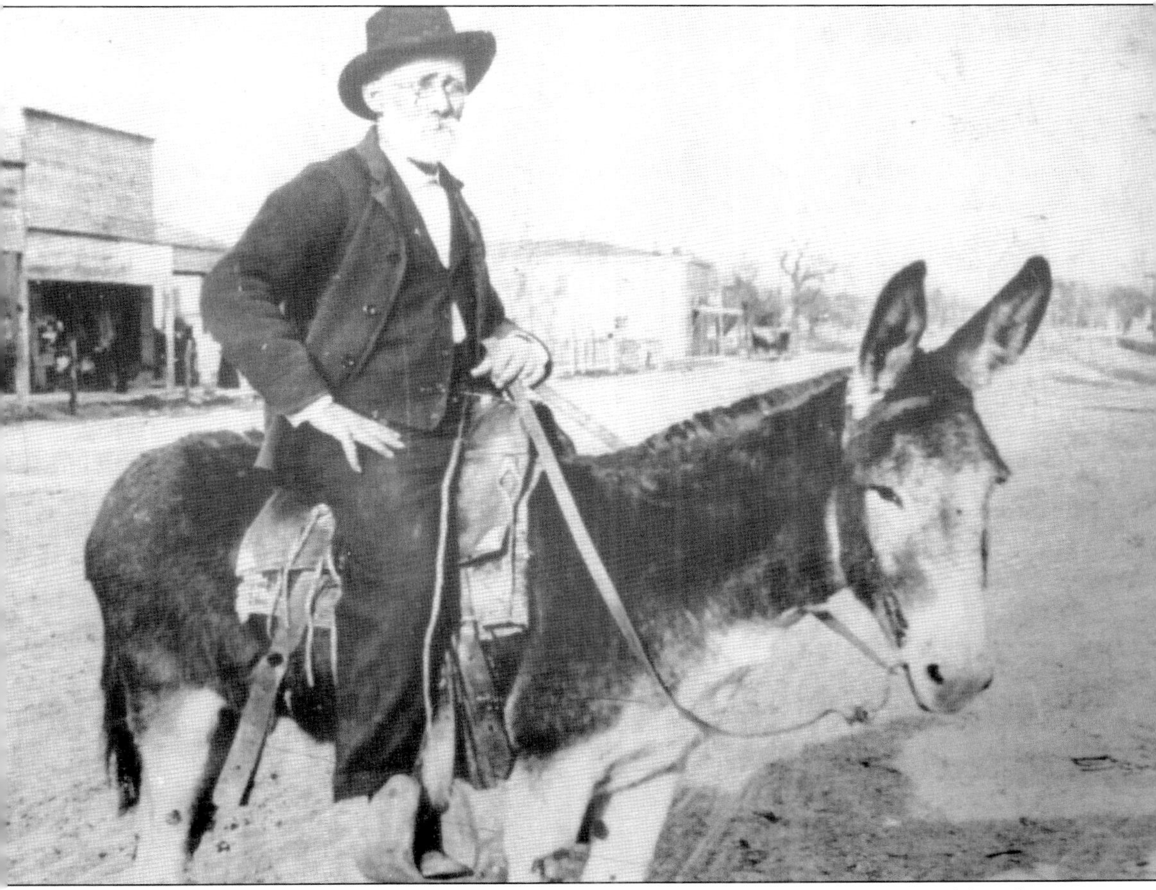

Navasota businessman Robert S. Brown is astride his trusty mule in the 1880s. Local lore has it that Brown and his mule inspired the name Brown's Mule, the chewing tobacco company. Some believe executives happened upon Brown and his mule, others believe Brown submitted a photograph to a contest. In a written response to a local inquiry, a Brown's Mule Company spokesman claimed to have researched the story and found no reference to the contest. (Courtesy Marcus Mallard.)

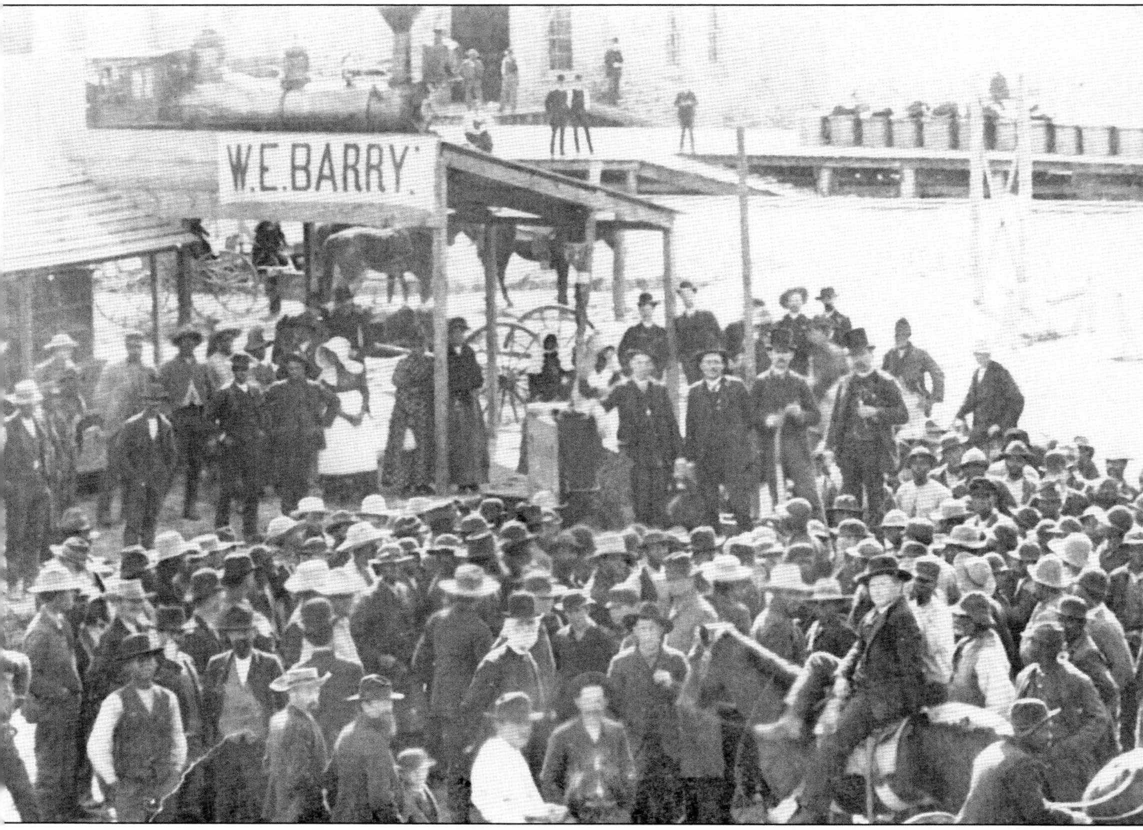

Pictured here is a political rally sometime in the late 1880s or 1890s. W.E. Barry was a confederate veteran running for office as a populist. During this era, the Populists were a strong, multiracial force. Shortly after this photograph, a shootout occurred in Anderson involving forces in opposition to the Populists. At the time, Populist sheriff Garrett Scott was in office. He is one of the men on the platform in this photograph. In that shootout, his brother, a Garret deputy, was killed, along with a few others. After this, Populist opposition formed a "white-man's union," a major political force for the next 50 years in Grimes County. (Courtesy Marcus Mallard.)

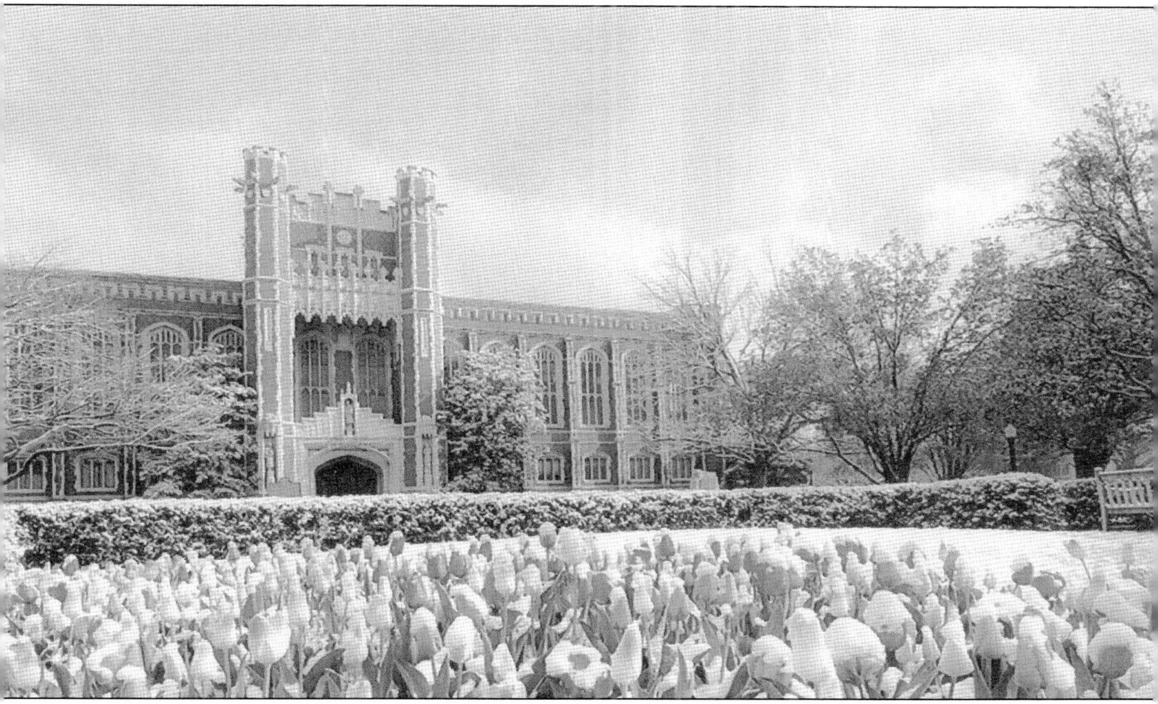

The library at the University of Oklahoma (OU) at Norman, Oklahoma, was named for William Bennett Bizzell. He was the university's fifth president. He had three doctorate degrees. Before he was president of OU, he was president of Texas A&M University and earlier president of the College of Industrial Arts in Denton, later Texas Women's University. Bizzell began his school administrative career as superintendent of schools at Navasota, Texas from 1900 to 1910. Doctor Bizzell was married to Carrie Wray Sangster of Navasota. They had two children. Among Doctor Bizzell's dizzying array of accomplishments, he started the OU Medical Center in Oklahoma City and was president of the National Association of State Universities. In 1936, he was inducted into the Oklahoma Hall of Fame. (Courtesy Prof. Rich Taylor, Dean of the Weitzenhoffer Family College of Fine Arts, University of Oklahoma.)

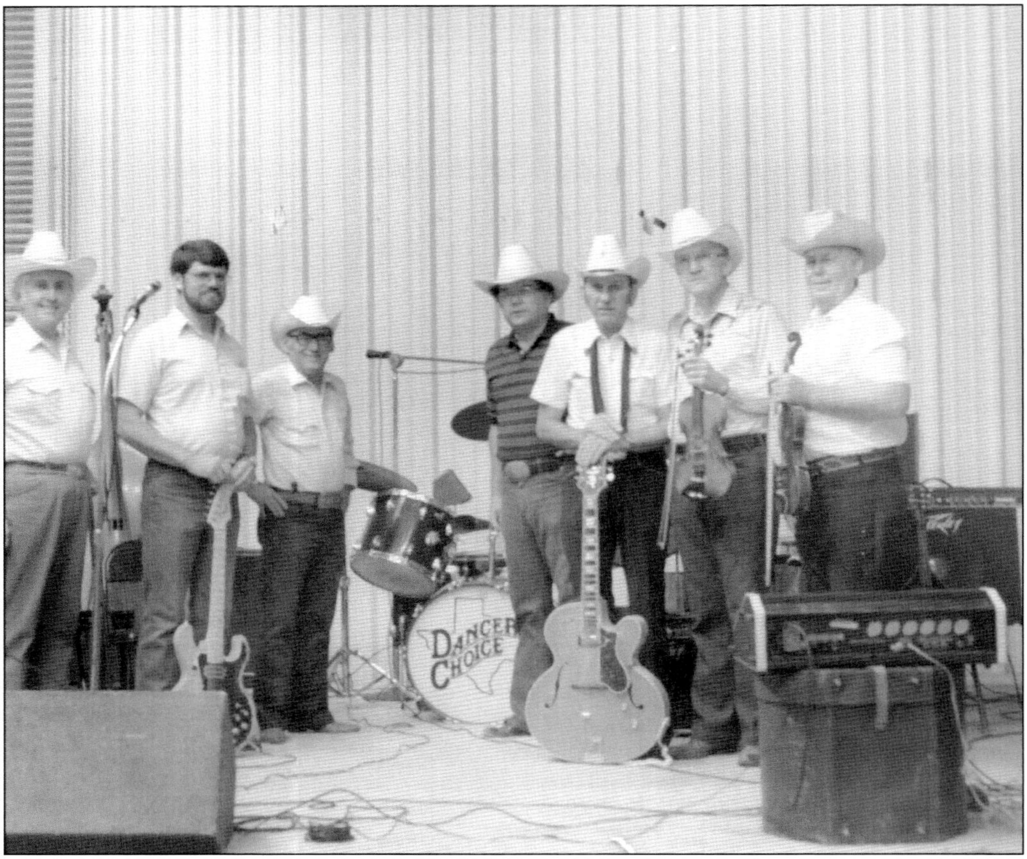

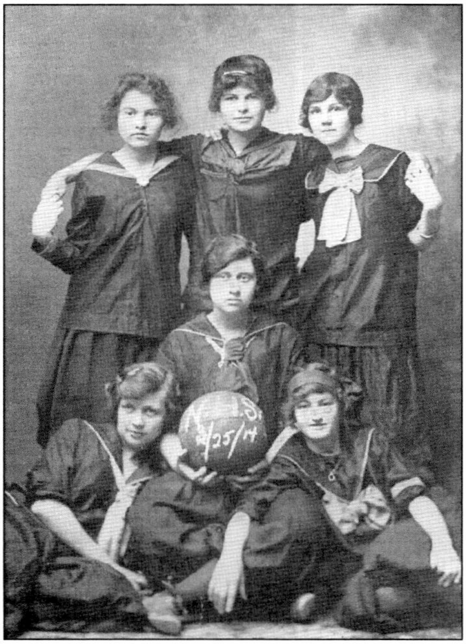

Drummer Marcus Mallard appears with the band Dancer's Choice. For many years, Mallard has been known as the "Historian of Grimes County." He is perhaps the best-known personality in the county. While collecting volumes of great historical data, he found time not only to play music but to serve as mayor of Navasota and county commissioner. (Courtesy Russell Cushman Collection.)

As the 20th century made its way, women were making a mark in multiple endeavors, including basketball. Featured here is the women's team of 1914, shortly after the dedication of Victoria Felder Manual Training School. The players are identified by last name as follows: (first row) Busby, Barton, and Sullivan; (second row) Steel, Ashford, and Van Pelt. (Courtesy Russell Cushman Collection.)

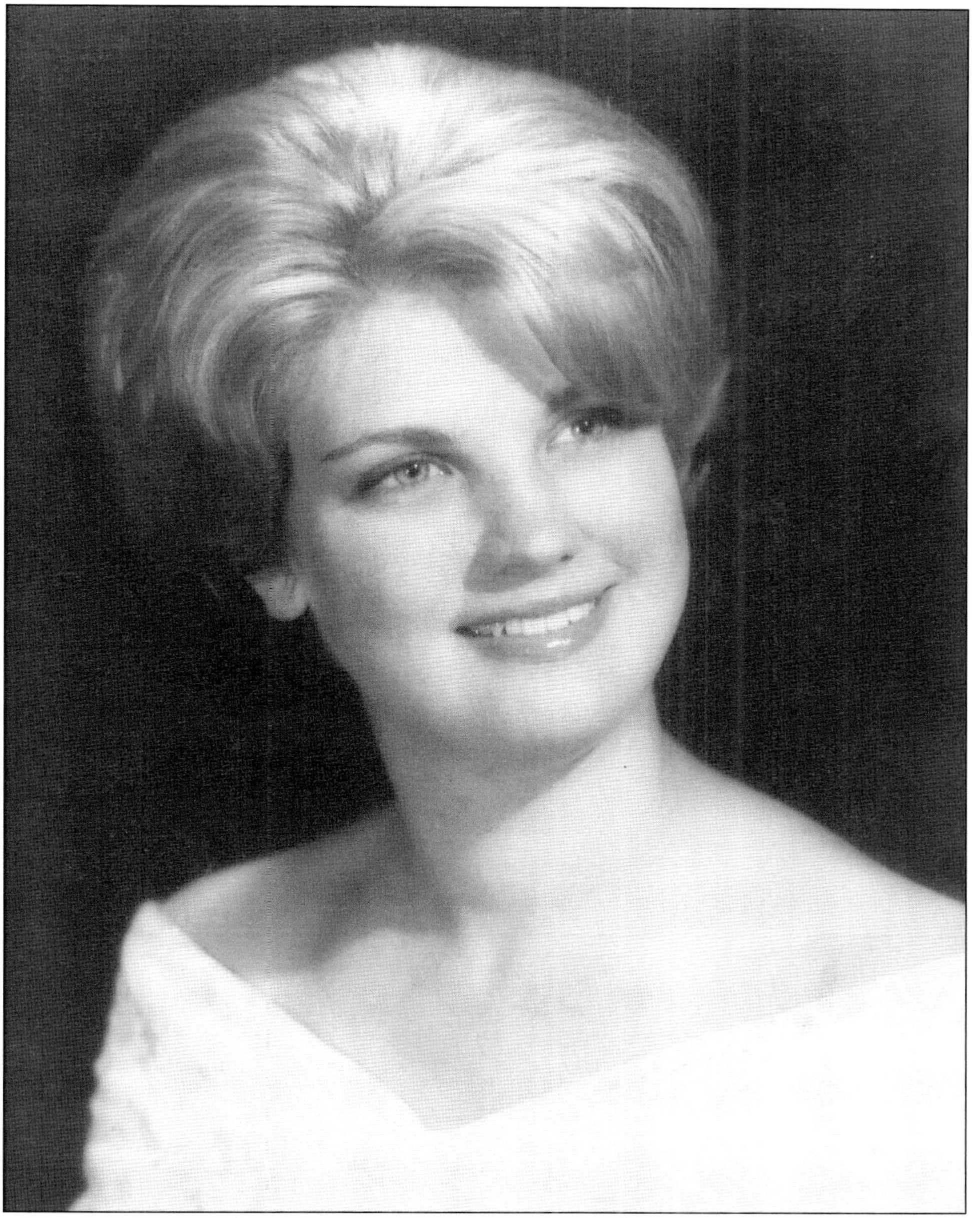

Pam Puryear (1943– 2005) is one of the more interesting personalities of Navasota's cultural history. The daughter of Orville and Laura Lott Puryear, she had a near master's degree in history from Texas A&M University. With Nath Winfield, she authored an important book on the subject of transportation, rivers, and ecology called *Sandbars and Sternwheelers: Steam Navigation on the Brazos*. She also authored an illustrated monograph titled *Dressing Victorian*, a brief overview of women's Victorian clothing in Texas. But, Puryear's passion was roses. She published articles in the *Heritage Rose Foundation News*. She was, furthermore, one of the three original founders of the Texas Rose Rustlers, associated with a national group called the Heritage Roses Group. Her discoveries were named for her, including "Pam's Pink" and "Climbing Lady Pamela." She often referred to herself as the "lily in the field." (Courtesy Russell Cushman Collection.)

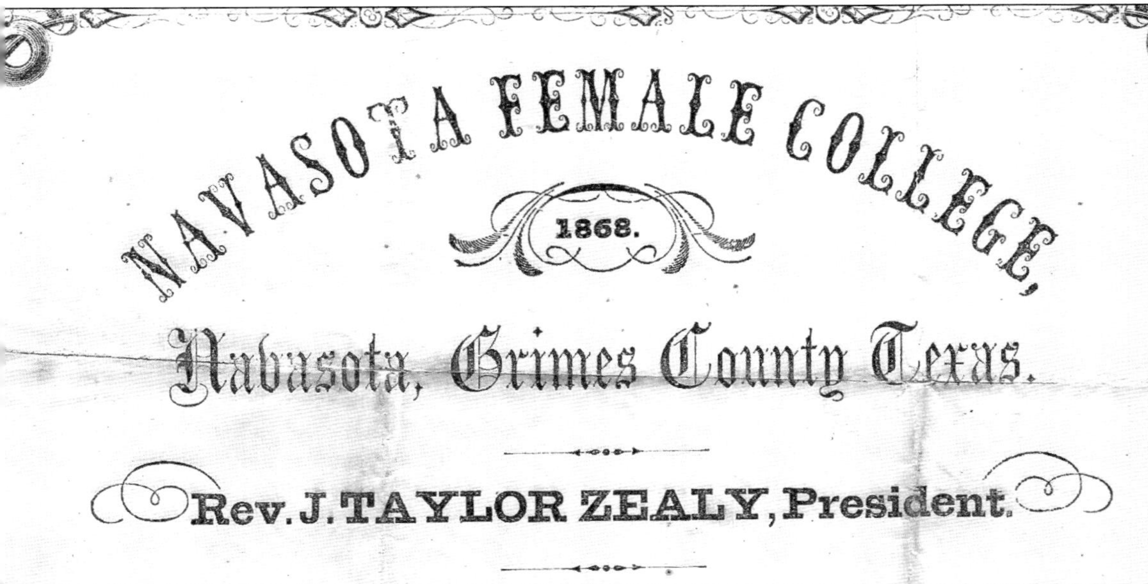
NAVASOTA FEMALE COLLEGE,

1868.

Navasota, Grimes County Texas.

Rev. J. TAYLOR ZEALY, President.

Evidence that women were early taking the initiative in bringing culture to Navasota is found in this 1868 document from the Navasota Female College, opened October 7, 1868. The document states that, "The system of instruction contemplates the development of the moral as well as the intellectual nature." Interestingly, while it stresses that the aim is to "habituate . . . [p]upils to independent thought," it emphasizes that "the management of the School is based upon the doctrine of implicit obedience to the authority of the Teacher, and nothing of a contrary character will be tolerated." The March 4, 1869 edition of the *Galveston News* stated, "Navasota boasts of a good school . . . under the management of Prof. J.T. Zealy" with "at present about fifty students—the school is likely to be a permanent institution." (Courtesy Texas Center for Regional Studies.)

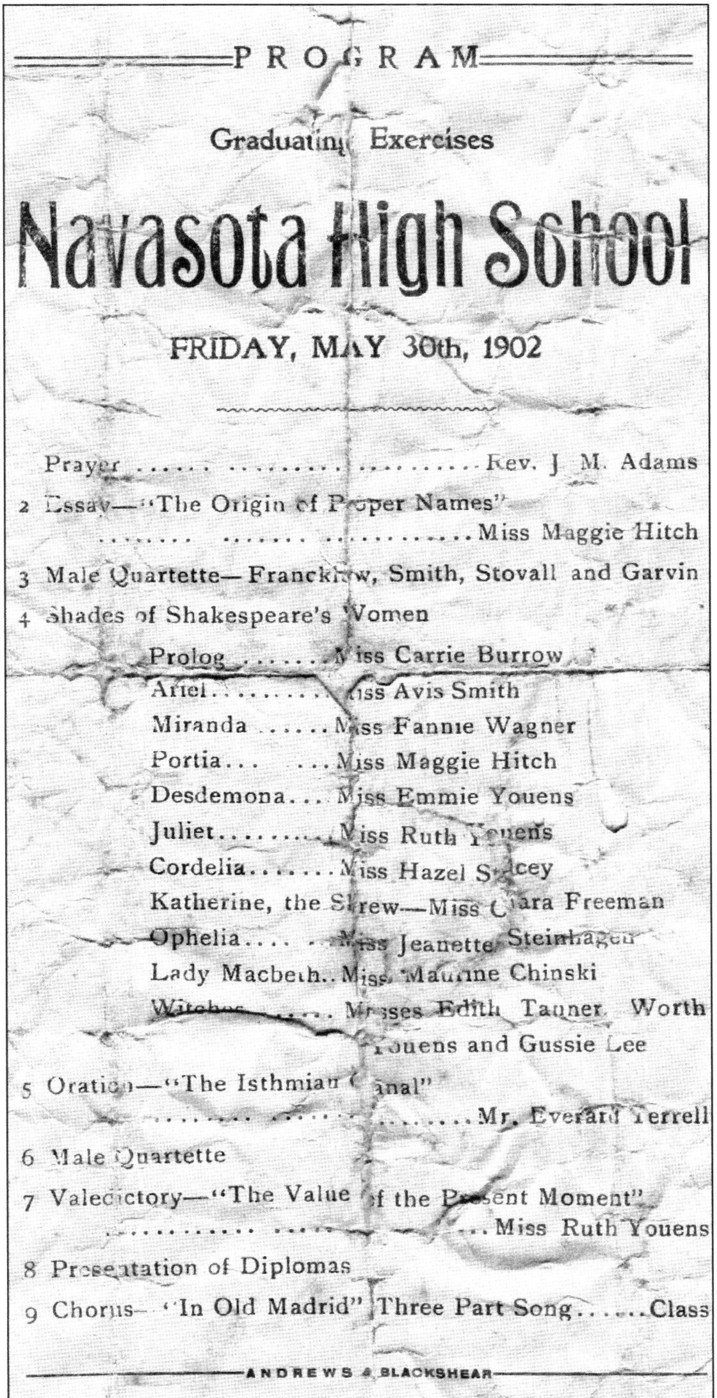

PROGRAM

Graduating Exercises

Navasota High School

FRIDAY, MAY 30th, 1902

Prayer .... Rev. J. M. Adams

2 Essay—"The Origin of Proper Names"
.... Miss Maggie Hitch

3 Male Quartette—Franckhow, Smith, Stovall and Garvin

4 Shades of Shakespeare's Women

Prolog .... Miss Carrie Burrow

Ariel......... Miss Avis Smith

Miranda ...... Miss Fannie Wagner

Portia... ...Miss Maggie Hitch

Desdemona.... Miss Emmie Youens

Juliet......... Miss Ruth Youens

Cordelia....... Miss Hazel Stacey

Katherine, the Shrew—Miss Clara Freeman

Ophelia.... ..Miss Jeanette Steinhagen

Lady Macbeth.. Miss Maurine Chinski

Witches ...... Misses Edith Tanner, Worth Youens and Gussie Lee

5 Oration—"The Isthmian Canal"
.... Mr. Everard Terrell

6 Male Quartette

7 Valedictory—"The Value of the Present Moment"
.... Miss Ruth Youens

8 Presentation of Diplomas

9 Chorus—"In Old Madrid" Three Part Song.......Class

ANDREWS & BLACKSHEAR

This program from the graduation exercises at Navasota High School in 1902 shows the emphasis on culture in Navasota Schools at the turn of the 20th century. Note, for example, the excerpts from Shakespeare that the students were asked to recite. (Courtesy Horlock History Center.)

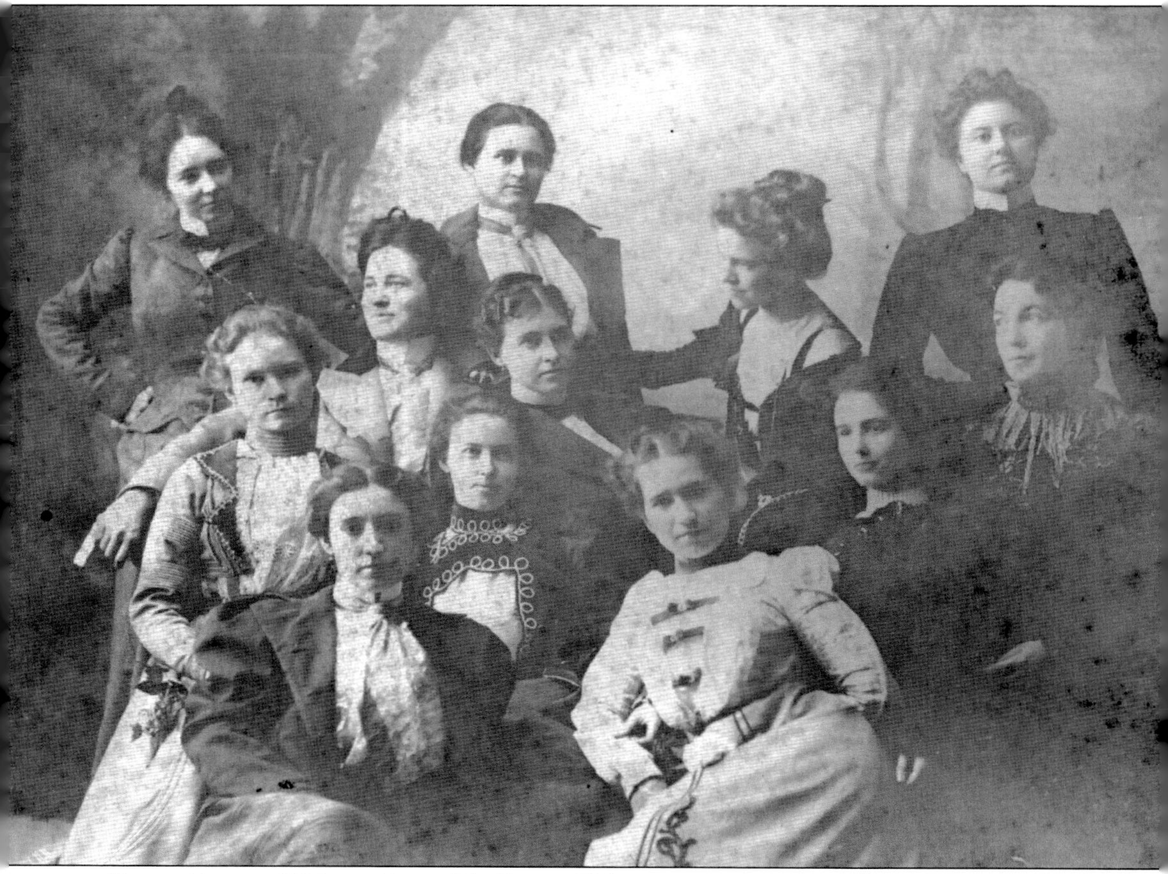

Pictured here in 1898, members of the Perian Club, a prominent women's discussion group of the late 19th century, attend a luncheon in honor of Bessie (Barry) Blackshear. From left to right are (first row) Nora (Wilkerson) Sangster and Zenobia (Daunis) Smith; (second row) Bessie (Barry) Blackshear, Katie Norwood, and Jessie (Lott) Peterson; (third row) Cara (Froehlich) Winter, unidentified, and Stella (Howell) Preston; (fourth row) Emma (Horlock) Harris, Mattie (Brosig) Norwood, Pearl (Garvin) Swanson, and Agnes (Horlock) Jackson. (Courtesy Texas Center for Regional Studies.)

Eight

Citizen Heroes of Our Wars

Navasota natives have served admirably in multiple wars, bringing pride to town. Not only have they been brave in battle, but also, they have been sensitive in peace. For instance, in August 1993, Navasota native and veteran of the Vietnam War Latham Boone III gave the following speech at the Vietnam Wall in Washington, DC. The occasion was a reunion of the 3rd Battalion, 1st Marines:

> We stand here today in memory of our comrades and friends whose names appear engraved upon this dark wall. The good times we shared together on liberty, at camp, and in the field, we now recall. We remember too those terrible days, their untimely deaths so far away. The blood, sweat, grime, and fear still come to mind as we think of Double Eagle, Utah, Texas Marble Mountain, Tet, the DMS, and other battles fought. In the reflection on this wall, we now see ourselves and them in another time, and wonder if what we did was all for naught. But looking back, we remember love of country, home, and friends and though some questioned, we did our duty even then. And in the heat and din of battle, we prayed for peace and God's will be done. Now in this moment of remembrance, let us pray for those whose blood was shed. As we ponder their loss, let us dedicate ourselves in their memory to preventing another wall of granite where young men's names are read. Finally, in their memory, let us set the record straight. It was others who made the decisions from afar. We won our battles, they lost the war.

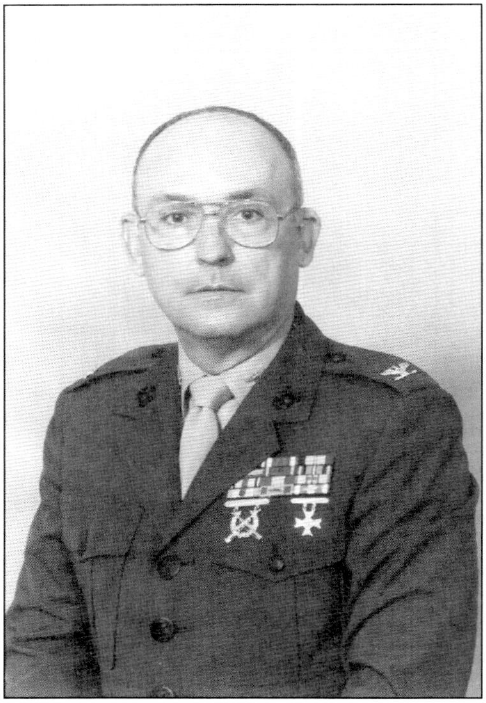

Besides receiving a Purple Heart with the Marines in Vietnam in 1966, Latham Boone III has had an illustrious political career. An attorney by profession, he has served as a state representative, district attorney, a special prison prosecutor, city attorney, and as interim city manager. Currently, he is serving as municipal court judge in Bryan. (Courtesy Latham Boone III.)

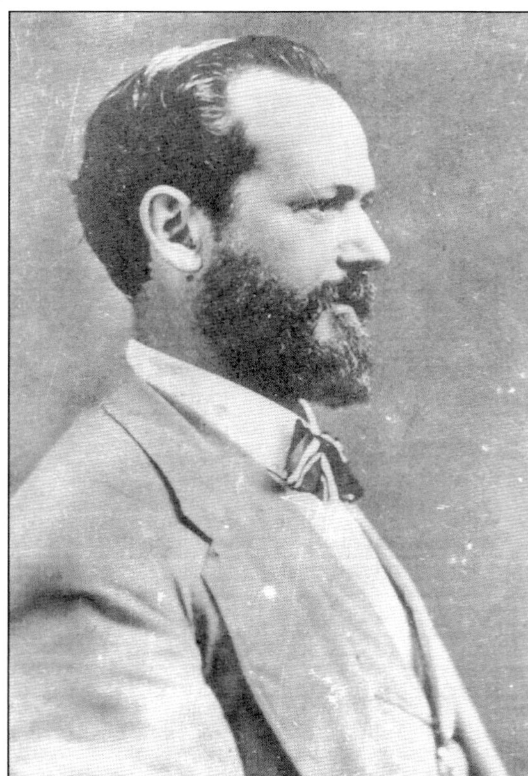

Col. William Harvey Sellers was assistant adjutant general of Hood's Brigade in the Civil War. Company H of that brigade was formed in Grimes County, a tri-county company. Sellers, at age 15, participated in the Mier Expedition, responding to Mexican efforts to reclaim Texas. (Courtesy *Navasota Examiner*.)

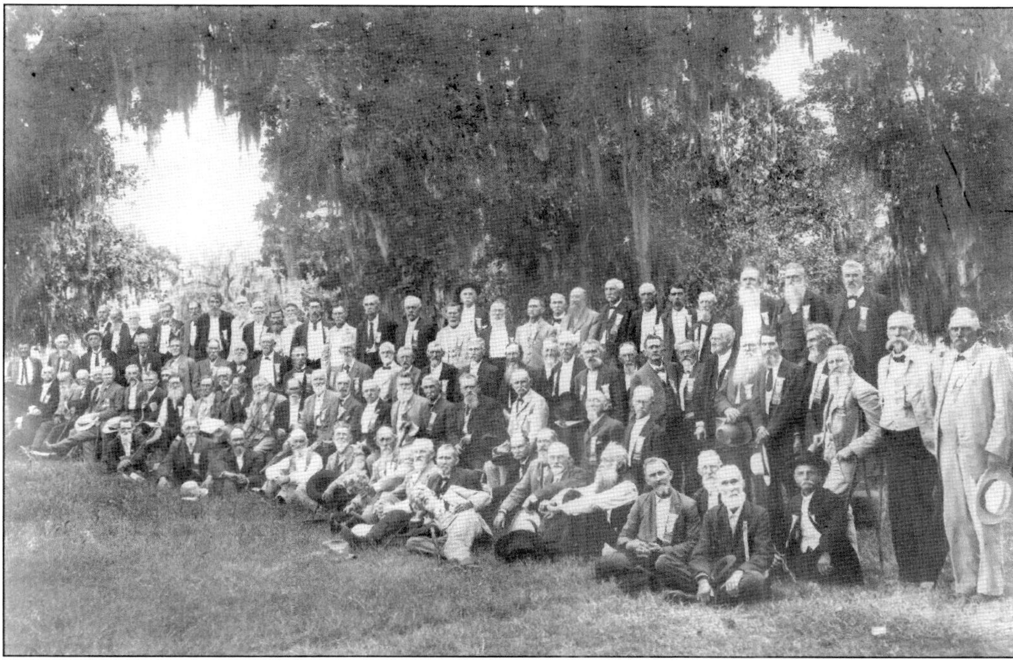

A reunion of the Hood's Brigade was held in 1907. The veterans gathered from the surrounding area to reminisce and share in the patriotism of the citizenry. Early on, Navasotans had an understanding of the significance of the history of their area and a feeling of deep respect for those who risked their lives for their beliefs. And Hood's Brigade remains special in the annals of military history, perhaps the most famous brigade to engage in the War between the States. It is interesting how well preserved the men appear in spite of the years and the psychological and physical grind of the Great War. Today, their memory is also well preserved, as there are Navasotans who, on a regular basis, tend the graves of Civil War veterans. (Both, courtesy Marcus Mallard.)

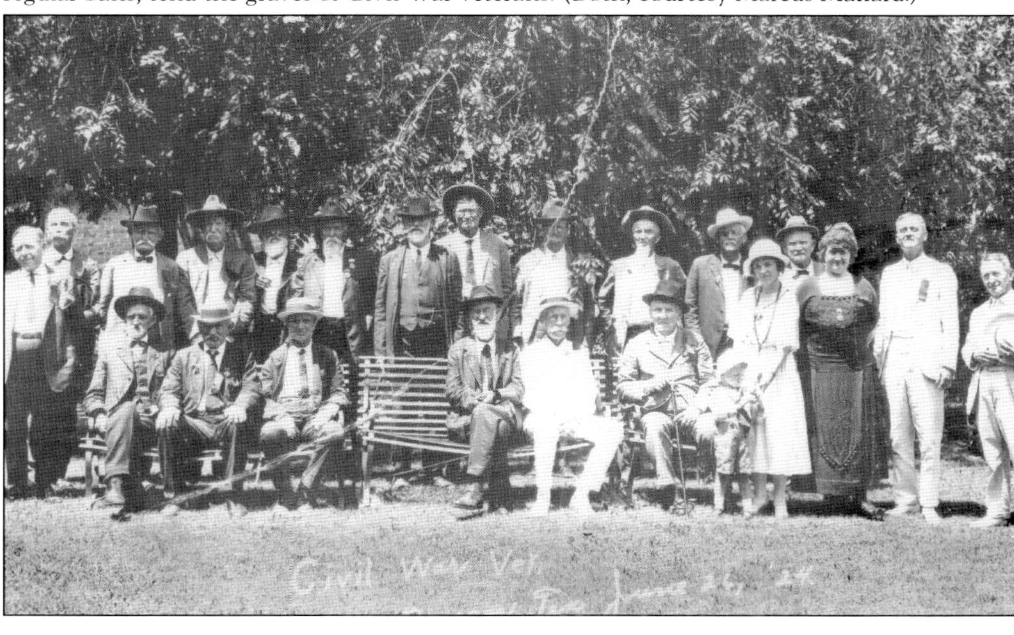

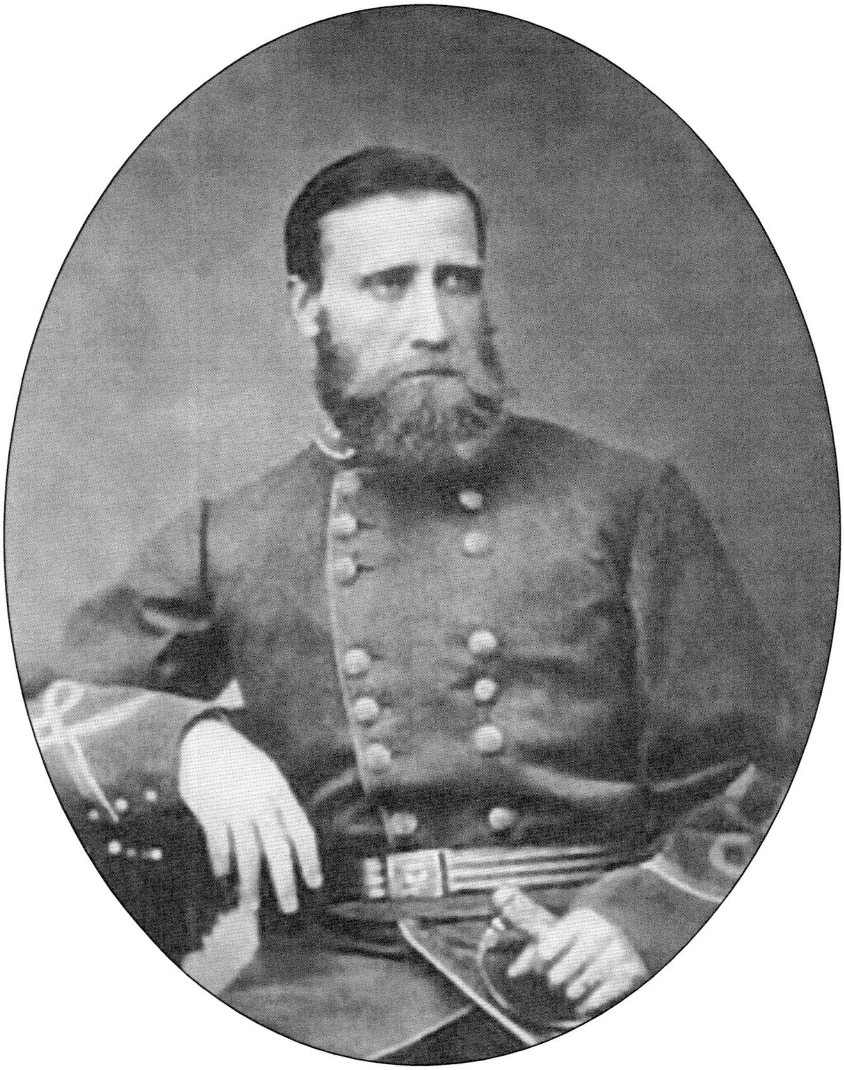

Pictured here is Gen. John Bell Hood, associated with the famous "Texas Hood's Brigade." The brigade was organized on October 22, 1861 in Richmond, Virginia. Initially, Brig. Gen. Louis Wigfall commanded the brigade that was composed of the 1st, 4th, and 5th Texas Regiments. These were the only Texas troops to fight in the Eastern Theater. Wigfall resigned his command on February 20, 1862, and on March 7, Hood received promotion to brigadier general and took command of the brigade. Because of his daring leadership, the brigade became known as Hood's Brigade, in spite of the fact that Hood served only six months as commander. On November 1, 1862, Brig. Gen. Jerome B. Robertson of Independence, Texas, assumed command of the brigade, with Hood becoming division commander. In September 1863, Hood was wounded at the Battle of Chickamauga and forced to leave the command. (Courtesy JohnBellHood.org.)

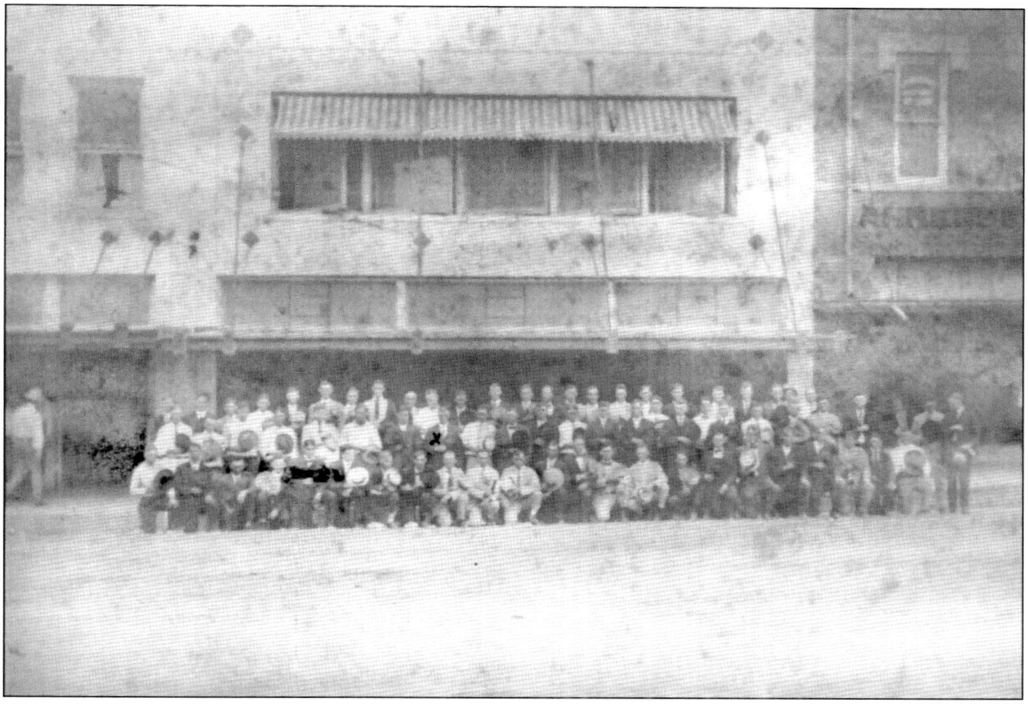

Navasotans were up for the Great War, the first major world conflict in modern times. This photograph features Grimes County men off Washington Avenue, posing before they muster to serve in World War I. Note the Wilson Building on the far right. (Courtesy Navasota Pubic Library.)

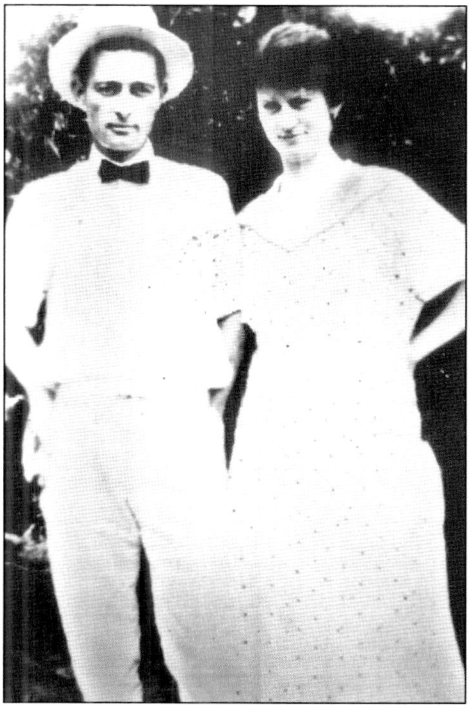

Seen here are Andrew "Buddy" and Artie Moore Fleming. Buddy was born in 1891 and Artie in 1894. A barber for many years in Navasota, Buddy served his time like so many loyal Navasotans; he was a veteran of World War I. (Courtesy Navasota Public Library.)

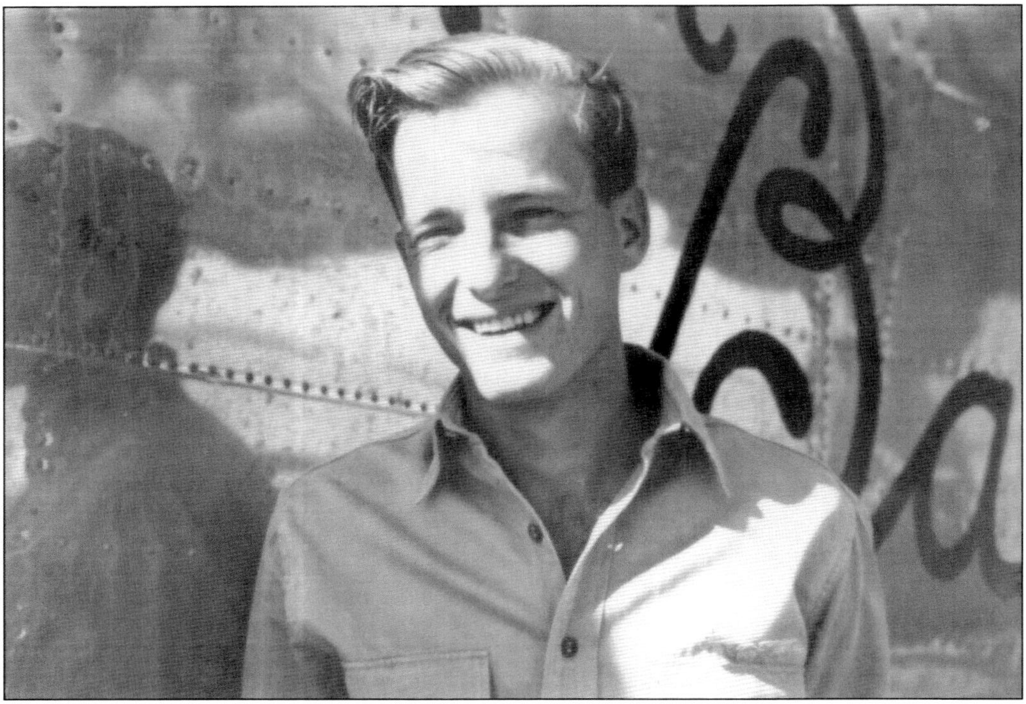

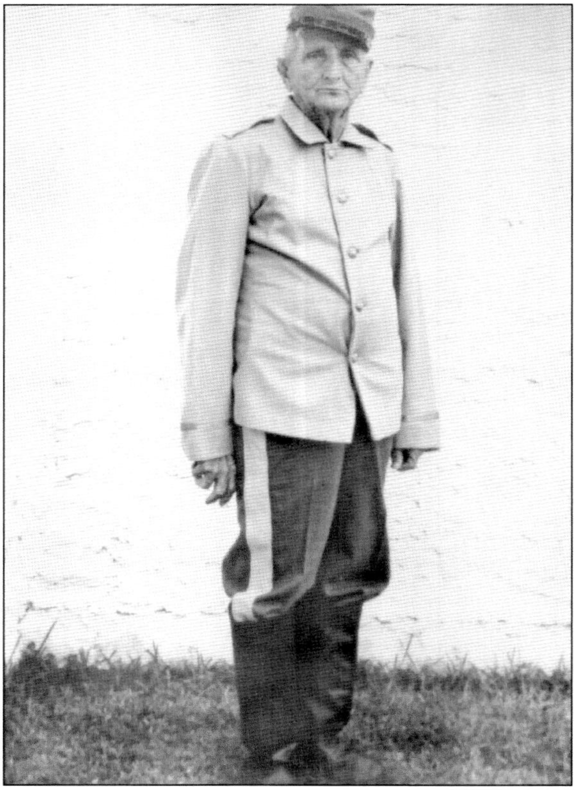

George F. Wingard Jr. was a true war hero. Born in 1924 in Shiro, his family moved to Navasota in 1929. During World War II, he served as the engineer top turret gunner on a B-24. Wingard flew 50 combat missions. (Courtesy Navasota Public Library.)

Navasotans served honorably at home with a unit called the Navasota Guards. Willie E. Backloupe, born in 1867, was part of the first militia after the Galveston Storm of 1900. Parenthetically, he received a diploma from the old Atchison Institute and played on a very good Navasota baseball team. (Courtesy Navasota Public Library.)

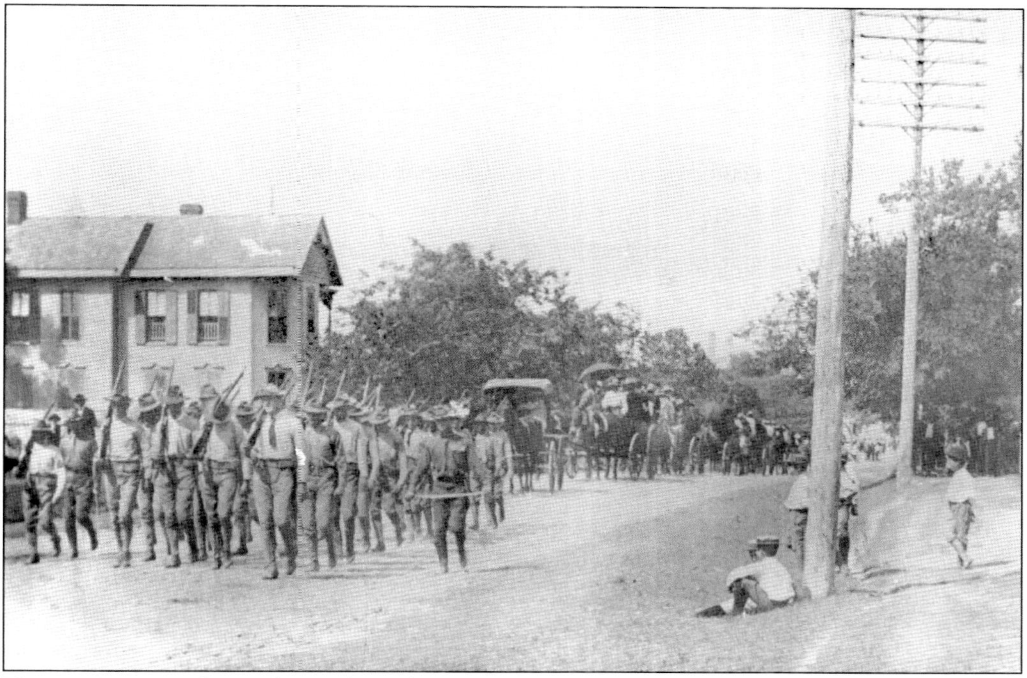

Navasota's National Guard Unit showed its colors in the 1907 Hood's Brigade Reunion Parade. They are shown here marching in file past the 400 block of East McAlpine Street. Note the long wagon train behind, and boys sitting on the sidelines in hats. (Courtesy Navasota Public Library.)

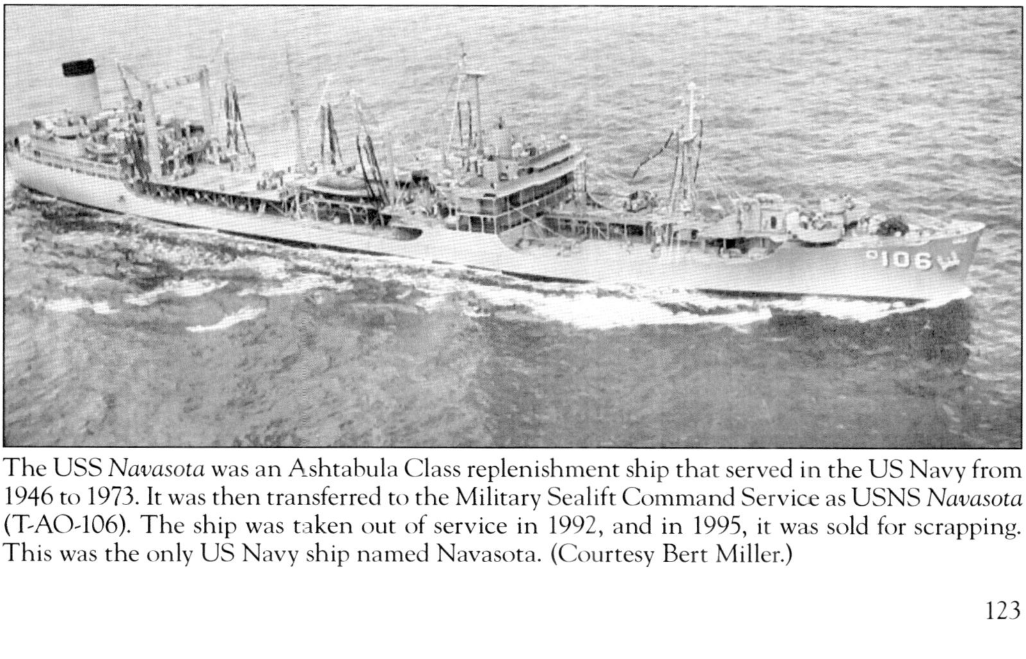

The USS *Navasota* was an Ashtabula Class replenishment ship that served in the US Navy from 1946 to 1973. It was then transferred to the Military Sealift Command Service as USNS *Navasota* (T-AO-106). The ship was taken out of service in 1992, and in 1995, it was sold for scrapping. This was the only US Navy ship named Navasota. (Courtesy Bert Miller.)

52 THE SACHEM

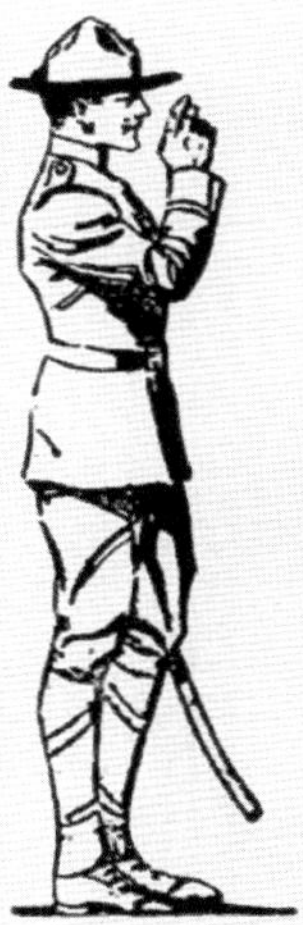

Soldier's Farewell

IN OLD MADRID Robin Adair Was Seeing Nellie Home to Our Mountains, from the Hiring Fair. When Coming Through the Rye, Robin Adair said: "Sing Love's Old Sweet Song, Sweet and Low, for I hear the Call to Battle."

"O Italia Beloved, exclaimed Nellie, will you have to Tramp, Tramp, Tramp, All Through the Night, my Warrior Bold?"

"No, My Bonnie, I must leave Columbia the Gem of the Ocean, and saii Out on the Deep."

"O take me to my Home, Sweet Home, My Heart is Bow'd Down."

"O Fair Dove, O Fond Dove, I must leave America, the Dearest Spot on Earth, and sail Over the Summer Sea to the Watch on the Rhine, Where Let Me, Like a Soldier Fall."

"Then you'll Remember Me On Billows Rocking Over There?" asked Nellie.

"Yes, Rosebud of the Wildwood. O How Can I Leave Thee? Still I must go to The Life on the Ocean Wave, but Believe Me, I fear not The Torpedo and the Whale, If All Those Endearing Charms Fly With Me."

She said "Farewell to One Who Treads the Path of Duty."

So he departed for The Gallant Ships of Uncle Sam with these words, "Keep the Home Fires Burning, Goodbye, Farewell."

L. H.

This "Soldier's Farewell" was taken from page 52 of the 1918 *Sachem*, the school yearbook. The poem illustrates the patriotism of the times and how it was inculcated into the public school system. Also, note the high romanticism and the optimism of the times. This was to be the "war to end all wars," or so it was hoped. The *Sachem* is a wealth of historical information; for instance, it was supported by advertisements from the local merchants. These pages are a who's who of the businesses of the times. (Courtesy Horlock History Center.)

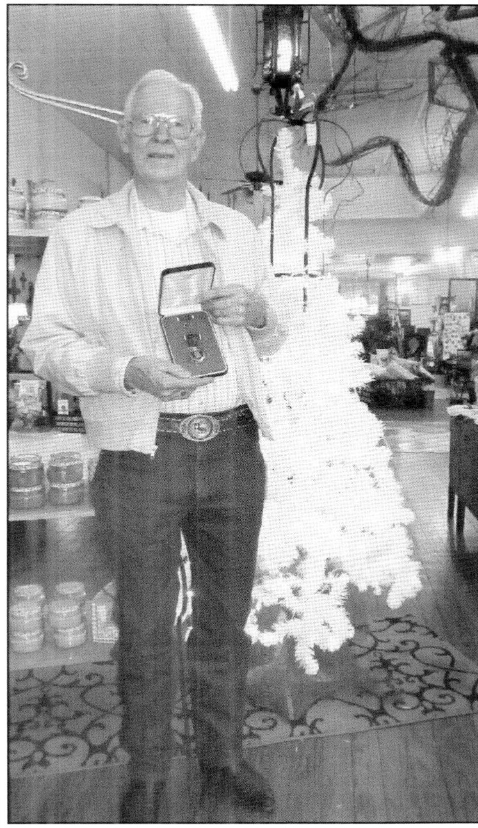

Alton Aga is one of six sons of the same Navasotan family to serve his country in war. Three of his brothers served with honor in World War II, while he and the remaining two brothers were in the Korean War of the 1950s. He served in three major invasions of Allied forces. On the last mission, with his feet frozen beyond an ability to maneuver, he was mercifully air lifted from the scene of a major battle. For his laudable service, he received the Purple Heart, shown in the photograph at right. Young Alga, during the era of his active service, appears below. (Right, courtesy Robin Montgomery; below, courtesy Alton Aga.)

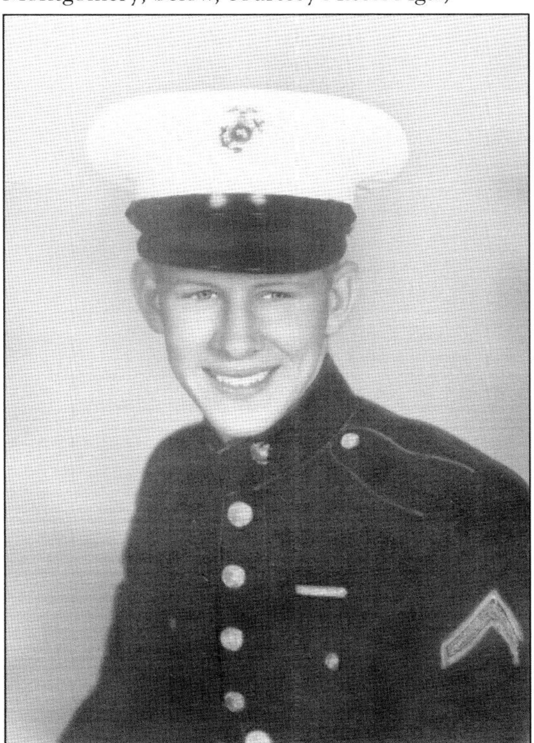

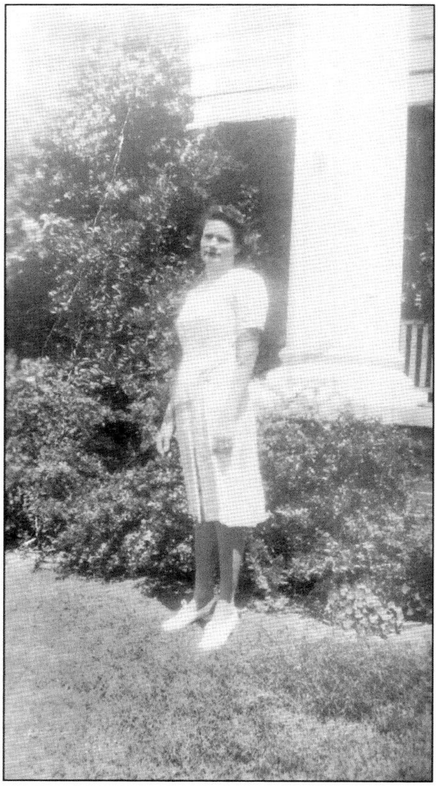

W.P. Keown was an Army flight instructor in Bryan during World War II, teaching basic and primary techniques at Easterwood Airport. He had been in the US Signal Corps in World War I. During his time in Bryan, there was difficulty finding lodging. Bryan was full, and in Navasota, troops were constantly camped on the field, presently occupied in part by the intermediate school. Keown finally found a temporary home, renting the Harry Moore Plantation house in the vicinity of the present Navasota High School. Shown in the photograph on the left is his wife, Virginia Keown, standing next to a pillar of the house, since moved to Conroe. The photograph below shows Johnny Keown, son of W.P. and Virginia, with his first grade class on the steps of the Atchison Institute. Miss Johnson was the teacher. (Courtesy Johnny Keown.)

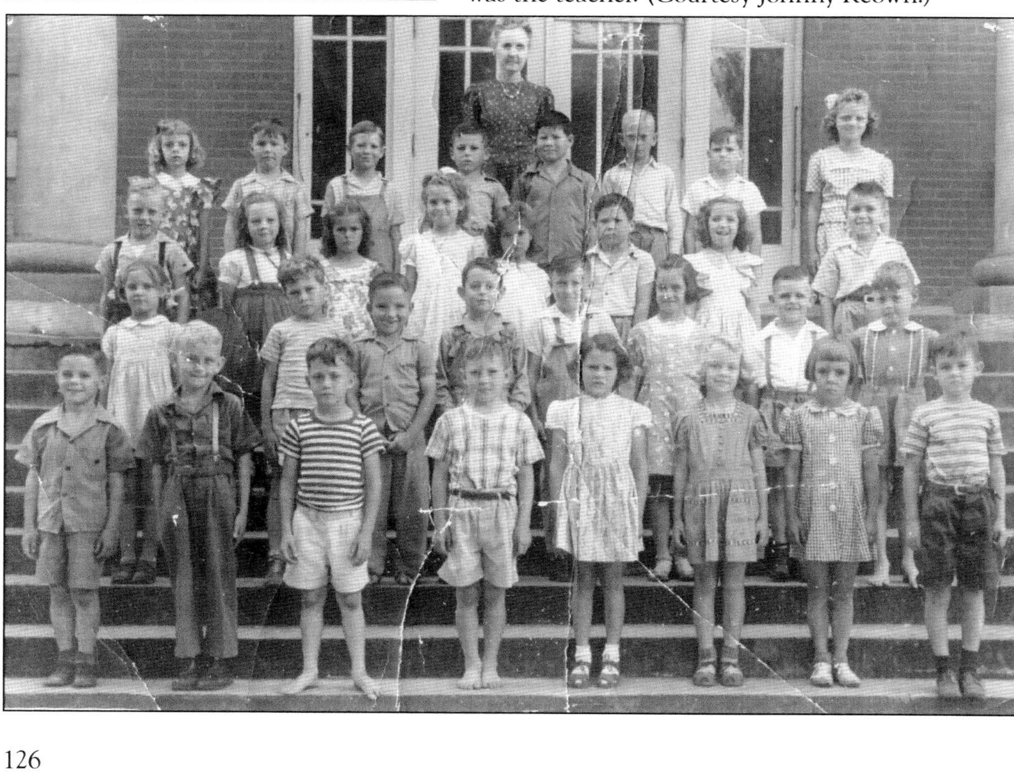

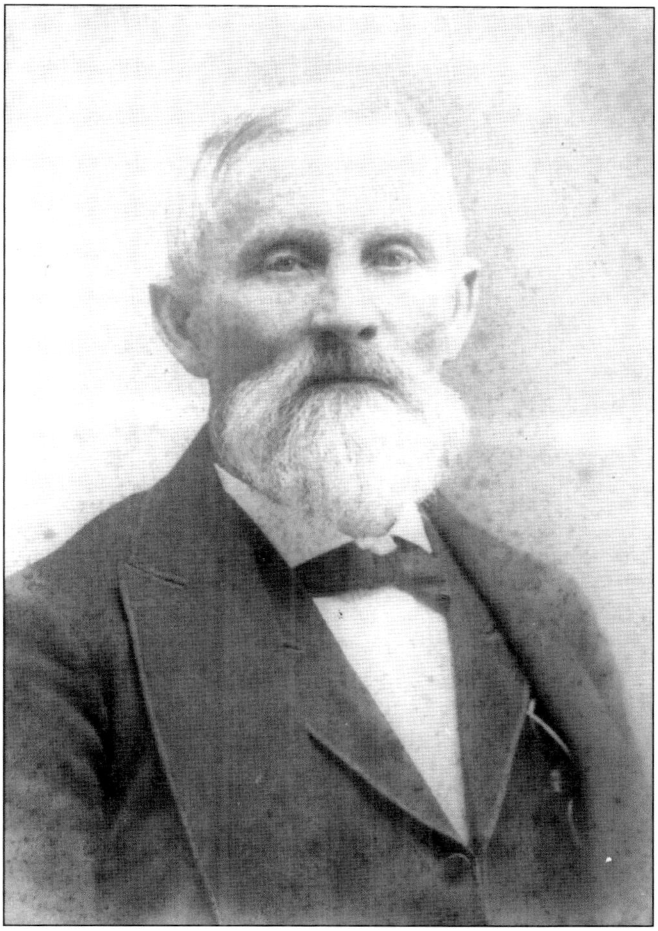

Capt. W.E. Barry started as a private in the 4th Texas Voluntary Regiment of Infantry, Company G, of the Grimes County Greys. He was wounded on May 6, 1864, at the Battle of the Wilderness. He was retired for disability on November 28, 1864. (Courtesy Russell Cushman Collection.)

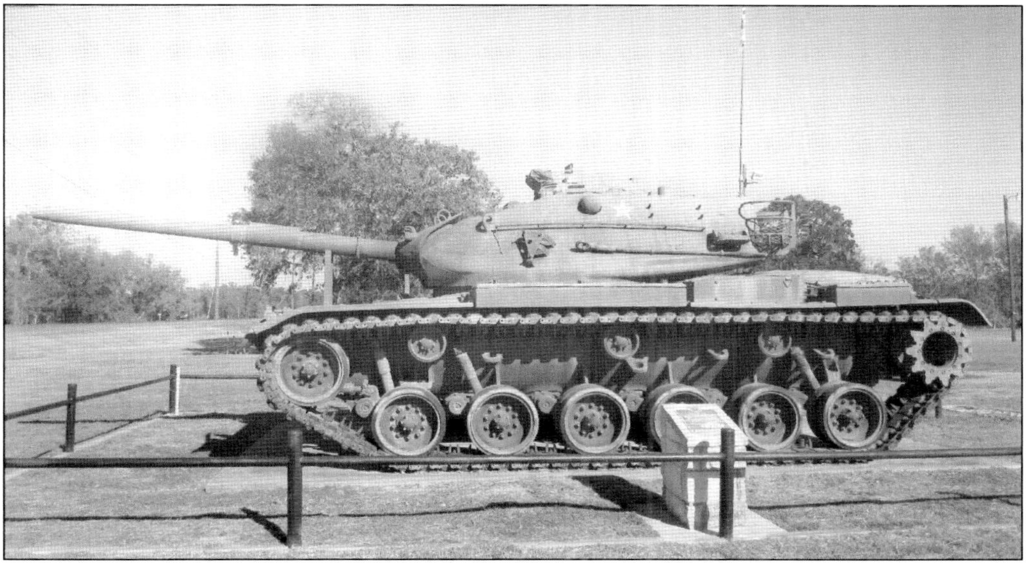

On March 23, 1999, the US Department of the Army delivered this model M-60 ATTS tank Serial Number 3757-A to the VFW grounds. The M-60 combat tank, equipped with a 105-milimeter cannon, was deployed in Vietnam and Desert Storm. The tank is dedicated to all members of VFW Post 4006 and to retired USN "Chief Bos'n Mate" Sam Corolla, who was instrumental in the tank's acquisition. (Courtesy Joy Montgomery.)

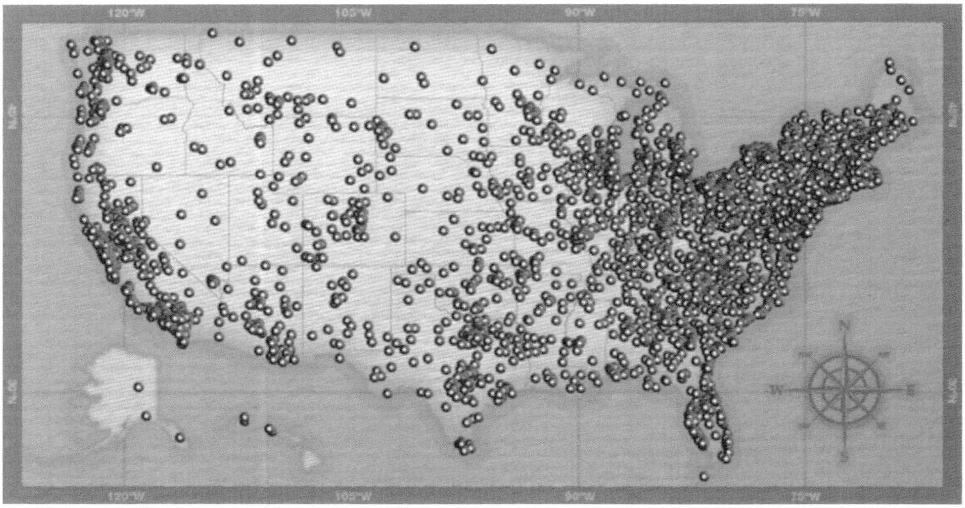